Book 2

Running the economy

Running the economy
Book 2

Edited by Cristina Santos with Martin Higginson, Susan Himmelweit, Peter Howells, Jonquil Lowe, Maureen Mackintosh, Wyn Morgan, Stuart Parris, Roberto Simonetti, Hedley Stone and Andrew Trigg

This publication forms part of the Open University module DD209 Running the economy. Details of this and other Open University modules can be obtained from the Student Registration and Enquiry Service, The Open University, PO Box 197, Milton Keynes MK7 6BJ, United Kingdom (tel. +44 (0)845 300 60 90; email general-enquiries@open.ac. uk).

Alternatively, you may visit the Open University website at www.open.ac.uk where you can learn more about the wide range of modules and packs offered at all levels by The Open University.

To purchase a selection of Open University materials visit www.ouw.co.uk, or contact Open University Worldwide, Walton Hall, Milton Keynes MK7 6AA, United Kingdom for a catalogue (tel. +44 (0)1908 858779; fax +44 (0) 1908 858787; email ouw-customer-services@open.ac.uk).

The Open University, Walton Hall, Milton Keynes MK7 6AA

First published 2013.

Copyright © 2014 The Open University

Edited, designed and typeset by The Open University.

Printed in the United Kingdom by Bell & Bain Ltd., Glasgow

ISBN 978 1 7800 7961 5

2.1

Contents

Part 4 Regulating markets, promoting growth

Chapter 11

Made in China: offshoring, production and cost

Stuart Parris

Contents

1   Introduction

> Companies that pursue well-crafted LCC [low-cost country] strategies are likely to see the landed costs of their products reduced by 20 to 40 percent, and service costs reduced by as much as 60 percent. The primary source of this advantage is lower wages and benefits, which translate into higher margins.
>
> (Bhattacharya et al., 2004)

Bhattacharya et al. (2004) highlight why in recent decades many manufacturing firms have moved operations to locations all over the globe to reduce costs. In many cases, firms choose to locate manufacturing activity in countries with cheap labour, like China, in the hope of obtaining a cost saving advantage over rivals. In addition, China has witnessed a growth in home-grown manufacturing firms – Chinese firms with the ambition to export goods overseas. The result has been a rise of manufacturing across low-cost countries. For instance, in 2002 approximately 45% of clothing, 60% of audio and video devices, and 70% of footwear sold in the USA were made in low labour cost countries such as China (Bhattacharya et al., 2004). Figure 11.1 (overleaf) shows how the real value of manufactured goods imported to the USA from China has risen steadily since the mid-1990s.

This chapter revisits the global imbalances story that you met in Chapter 2. That story focuses on macroeconomic issues, explaining how the rapid growth of Asian export activity increased the current account surplus in China. In contrast, heavily importing Chinese goods has built up large current account deficits in countries like the UK.

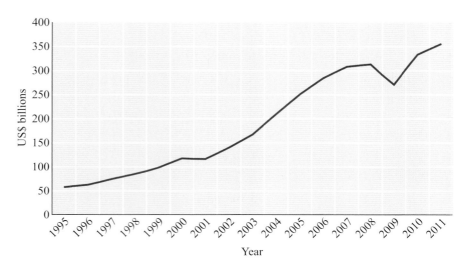

Figure 11.1   Value of manufacturing imports to the USA from China

(Source: United Nations Conference on trade and Development (UNCTAD), 2012; series adjusted with IMF GDP deflator using a base year of 2005)

Microeconomics

Microeconomics is the branch of economics that studies individuals, households, firms, markets and institutions.

The corresponding **microeconomic** story told in this chapter is how, over recent decades, European and US firms have offshored manufacturing activity from domestic locations to Asia, especially China. Firms have relocated production abroad to cut costs to face international competition, so it is necessary to understand how firms compete and, in particular, how costs influence firms' decisions. This chapter starts the analysis of firm behaviour by looking at how economists model firms and their costs, and how costs and technology shape firms and industries. It lays the basis for the analysis of markets and competition that will follow in the next three chapters of Part 4.

Section 2 of this chapter examines some of the motives for offshoring production by looking at the cost of labour in China. Then Section 3 explains how firm production can be modelled, and Section 4 shows how costs per unit vary as output changes. Sections 5, 6 and 7 highlight different challenges faced by firms when attempting to produce at the lowest possible cost. Section 8 turns again to China and reflects on the economic theories discussed in this chapter. Section 9 concludes.

The learning outcomes for this chapter are:

- to understand how economists model firms' technology and costs
- to understand economic models of the relationship between firms' costs and output
- to appreciate the various factors that shape firms' costs, such as technology and factor prices
- to understand the difference between the short run and the long run as used in microeconomic models
- to understand the concepts of marginal cost and marginal product.

2   The search for lower costs: Chinese wages

Low wages in Asian countries such as China explain much of the increase in both offshoring and outsourcing of production from Europe and the USA. As a survey of top US executives indicates, firms that manage production costs will be able to gain advantage over rivals:

> Among industry-leading companies, more than 40% of executives say their key competitive advantage is their ability to keep costs low. And not just during a downturn. Companies with consistently lower costs can out-invest rivals in R&D and marketing, compete on price, and quickly shift resources to gain market share, all while maintaining strong margins.
>
> (Guarraia and Saenz, 2011)

If goods can be produced in locations with a large supply of labour with the necessary skills and a willingness to work for low wages, then this can considerably reduce production costs. In fact, since the 1960s manufacturing activity in Asian countries such as Korea, Taiwan and Singapore has risen. The availability of cheap Asian labour encouraged firms to offshore manufacturing activities (Nelson and Pack, 1999). Later, in the 1980s, China emerged as a major destination for offshoring activity because the price of labour relative to that in countries in Europe and the USA was very low. Even in 2011 the average hourly wage in US manufacturing was $36, compared with $47 in Germany and $36 in Italy. In contrast, in countries such as Taiwan, hourly wages were $9 (Bureau of Labor Statistics, 2012), and estimates of Chinese hourly wage rates vary between $1 and $2.5 depending on industry and region (Wright et al., 2011). Figure 11.2 highlights the considerable difference in mean hourly wages in different parts of the world as measured in 2008, compared to the USA.

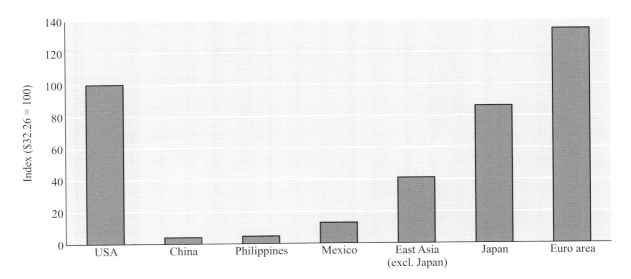

Figure 11.2   Average hourly compensation costs of manufacturing employees in selected economies and regions, 2008. Note that the group labelled 'East Asia excluding Japan' consists of an average of wages in Hong Kong, the Republic of Korea, the Philippines, Singapore and Taiwan. The US average wage in 2008 was $32.26.

(Source: Banister and Cook, 2011)

Even high-technology companies such as Apple Inc. rely on low Chinese wages to contain costs. Figure 11.3 (overleaf) shows how some of the components of the iPhone are purchased from manufacturers worldwide. A significant number of key iPhone components produced in Asia are manufactured (at the time of writing) by another firm, Foxconn. Foxconn's assembly plant in Shenzhen, China, employed approximately 230 000 staff in 2012 (Duhigg and Bradsher, 2012), many of whom assemble the iPhone and iPad for Apple.

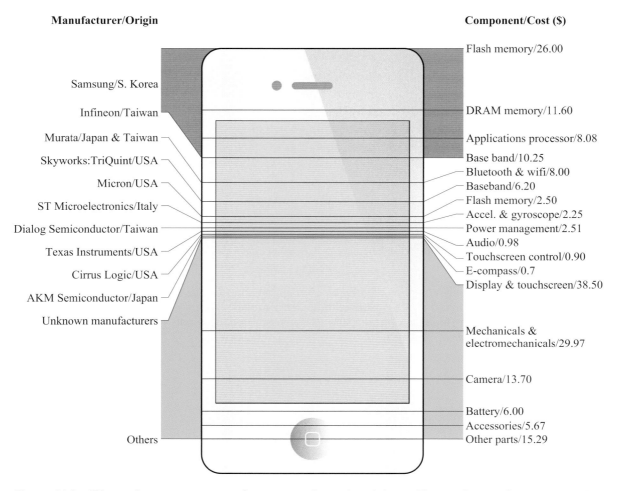

Manufacturer/Origin

Samsung/S. Korea

Infineon/Taiwan

Murata/Japan & Taiwan

Skyworks:TriQuint/USA

Micron/USA

ST Microelectronics/Italy

Dialog Semiconductor/Taiwan

Texas Instruments/USA

Cirrus Logic/USA

AKM Semiconductor/Japan

Unknown manufacturers

Others

Component/Cost ($)

Flash memory/26.00

DRAM memory/11.60

Applications processor/8.08

Base band/10.25
Bluetooth & wifi/8.00
Baseband/6.20
Flash memory/2.50
Accel. & gyroscope/2.25
Power management/2.51
Audio/0.98
Touchscreen control/0.90
E-compass/0.7
Display & touchscreen/38.50

Mechanicals & electromechanicals/29.97

Camera/13.70

Battery/6.00
Accessories/5.67
Other parts/15.29

Figure 11.3   iPhone 4 component manufacturers and cost breakdown. The total cost of components is US$178, with an average sale price of US$560.

(Source: The Economist, 2011a)

2.1   Rising wages in China

An emerging challenge for firms offshoring or outsourcing to China is rising labour costs. For instance, in 2011 the cost of assembling an iPhone was estimated at US$7 per unit (*The Economist*, 2011a). However, in 2012 Foxconn workers received significant wage increases after a period of severe criticism in the media of the treatment of Foxconn staff. The media focus followed a series of suicides of company workers, as well as complaints about low pay, excessive levels of overtime and abusive treatment of workers.

Foxconn responded by increasing the wages of some staff as well as improving working conditions by reducing excessive overtime. For Apple, the rise in the cost of labour at the Foxconn facility may contribute to higher production costs because Foxconn may have to demand a higher price from Apple for each iPhone assembled. Wage rises of staff at Foxconn reflect a trend of increasing wages in industrial regions of China. For example, manufacturers in Shenzhen report labour shortages and higher wage demands as a result of competition for labour between firms and changing attitudes of workers (Hunt, 2012). In addition, the Chinese government has increased the minimum wage rate in some regions. In 2012 the US federal minimum wage was just four times the minimum wage in Shenzhen, compared to twelve times larger in 2004 (Tsui and Rabinovitch, 2012).

Finally, firms offshoring production to China from the USA are exposed to changes in value of the Chinese renminbi (of which the yuan is the principal currency unit) against the US dollar. The number of yuan that can be purchased with $1 has fallen over time, particularly since 2006, as shown in Figure 11.4.

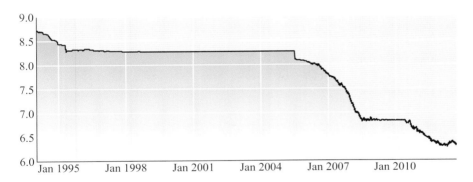

Figure 11.4   Number of yuan that can be purchased with US$1

(Source: Trading Economics, 2012)

Activity 11.1

What is the impact of the appreciation of the yuan against the dollar on US firms' incentives to offshore to China?

Answer

Of course, at the time of writing, China still has low wages compared to developed countries, so the actual cost of labour remains comparatively low, despite the trend increase.

However, rising wages in industrial parts of China have prompted some firms to relocate manufacturing activity to less developed areas. This is particularly true of industries where labour contributes a large proportion of production costs, for example in the production of clothing. Some firms have relocated to other low-wage countries like Indonesia, where wages are lower than in China. This shows that firms are constantly looking for ways to contain their costs, and many pay close attention to wage levels.

3   Modelling the firm: production, technology and factor inputs

Although labour costs are important, labour is not the only input into the production process. Figure 11.3 shows how complex the production of modern goods and services can be. To produce the different goods and services consumed in an economy requires a variety of different firms. Often, many firms – some based in several countries – are involved in different stages of the production and distribution process for an individual good, in what is known as a value chain. You saw an example of a value chain for the production of sandwiches in Chapter 1, Section 4.2.

Value chains, which focus on relationships between firms, often across countries, are one representation of the complexity of the production process. But looking at value chains neglects what goes on inside firms, that is, how firms combine various inputs into the manufacturing process, such as the raw materials used by the component manufacturers, the labour used in the various factories, and the capital (the equipment required to produce components). When you purchase a new iPhone, your purchase includes some form of customer support – a service element that will also require factor inputs, predominantly in the form of labour, perhaps based in a call centre. I could list all the inputs required to produce the iPhone (i.e. including service components), but without knowing how to organise them, I wouldn't be able to produce and sell smartphones. The role of the **firm** is to purchase the necessary inputs and combine them in the right way, using the best techniques available, to produce the final products. I can use this idea to provide a formal definition of the firm, as an organisation that purchases and combines factor inputs, such as land, labour and capital, in order to produce goods and services. These inputs to the firm's production process are called *factors of production*. This definition also encompasses firms that focus on the delivery of services where no manufactured goods are sold, but which nevertheless provide valuable output such as accountancy, marketing, and consultancy.

Firm
A firm is an organisation that purchases, combines and transforms factor inputs (land, labour and capital) into outputs of goods and/or services for sale.

3.1   Modelling the firm: the production function

A firm can combine factors of production in various ways and in various proportions to create output. For example, some labour might be replaced by capital in the production process – certain manufacturing

Production function
The production function specifies the maximum output that a firm can obtain from each available combination of inputs. It represents the technology used by the firm in the production process.

stages could be automated using machinery to replace the employees' hours of work. Depending on the type of good produced and the availability of technology, firms may face a choice about the production method used. The best production methods available to the firm can be summarised in a **production function**, which identifies the maximum output that a firm can produce from each available combination of inputs. This view offers an 'engineering' representation of the production process that focuses on the inputs used and outputs produced by the firm. It measures the flow of the quantity of inputs into production over a period of time necessary to produce a certain quantity of output. The production function, which complements the value chain view of production, represents the technology used by the firm in the production process and is my starting point in modelling the firm and its costs.

The production function is usually represented algebraically.

$$Q = f(F_1, F_2, \ldots, F_n)$$

The firm's output (Q) is dependent on (i.e. is a function of) how the various factors of production (the different Fs, up to any number n of them), such as land, different types of labour and machinery (usually called capital, or capital goods) and raw materials, are combined. Chapter 1 also introduced the idea of intermediate goods, which are another possible input into the production function. The lower case 'f' represents the function (a mathematical relationship) that specifies how the inputs are combined to produce output Q:

Technical efficiency
A firm is technically efficient if it is using the minimum quantity of inputs required to produce a given output for each technique of production.

The production function assumes that the firm is **technically efficient**, that is, it does the best it can with its chosen technique of production when it combines its inputs, without waste.

While production functions can be complex, for the purpose of this chapter I need only a simplified version with two inputs, labour and capital services (often referred to as just labour and capital), which I represent by the letters L and K, respectively. So the production function becomes

$$Q = f(L, K)$$

The production function shows how much output will increase if a greater quantity of inputs is used. Many firms are motivated to grow larger and produce more goods or services (increase output). For example, to increase output, a manufacturing firm could recruit more workers (labour) to assemble more components or help maintain equipment on the production line. It might also use more equipment (capital), such as engineering tools, and it might need to rent or build more production space, or add new assembly lines.

To illustrate how a production function works, I will use an example with a production function that takes the form

$$Q = 2L + K$$

In this example I measure units of labour in hours worked, and units of capital as the number of hours of automated machine use.

Activity 11.2

If a firm with the above production function can input 10 units of labour and 10 units of capital per day, how much output can be made in one day?

Answer

The production function tells you that 10 units of labour and 10 units of capital can be combined to produce 30 units of output
(2 × 10 + 10 = 30).

Notice that the firm could produce the same level of output (30 units) using a different technique that requires more capital and less labour. For example, it might use 5 units of labour and 20 units of capital
(2 × 5 + 20 = 30), or any other combination of capital and labour that produces 30 units of output.

In this example, the production function allows capital to be substituted for labour at a rate of 2 units of capital for 1 unit of labour.

A firm's production function represents its technology, so a change in a production function reflects a change in the firm's technology – technological change. Generally, technological change increases the productivity of inputs. Indeed, one important source of productivity growth results from technological change, which is discussed in Section 6.

4 Modelling a firm's costs: total and average costs

The production function is the starting point for the analysis of a firm's costs as it indicates the quantities of factors of production needed for each level of output. If a firm produces more output, then it will need more inputs, and therefore its costs will rise. However, the production function alone cannot tell me the costs faced by the firm because it ignores the prices of the factors of production. As you saw in Section 2, managing the cost of inputs, such as labour's wages or prices of raw materials, is important. Capital has a cost too: it must also be purchased or rented.

Total costs
The total costs of a firm are the expenses incurred in buying the inputs necessary for production.

In order to analyse costs, therefore, I need to take into account both the quantities of factors of production, whose relationship with output is modelled by the production function, and their prices. For each level of output, **total costs** (TC) are given by the sum of the costs of inputs used. The cost of an input is given by the number of units of input used multiplied by their unit price.

For a given quantity of output Q, the production function tells you the quantity of labour L and capital K needed:

$$Q = f(L, K)$$

The total costs for each level of output can be found by multiplying the quantity of each factor by its price, and can be written as

$$TC = p_L L + p_K K$$

where the price of a unit of labour is given by p_L, and the price of a unit of capital is given by p_K. In this case the price of labour is the hourly wage, and the price of capital is the hourly cost of renting machinery.

This equation tells me something important: total costs will change if either the prices of inputs (p_L or p_K) or the quantities (units) of inputs (L or K) change, or both. If prices fall and the numbers of units of each input stay the same, then total costs will fall. Section 2 showed that many western firms follow this strategy by offshoring to low-wage locations. Alternatively, instead of offshoring to low-wage locations, a firm might prefer to focus on cutting costs by improving its technology and reducing the quantity of inputs used even if factor prices stay constant. Some firms have focused on cutting costs by improving productivity instead of locating production in low-wage countries. Indeed, some firms have reversed previous offshoring decisions and switched to local suppliers because the cost advantages arising from low foreign wages were less than the disadvantages arising from poor quality of components and low productivity.

The introduction of technological change modifies the production function so that inputs are used more efficiently and the firm reduces total costs. Section 6 examines technological change in detail. Until then, I analyse costs assuming that technology is fixed.

Knowing the total costs for each level of output is useful in order to check that costs are below revenues and the firm is profitable. However, total cost does not say whether the firm produces efficiently. If a firm decides to increase output, and prices and productivity remain constant, then total cost will naturally rise because more inputs will be used. So firms find it useful to calculate unit cost, that is, the average cost of each unit of output. **Average cost** is calculated by dividing total cost by the number of units produced, i.e.

$$\text{average cost} = \frac{\text{total cost}}{\text{quantity of output}}$$

and gives firms an indication of their cost-efficiency for each possible level of output.

Depending on the technology used and the type of goods or services produced, a firm's average cost will vary with its scale (the quantity of output produced), so setting the level of output is a key decision for the firm when it tries to manage its costs, as you will see in the following sections.

4.1   Short run and long run

To model how cost changes with output, I need to consider the implications of time. It is reasonable to think that in the short term, firms can make only limited choices about how to produce goods and services to sell. For instance, firms can decide how much to produce and try to optimise existing equipment and processes. However, expanding factories or implementing new production methods requires time. Economists model time by distinguishing between the short run and the long run. You have read about the short and long run in macroeconomics in Part 3 (see Chapter 4, Section 2, and the whole of

Average cost
The average cost of production is the total costs of production divided by the number of units produced. The average cost can be interpreted as the average cost of producing a unit of output. This is the same as 'unit cost'.

Short run
A firm is operating in the short run when it is unable to change the quantity that it uses of at least one of its factors of production.

Long run
In the long run, a firm is able to change the quantity of all of its factors of production.

Chapter 10). Here I define what **short run** and **long run** mean in microeconomics for an individual firm.

The short run denotes a constraint on firm behaviour rather than a particular period of time. In the short run, a firm is unable to change the quantity of at least one input in the production function. The quantity of at least one factor input is fixed no matter how much the firm decides to produce.

Take the example of a firm manufacturing technology goods. In the short term, the firm may increase the number of hours worked by introducing overtime. However, the machinery and size of the premises would, in the short term, be considered a fixed input; the quantity of capital input into production is fixed. In the long run, the firm could open new manufacturing sites or construct new buildings – but this would be expected to take several months to achieve. In this example the firm's short run is perhaps a period of months.

In contrast, if a firm is managing an airport, then the short run might be a period of several years. The terminal space – a fixed factor of production determining the capacity of an airport in terms of flight departures, arrivals, cargo and other retail space – takes many years to increase in size.

Of course, capital can sometimes be treated as a variable factor. For instance in a small services firm, capital such as the firm's computers, phones and office space could be rented at short notice, and so be treated as variable. Whereas if staff were employed on fixed-term contracts, in the short run labour would be treated as the fixed factor. In this example the short-run period would be determined by the length of the fixed term in the employment contract.

In the *long run*, firms can vary *all* factor inputs as they wish. So a firm has the greatest opportunity to reduce average cost in the long run. In the long run, there is no fixed factor of production and the firm is free to adjust the quantities of all inputs to find the cheapest mix. Firms may recruit more key personnel, invest in items of capital equipment such as new factories or warehouses, or buy a 'greenfield' site for a new factory. In modelling firms in the long run, it is still assumed that each firm is operating with a *given* technology available to all firms.

In the *short run*, the firm is constrained; some inputs are fixed that may reduce its ability to minimise average cost. If a factor is fixed, then the cost associated with using that factor will not change with output. A cost that does not change with output is called a **fixed cost**. In the short run, therefore, the firm's costs can be separated into two categories: fixed costs and **variable costs**. Variable costs change with output. They include the cost of factors that increase with a rise in output or decrease with a fall in output, such as raw materials and hours of labour.

Fixed costs
Fixed costs are costs that do not vary with the level of output.

Variable costs
Variable costs are costs that vary with the level of output.

To understand how costs of production change with output, one needs to know how average cost can change in the short run and in the long run. To do this, I will examine short-run average cost (SRAC) and long-run average cost (LRAC). The next section analyses costs in the long run, when all factors of production can change and therefore the firm has no fixed costs. Section 7 will investigate costs in the short run.

5   Long-run average cost curves

To help to analyse a firm's costs, economists use graphs called cost curves. Cost curves are a method of representing how production costs, such as LRAC, vary with quantity of output. The cost curves show how cost, on the vertical axis, changes with the quantity of output, on the horizontal axis. As used here, 'quantity of output' means the quantity produced in a given period, for instance the number of units produced per day or per week. So moving along the horizontal axis from left to right shows how the firm's costs change for increasing quantities of output. Cost curves are usually drawn using smoothed curves suggesting that costs change gradually with increases in output, although in practice their behaviour might be less smooth.

The LRAC curve in Figure 11.5 shows one example of how a firm's average cost can change with output. The exact shape of the LRAC curve will vary with the technology used by a firm. In the example shown in Figure 11.5, as output increases, the average cost of production falls continuously, so the LRAC curve slopes down over the whole output range. The firm benefits from a reduction in average cost as the level of output increases.

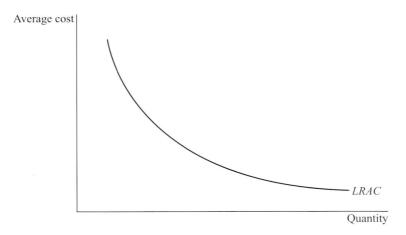

Figure 11.5   A long-run average cost curve showing cost falling as output increases

5.1   Economies of scale

If the LRAC curve slopes downwards over a range of output, it is said that over that range of output, the firm is benefiting from economies of scale. In Figure 11.5, the firm is benefiting from economies of scale over the whole output range shown. Economies of scale imply that as output increases, LRAC falls.

I will discuss two examples of how firms can achieve **economies of scale**, first through specialisation and second through economies of increased dimensions. Achieving economies of scale via specialisation occurs when there is a division of labour in a firm, so that the production process is divided into narrowly defined discrete tasks. Discrete tasks can be allocated to individuals or groups of workers who learn to become highly proficient in their set task. The firm gains because each worker becomes a specialist in a particular task, and will be more efficient than an unspecialised 'jack of all trades' worker. Specialised workers increase efficiency; the firm becomes more productive and average cost falls. The firm also gains from a reduction in training costs, as it is no longer necessary to train each worker on all stages of the production process. Economies of scale arise from specialisation because as output increases, it is possible to break up the production process into smaller and smaller tasks, so that workers become increasingly specialised and efficient, reducing average cost.

Economies of scale
Economies of scale exist when LRAC falls as output increases.

Economies of scale via specialisation are one reason why a firm like Apple outsources assembly of their products. In addition to the cost saving from low wages, the outsourcing of the assembly process to vast production sites means that the division of labour in the production process results in factory workers specialising in discrete stages of the assembly process. In this case, specialisation increases the speed of production, as workers become faster at assembling different parts of the final product. Other efficiencies are gained from another type of division of labour: a large number of assembly line workers can be managed by relatively few staff.

Foxconn iPhone assembly line

(Source: Naseer, 2012)

Another example of economies of scale is a concept known as *economies of increased dimensions*. For example, enormous container ships and very large lorries can transport goods at lower average cost per unit than is possible using smaller ships and vehicles. As the size of the ship or lorry increases, its carrying capacity rises by a greater factor than the materials needed to make and run it. Industrial plant displays the same effect: an extension to a factory that doubles the output capacity of the firm may be possible without doubling the maintenance and usage costs.

Container ships are a good example of how firms can achieve economies of increased dimensions. For instance, *The Economist* (2011b) reported that the Maersk Line container ship *Eleonora*, which is over four football pitches long with an engine as powerful as 1000 family cars, was one of the largest ever built. The 7500 containers aboard could be transported with a minimum of 13 crew. At the time of launch, analysts predicted that other shipping firms with smaller vessels would struggle to match the lower costs attainable from such economies of scale. As each container on board can hold 70 000 T-shirts, when fully loaded the average cost of transporting an individual T-shirt on the *Eleonora* from China to Europe was estimated at only 2.5 US cents

Top: the *Eleonora Maersk*, one of the world's largest container ships.
Bottom: a supermarket warehouse at Christmas.

(Sources: Johnston, 2011; Bazley, 2010)

(Johnston, 2011). In response, other shipping firms subsequently placed orders for even larger vessels.

If a firm offshores production, then it may need to transport goods to markets that are a large distance away. The price of transporting goods from China to the USA or Europe is part of the cost of offshoring production. Rises in the cost of fuel increase transport costs and make offshoring more expensive. Economies of increased dimensions help to reduce transport costs and reduce average cost. This has been an advantage for firms that offshore production of electronics and clothing goods to China. Provided that firms ship their product at a large enough scale, the cost of transporting goods from China to Europe and the USA remains relatively low.

5.2   Limits to economies of scale

Figure 11.5 illustrates a firm achieving continuous economies of scale. In this situation there is every incentive, in the form of ever lower average cost, for the firm to continue to expand output. In such a case, it is plausible that a single firm could supply the whole market at a lower cost than could be achieved by a number of firms in competition with each other. Chapter 14 examines situations when a single firm does in fact supply the entire market. In such cases, a single firm can have significant control of how a market operates, so such a firm often attracts careful oversight from governments.

Minimum efficient scale

Minimum efficient scale refers to the output at which long-run average cost first reaches its minimum level as output rises.

Diseconomies of scale

Diseconomies of scale exist when long-run average cost rises as output increases.

Industry

An industry is a group of firms producing a broadly related range of goods using similar technologies.

However, for most firms there are limits to economies of scale. The LRAC curve depicted in Figure 11.6 shows a more typical scenario for a firm. As the firm's output increases from a low level, average cost decreases because of economies of scale. As output continues to increase, the curve flattens; average cost remains constant as output increases. The flattening of the curve indicates that economies of scale have been exhausted; increasing output will not reduce the unit cost. The flat part of the curve shows that unit cost is constant as output increases. The level of output at which the curve becomes flat, Q_{MES}, is known as the **minimum efficient scale (MES)**. The MES marks the size of the firm beyond which there are no cost advantages to be reaped from operating at a larger scale; it is the point at which all economies of scale have been taken up. Figure 11.6 shows that as the firm produces higher levels of output, average cost starts to rise. The firm is now experiencing diseconomies of scale. **Diseconomies of scale** arise from the disadvantages that large-scale production may entail. The major sources of diseconomies of scale are coordination problems that beset management in large bureaucratic organisations.

The MES will vary across different **industries** and has important consequences for the structure of the market, particularly regarding how many firms operate in that market. To see why, first I need to

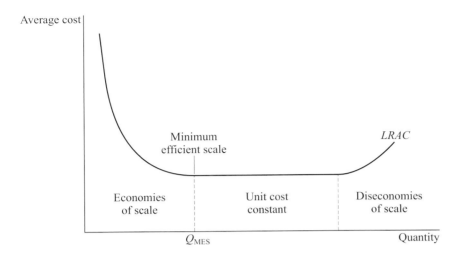

Figure 11.6   LRAC curve displaying economies and diseconomies of scale

determine the total output of a particular good or service (the market size) and then compare it to the MES for a firm. For example, the total production of electricity is determined by summing the output for every firm producing electricity. Suppose that the MES for an electricity producer is relatively high compared to the total output of electricity production. To achieve MES, an electricity producer needs to produce a high level of output relative to the total size of the market. In such a situation, there is little room for other producers; it is more efficient for a few firms to generate all the electricity required. In fact, in 2008 the UK's retail electricity market, from which most households buy electricity, was dominated by six firms accounting for 99% of electricity sold (Department of Energy and Climate Change (DECC), 2010). As the MES is high relative to the market size, each firm produces electricity for a large proportion of the electricity market.

Activity 11.3

Suppose that the MES is low relative to the size of the market. Would production be shared between a few firms, or many firms?

Answer

If the MES is low relative to the size of the market, then as no cost saving advantage can be gained from producing beyond the MES, the market is likely to include many firms. Increases in output beyond the MES not only produce no reductions in average cost, but could result in rising average cost if the firm encounters diseconomies of scale. For example, consider the market for hairdressing in the UK. The market is dominated by many small firms (i.e. many small independent salons); the MES is low relative to the total market.

6   Technological change

> An essential question for the economic future of a country is not
> only what it produces, but how it goes about producing it.

(Lerner, 2009, p. 44)

The analysis in the previous section assumed a given technology.
However, Sections 3 and 4 described how advances in technology can
increase a firm's productivity, such that existing levels of output can be
achieved with lower inputs and reduced total cost. Technological change
can be represented diagrammatically as a *downward shift* in the LRAC
curve as shown in Figure 11.7. This might occur when the firm
upgrades by investing in more advanced machinery that needs less
electricity, fewer operators and fewer raw materials to produce the same
output. The shift of $LRAC_0$ downwards to $LRAC_1$ in Figure 11.7
shows that long-run average cost has fallen at each and every level of
output, or scale of production. For instance, at output Q_0, a shift from
$LRAC_0$ to $LRAC_1$ results in a fall of average cost from C_0 to C_1. Firms
may expect average cost to fall in the long run, provided that they are
prepared to make the necessary investment in new production
processes.

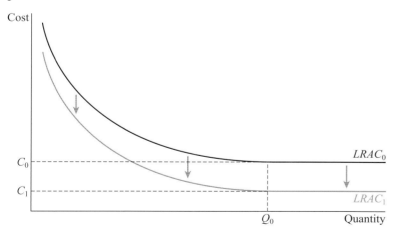

Figure 11.7   A downward shift in LRAC

6.1   Learning processes and the firm's learning curve

You saw in Section 2.1 that even Chinese producers face increasing labour costs. In response to rising wages, some firms – such as Foxconn itself – are planning to replace workers with high-tech automated machinery, which could assemble final goods more quickly than existing workers could. As Figure 11.7 illustrates, introducing an automated process might reduce average cost, even after allowing for the cost of the new technology.

> The rows of rectangular capsules lined up in a factory in Dongguan in southern China look like sleeping compartments for astronauts. The 24 Japanese-made knitting machines in the factory of Hong Kong-based Milo's Knitwear will soon be joined by four more. In total, the machines cost the family-owned company $1.8m.
>
> A factory with neat rows of machines and just two workers is the antithesis of the typical image of Chinese manufacturing. At other facilities in the industrial province of Guangdong, just across the border from Hong Kong, thousands of workers are typically hunched over their work stations making everything from iPhones to running shoes.
>
> [...]
>
> Last year, Terry Gou, the boss of Foxconn, the Taiwanese company that makes iPhones and iPads, which employs about 1m people in China, interrupted a party for his workers to say he planned to introduce 1m robots across the company's Chinese factories in three years. While few bosses are making such grand pronouncements, more and more are weighing the pros and cons of automation.
>
> (Jacob and Mishkin, 2012)

Activity 11.4

If production technology is available that reduces unit costs, why couldn't all factories in China upgrade?

Answer

It is likely that many Chinese factories will upgrade production processes. However, while the production function approach assumes that new technology can immediately be adopted by firms once available, in practice it often requires time to learn how to operate new tools or machinery processes. Historically, Chinese manufacturing has specialised in labour-intensive processes, obtaining economies of scale from building vast factories using a large supply of cheap labour. As labour becomes more expensive, manufacturing in China may become more capital-intensive, increasing the input of new machinery and technology, reducing the input of labour in the production process. However, a vital element of technology is the knowledge of how to exploit its potential.

The example in Figure 11.7 implicitly assumes that firms know how to use new technology, i.e. the more sophisticated machines. However, do firms always know how to obtain maximum efficiency from new technology?

Technology can be viewed as consisting of bodies of knowledge that are necessary to produce particular artefacts. The hardware (for example, physical machinery) is important, but human knowledge of how to operate the hardware is also very important and is included as part of a firm's 'technology'. Learning how to use the hardware most effectively is therefore a crucial capacity for firms. It is likely that the downward shift in the LRAC curve shown in Figure 11.7 occurs only incrementally over time as engineers learn to operate the new machinery effectively. The *learning curve* in Figure 11.8 (overleaf) captures the idea that turning technological change to competitive advantage is a skill that needs to be learned like any other with practice over time, through a process that economists call **learning-by-doing**.

The learning curve in Figure 11.8 indicates that productivity benefits from new technology take time to be fully realised. Once a worker has practised a task, he will make fewer mistakes, reduce wastage and incrementally modify or improve processes, such that average cost falls as output per worker increases. Whenever there is repetition of activities, whether producing goods or services, there is potential to be gained from learning how to improve. Figure 11.8 depicts the idea of a learning curve. It shows a fall in average cost that occurs as learning

Learning-by-doing
Learning-by-doing refers to a fall in unit costs as cumulative output increases over time.

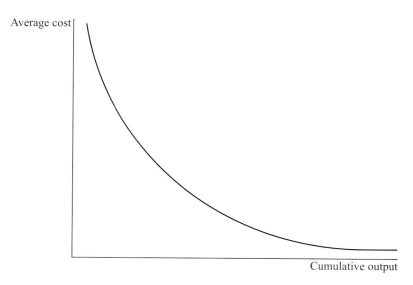

Figure 11.8   A learning curve

takes place cumulatively. Average cost falls as the firm accumulates experience of producing output *over time*.

Activity 11.5

What is the main difference between the learning curve in Figure 11.8, and Figure 11.5 that showed economies of scale?

Answer

Figure 11.8 plots average cost against *cumulative output*, the idea being that *over time*, the more output a firm produces the better or the more efficient it will become at producing a particular good or service. The costs per unit of output will fall as firms learn by doing. The expectation of the learning curve is that over time a firm will progressively move along the curve to the right – average cost will fall as experience of production process increases with output. The learning curve is not the same as the LRAC curve shown in Figure 11.5; the LRAC curve represents average cost for a *possible range of output in a given time*. In Figure 11.8, the benefits of learning occur cumulatively as experience of the production process grows *over time*.

---

7   Costs in the short run

This section looks at how costs are modelled in the short run, when at least one factor input in the production function is fixed in amount. A firm may still change the level of output, but it cannot change the input of its fixed factors. Therefore the firm is constrained by its inability to change its fixed factors, and the mix of inputs into the production process is not necessarily optimal.

The challenge of dealing with short-run constraints is a situation that was faced by US company DuPont in the period following the economic crisis of 2008. Part of DuPont's business provided paint for 30% of automobiles produced in the USA. The automotive industry was quickly hit by the financial crisis, as orders for new cars fell rapidly in response to a drop in consumer confidence and restrictions to consumer credit.

Activity 11.6

Imagine that you are the CEO of DuPont. How could you reduce average production costs in response to a sharp reduction in orders?

Answer

A reduction in orders is likely to mean that firms reduce output too. If output falls, then fewer inputs are required. In the long run, all inputs can be reduced and costs minimised for any level of output. The problem is that long-run changes require time. If a firm has a rapid reduction in orders, then it may wish to reduce output immediately; the changes are made in the short run. In the short run, only the firm's variable costs can be changed. The fixed costs in the short run will remain constant.

In the short run, DuPont targeted production inputs that could be cut quickly in response to falling order books. Cost-cutting focused on reducing the variable cost that would not be fully utilised as output fell. Raw material costs reduce as the level of output falls, and small savings were made from reducing expenses budgets and travel costs, but the bulk of cost savings were made from laying off short-term contract labourers, dismissing thousands of workers, and asking others to take several weeks of unpaid leave (Charan, 2009; Loomis and Burke, 2010).

Many of the costs associated with labour can be considered variable. In the DuPont example, the firm could adjust its labour input much faster than it would be able to reduce the fixed costs of the business, by reducing factory spaces and buildings. In the long term, plans were developed to reduce the costs of fixed factors of production in the business, which meant reorganising its manufacturing plants. DuPont saw cost-cutting as vital for its survival, but many other businesses, large and small, have followed a similar cost-cutting strategy of asking staff to work fewer hours or take unpaid leave to cope with falling revenues in the short run.

7.1 Analysing short-run constraints

The production function tells us that firms must use more inputs to increase their output. In the short run, a firm can change the input of only its variable factors. For instance, imagine a firm that combines raw materials, labour and machinery on an assembly line to manufacture a good. In the short run, the firm's machinery is a fixed factor of production. It would take several months to change the firm's manufacturing machinery and processes. In the short run, weekly output can be increased only if the firm combines more materials and labour with the existing machinery. The firm will need to hire more workers to increase the hours of work and increase its weekly output, for instance by speeding up the assembly line.

7.2 Returns to labour

Activity 11.7

Based on what you have read about the short run, if a firm recruits an additional worker at the start of every week and measures the increase in weekly output, would you expect the output to rise by the same amount each week?

Answer

When a firm has very few employees, adding additional workers may mean that the production and assembly line can run faster and, up to a point, extra workers can share equipment. Initially, as the firm adds more employees, each employee contributes progressively more to total output. If you start with one worker producing 4 units, adding a second may increase total output by 5 units and adding a third may increase total output by more than 5 units. The firm would then be said to be experiencing *increasing returns to labour*.

This can arise when initially equipment is underutilised. For instance, in 2012 Jaguar Land Rover would have expected to gain increasing returns to labour by switching to a 24-hour production process, introducing a night shift and recruiting 1000 new workers to make use of the firm's existing capital (Kollewe, 2012).

Table 11.1 shows an example of increasing returns to labour. The first two columns of the table show how changes in the number of workers influence total output; I have assumed that adding a third worker results in an increase of 6 units.

Table 11.1   An example of increasing returns to labour

Number of workers (units) (a)	Total output per week (units) (b)	Increase resulting from additional worker = marginal product (c)	Average product (units per worker) (d) = (b) / (a)
0	0	0	0
1	4	4	4 (= 4/1)
2	9	5	4.5 (= 9/2)
3	15	6	5 (= 15/3)
4	25	?	?

Notice that the third column shows how much each *additional* worker increases total output. This is an example of marginal analysis – the *change* in output for a *unit change* in labour input (where a unit is defined here as the number of workers) is known as the marginal product of labour. For example, when the firm adds a second worker, output increases from 4 units to 9 units, output increases by 5 units. The **marginal product of labour** for adding a second worker is 5 units, as shown in column (c). I have also calculated the average product of labour, i.e. the total output divided by the total labour input. Average product of labour can be used as a measure of average worker productivity. If the average product of labour increases, then on average each worker is producing greater output.

Marginal product of labour
The marginal product of labour is defined as the additional units of output gained from the input of one more unit of labour.

Activity 11.8

Complete Table 11.1 to show the marginal and average product of labour when a fourth worker is added to the firm.

Answer

The data show that adding a fourth worker causes output to rise by an additional 10 units (i.e. 25 − 15); the marginal product of adding a fourth worker is 10 units. Together, four workers produce a total of 25 units, so the average product per worker is 6.25 units (= 25/4). Using marginal analysis, the firm can see whether it is benefiting from adding labour input; it can analyse whether it has increasing returns to labour.

Unfortunately, increasing returns to labour usually have limits. In the short run, as the firm continues to increase labour, a point will be reached after which adding more workers brings successively smaller increases in output. For example, if output rises by 10 units after adding a fourth employee, but then rises by only 8 units for a fifth employee and by 6 units for a sixth employee, then the output gained from adding each extra labourer is decreasing. Although total output has risen by a further 24 units (i.e. 10 + 8 + 6), output is rising by progressively smaller amounts with the addition of each new worker. The marginal product of labour is decreasing with each additional worker. In this situation the firm is experiencing *diminishing returns to labour*.

Diminishing returns to labour can occur once too many workers try to operate a single assembly line and end up getting in each other's way. One way to think about this situation is that diminishing returns to variable factors arise as the use of fixed factors of production (machinery in this example) becomes less efficient. Ideally, the firm would invest in more machinery, but in this example capital is a fixed factor, so diminishing returns to variable factors (in this case labour) pose a serious constraint on the expansion of output for the firm in the short run.

7.3   Marginal cost

Just as marginal analysis can be used to see how the marginal product of labour changes when workers are added to the production line, a marginal cost analysis can be used to examine how costs change with output. **Marginal cost** analysis examines how much it costs a firm to produce an additional unit of output.

If the firm has increasing returns to labour, then assuming that all workers are paid the same, adding each additional worker results in progressively greater increases to output *and a fall* in marginal cost; the cost of producing one extra unit of output is falling. The formula for calculating marginal cost is

$$\text{marginal cost} = \frac{\text{change in total costs}}{\text{change in quantity of output}}$$

Table 11.2 shows how the weekly costs for my example firm change with different levels of output. I have assumed a fixed cost of £500, and shown how variable costs change with each unit of output produced.

Marginal cost
Marginal cost is the increase in total costs as a result of producing one additional unit of output.

Table 11.2   Short-run cost calculation (figures rounded to nearest whole £)

Fixed cost (£)	Variable cost (£)	Total costs (£)	Total output (units)	Marginal cost (£/unit)	Average cost (£/unit)
500	0	500	0	–	–
500	100	600	1	100 = (600–500)/ (1–0)	600 = 600/1
500	195	695	2	95 = (695–600)/ (2–1)	348 = 695/2
500	285	785	3	90	262
500	370	870	4	85	218

Activity 11.9

Check that you understand how to calculate the marginal cost in Table 11.2.

Answer

For example, the marginal cost for producing the fourth unit of output is shown as £85 – i.e. the change in total cost resulting from a change in production from 3 to 4 units is £85. This can be confirmed using the formula

$$\text{marginal cost of producing 4th unit} = \frac{\text{change in total costs}}{\text{change in quantity of output}}$$
$$= \frac{870 - 785}{4 - 3}$$
$$= 85$$

Notice that Table 11.2 shows how costs change for *each unit* of output, so I can calculate marginal cost by subtracting from each value of total costs the value shown in the previous row. This is because in this example the change in quantity of output is always one unit. However, in practice firms may not have such detailed data, in which case the formula above can be used to estimate the marginal cost of producing an additional unit of output.

7.4   The relationship between marginal and average cost

Table 11.2 shows that when marginal cost is less than average cost, average cost also falls. It makes sense that if the cost of producing an extra unit of output is less than the existing average cost, then the average cost of production will also fall as output increases.

However, if output continues to rise, then in the short run this firm will encounter diminishing returns to labour. Each new worker added to the firm will contribute a progressively smaller rise in output. Marginal cost will also start to rise: the cost of producing an extra unit of output increases because each additional worker added to the firm contributes progressively less to total output.

But what happens to average cost when marginal cost starts to rise?

This is best explained using Figure 11.9. The blue line shows the short-run marginal cost (SRMC) curve for a firm, plotting how marginal cost changes with output. This line reflects the discussion above: when the firm has increasing returns to labour, marginal cost falls as output increases. Once output is greater than Q_1, the firm encounters diminishing returns to labour and marginal cost rises: each additional unit of output costs more than the previous one.

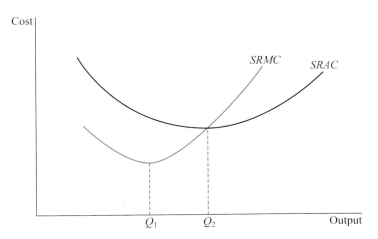

Figure 11.9 Short-run average cost (SRAC) and short-run marginal cost (SRMC) curves

The black line in Figure 11.9 is the short-run average cost (SRAC) curve, which has a distinctive U-shape. The shape of the SRAC curve is related to the shape of the SRMC curve. Initially, the SRAC decreases as output increases. This is because marginal cost is *less* than average cost, so every additional unit of output produced costs less than average, thus as output increases, average cost falls too. Marginal cost is at a minimum at Q_1, but the SRAC continues to fall until output reaches Q_2. As output increases from Q_1 to Q_2, average cost continues to fall because marginal cost, although it is rising, *is still lower than average cost.*

The minimum value of average cost occurs when marginal cost and average cost are equal. This is shown in Figure 11.9 at the point where the SRAC and SRMC curves cross. Average cost and marginal cost are equal when output is Q_2 (this occurs at the minimum SRAC). Once marginal cost is greater than average cost, producing more output will cause average cost to increase.

A general way to think about the SRAC curve in Figure 11.9 is that average cost decreases as the firm produces more efficiently. At low levels of output, the firm has fixed factors that are underutilised and not being used efficiently. For instance, if output is low, machinery might sit idle. However, the cost of machinery is fixed, and the firm still has to pay for it even if it sits idle. As output increases, the firm can make better use of fixed factors, they are being used more efficiently, and average cost falls. Once output passes Q_1, gains from efficiency progressively decrease, but nevertheless there are still gains, so efficiency continues to rise until Q_2. Once output passes Q_2, expanding output becomes less efficient given the fixed factors available, and average cost begins to rise.

7.5   The relationship between SRAC and LRAC

The previous subsection showed how a firm's ability, in the short run, to change average cost in response to output is constrained by fixed factors giving rise to a distinctive U-shaped SRAC curve. However, in Section 5, I modelled average cost in the long run, when the firm can minimise costs because even factors that were fixed in the short run can be varied. In the 'here and now', a firm must operate on its SRAC, even if it plans to reduce costs in the future. So what is the link between short-run and long-run average costs?

One way to link LRAC and SRAC curves is to imagine that the LRAC curves connect together a series of SRAC curves representing different levels of inputs of fixed factors of production, or in other words different scales of production. For instance, Figure 11.10 shows the cost curves for a firm that initially has a single small factory, and operates in the short run on $SRAC_1$. In the long run, the firm increases factory space on two different occasions. After each expansion, the factory will operate with a new SRAC curve. If the expansion is associated with economies of scale, as represented in Figure 11.10, then the SRAC curves will shift down and to the right.

Imagine that the firm starts with $SRAC_1$. Then after the first expansion, it moves to $SRAC_2$, and the second expansion results in $SRAC_3$. Over time, as all factor inputs can be varied (including the size of the factory), the firm will move along the LRAC curve. In the present, the firm must work with its existing SRAC curve related to existing fixed factors of production.

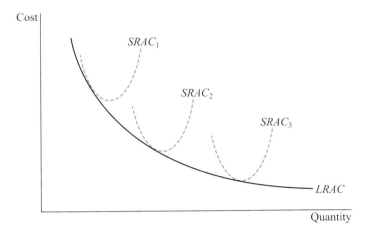

Figure 11.10   The relationship between LRAC and SRAC curves, in the case of economies of scale

Notice that each SRAC curve in Figure 11.10 is tangential to the LRAC curve – that is, it just touches the LRAC curve without crossing it. Also, each SRAC curve does not necessarily touch the LRAC curve at the minimum value of the SRAC curve. In the long run, the firm can find the optimal amount of labour and capital to produce any given output, so in effect the LRAC curve shows the minimum average cost possible at every level of output.

In drawing a smooth LRAC curve, I have assumed that firms can incrementally (or continuously) change inputs of all factors of production – in reality, it is often the case that some factors (like the size of a building), must be varied in distinct stages. So in practice, it is useful to think of the LRAC curve as a line connecting together a series of points related to different stages of a firm's expansion.

8   China in context: a firm's costs and its environment

The formal analysis of costs in the previous three sections has looked inside firms. However, firms' costs are influenced by the external environment. For example, being located in China offers firms a cost advantage simply because of the low wages in that country. But low wages are not the only reason for the Chinese success story. The creation of a successful business environment has required heavy and rapid investment in infrastructure. The pace of change in China in the last 30 years has rarely been far from the news. Vast construction projects, such as those detailed in reports on the number of power stations completed per week or the number of planned airports, capture the imagination:

> China is building and expanding airports at an unprecedented pace, one that matches its roaring economy. The country will spend $17.4 billion over the next five years to build 42 airports in cities stretching from the Russian border in the northeast to the high Tibetan plateau in the southwest. Chinese planners have orders to expand 73 airports and to move 11.
>
> (MacLeod, 2006)

Much of the change in China's infrastructure and the pace of development has been strongly supported by state investment. China's government has encouraged a rapid development of industrial locations, encouraging firms to offshore to China, relaxing planning restrictions and providing tax incentives for firms to locate activity in coastal regions. The pace of change has been rapid for industrial locations, and China's GDP growth performance has been strong. Firms operating in China have taken advantage of economies of scale arising from the large Chinese economy, and have undergone rapid expansion in output, resulting in low unit costs.

China's business environment has also benefited from access to advanced technology imported through investment by foreign firms. Firms offshoring to China have brought both the technology hardware and experience of production processes to Chinese locations. Local factors such as a supply of greenfield land, skilled labour and government support have helped to accelerate long-run changes, to help facilitate catch-up. Many firms offshoring to China have used knowledge and experience from previous endeavours to maximise advantages from economies of scale; rather than firms incrementally expanding existing production sites, vast new purpose-built sites in coastal regions of China have been developed.

The process of developing industrial regions in China has an additional benefit shared by all firms located in these areas, known as external economies. Firms sharing close geographical locations, particularly those producing related products and services, can gain cost-saving advantages from sharing experiences with learning new technology or sharing use of infrastructure, such as improvements to transport networks and other utilities. In addition, the geographical closeness of firms engaged in similar types of production can generate mutual benefit because they are able to access a pool of specialised labour. By locating in the same area, firms create a skilled workforce that can meet the needs of an industry and reduce the cost of recruitment and training for all firms.

Economists have long recognised that firms can benefit from external economies that arise from sources outside the firm (Marshall, 1920). External economies often arise in industries that are expanding because it becomes easier for firms to source different inputs into the production process. External economies contributed to the development of high-technology areas like Silicon Valley in California, and played an important role in establishing the microcomputing industry that later helped to generate firms like Microsoft and Apple (Langlois, 1992).

As the concentration of an industry in a region of China grows, all firms in that location can potentially share the benefit of external economies. For example, the availability of qualified engineers in industrial areas of China helps to provide access to specialised labour input into the firm. The *New York Times* analysis 'How the U.S. lost out on iPhone work' observed that:

> Another critical advantage for Apple was that China provided engineers at a scale the United States could not match. Apple's executives had estimated that about 8,700 industrial engineers were needed to oversee and guide the 200,000 assembly-line workers eventually involved in manufacturing iPhones. The company's

analysts had forecast it would take as long as nine months to find that many qualified engineers in the United States.

In China, it took 15 days.

(Duhigg and Bradsher, 2012)

Some locations offer attractive rewards

Similarly the Foxconn facility that assembles iPhones in Shenzhen, China, benefits from agglomeration economies due to the scale of other manufacturing activity nearby. For instance, the proximity of suppliers to the Foxconn operation helps to reduce transport costs, but also reduces the time cost of searching for suppliers of raw materials or intermediate goods:

'The entire supply chain is in China now,' said [a] former high-ranking Apple executive. 'You need a thousand rubber gaskets? That's the factory next door. You need a million screws? That factory is a block away. You need that screw made a little bit different? It will take three hours.'

(Duhigg and Bradsher, 2012)

These examples suggest that locating production in China offers firms not only lower labour costs but also efficient management of their production costs. Producing in the USA would mean that Apple should treat industrial engineers (and many other inputs) as a fixed factor in the short run because it is difficult to recruit them quickly, whereas in areas of China benefiting from external economies, varying the quantity of engineers is quick and the firm can operate on its long-run cost curves, without short-run inefficiencies.

As areas of China become increasingly developed, the cost of factors will likely rise (for instance, wages and land prices at the time of writing are increasing, while their availability is decreasing), although production processes will change; for instance, some labour may be replaced by machinery, and the best available technology may be installed. External economies also have limits; for instance, road networks can become congested if the concentration of industry is too high. It may prove difficult to maintain a rapid movement along the LRAC curve as firms encounter rising constraints.

9   Conclusion

This chapter has examined how processes occurring within a firm can be captured in economic models. It outlined economic theory related to production and cost, paying special attention to average cost. It also introduced some basic microeconomic concepts in the supply side of the economy, such as the production function and cost curve analysis. It has shown how the production process can be modelled in terms of long-run and short-run cost curves, and shown how different types of factor inputs influence the opportunity firms have to manage their production costs.

Most importantly the chapter has introduced the use of average and marginal analysis – two important techniques that will be required in the remainder of Part 4. However, this chapter has not considered the price of goods and services, or the price of production inputs that are determined by market forces. The next chapter will look at the interaction between output and price by evaluating supply and demand together.

References

Banister, J. and Cook, G. (2011) 'China's employment and compensation costs in manufacturing through 2008', *Monthly Labor Review*, March, pp. 39–52; available online at www.bls.gov/opub/mlr/2011/03/art4full.pdf (Accessed 28 December 2012).

Bazley, L. (2010) '24 million customers, three million cases and four-and-a-half miles of conveyer belts', *Daily Mail*, 14 December, [online] www.dailymail.co.uk/news/article-1338281/24-million-customers-million-cases-half-miles-conveyor-belts-The-supermarket-warehouse-thats-gearing-Christmas-rush.html (Accessed 28 December 2012).

Bhattacharya, A., Bradtke, T., Hemerling, J., Lebreton, J., Mosquet, X., Rupf, I., Sirkin, H.L. and Young, D. (2004) *Capturing Global Advantage: How Leading Industrial Companies are Transforming their Industries by Sourcing and Selling in China, India, and Other Low-cost Countries*, Boston, MA, Boston Consulting Group.

Bureau of Labor Statistics (2012) *International Comparisons of Hourly Compensation Costs in Manufacturing*, [online] www.bls.gov/web/ichcc.supp.toc.htm (Accessed 2 February 2013).

Charan, R. (2009) 'DuPont's swift response to the financial crisis', Bloomberg BusinessWeek, 7 January, [online] www.businessweek.com/stories/2009-01-07/duponts-swift-response-to-the-financial-crisis (Accessed 28 December 2012).

Department of Energy and Climate Change (DECC) (2010) *Energy Market Assessment*, [online] www.decc.gov.uk/assets/decc/1_20100324143202_e_@@_budget2010energymarket.pdf (Accessed 28 December 2012).

Duhigg, C. and Bradsher, K. (2012) 'How the U.S. lost out on iPhone work', *New York Times*, 21 January, [online] www.nytimes.com/2012/01/22/business/apple-america-and-a-squeezed-middle-class.html?_r=4&ref=general&src=me&pagewanted=all (Accessed 28 December 2012).

The Economist (2011a) 'Slicing an apple', 10 August, [online] www.economist.com/blogs/dailychart/2011/08/apple-and-samsungs-symbiotic-relationship (Accessed 28 December 2012).

The Economist (2011b) 'Economies of scale made steel', 12 November, [online] www.economist.com/node/21538156 (Accessed 2 February 2013).

Guarraia, P. and Saenz, H. (2011) 'Delivering savings that stick', *CFO Journal*, 27 September, [online] http://webreprints.djreprints.com/2901440484220.html (Accessed 28 December 2012).

Hunt, K. (2012) 'Apple and Foxconn plan raises bar for Chinese factories', BBC News, 4 April, [online] www.bbc.co.uk/news/business-17584523 (Accessed 28 December 2012).

Jacob, R. and Mishkin, S. (2012) 'China turns to robots as labour costs rise', *Financial Times*, 4 October, [online] www.ft.com/cms/s/0/2a804e04-0c95-11e2-

a776-00144feabdc0.html?ftcamp=published_links%2Frss%2Fworld_asia-pacific_china%2Ffeed%2F%2Fproduct (Accessed 2 February 2013).

Johnston, M. (2011) 'Economies of scale: sending a T shirt from China to Europe for 2.5 cents', Econfix, 21 November, [online] http://econfix.wordpress.com/2011/11/21/economies-of-scale-sending-a-t-shirt-from-china-to-europe-for-2-5-cents (Accessed 28 December 2012).

Kollewe, J. (2012) 'Jaguar Land Rover shifts to 24-hour production to keep pace with demand', *The Guardian*, 14 August, [online] www.guardian.co.uk/business/2012/aug/14/jaguar-land-rover-24hour-production-jobs (Accessed 28 December 2012).

Langlois, R.N. (1992) 'External economies and economic progress: the case of the microcomputer industry', *Business History Review*, vol. 66, no. 1.

Lerner, J. (2009) *Boulevard of Broken Dreams: Why Public Efforts to Boost Entrepreneurship and Venture Capital have Failed and What to Do About It*, Princeton, NJ, Princeton University Press.

Loomis, C.J. and Burke, D. (2010) 'Can Ellen Kullman make DuPont great again?', *Fortune*, vol. 161, no. 6, pp. 156–63.

MacLeod, C. (2006) 'China in a flurry of airport construction', *USA Today*, 2 October, [online] www.usatoday.com/travel/flights/2006-10-02-china-airports-usat_x.htm (Accessed 28 December 2012).

Marshall, A. (1920) *Principles of Economics*, London, Macmillan and Co. Ltd; available online at www.econlib.org/library/Marshall/marP.html (Accessed 28 December 2012).

Naseer, A. (2012) 'Apple gives ABCNews "unprecedented" access to Foxconn factories in China', 22 February, [online] http://jailbreakstory.com/2012/02/apple-gives-abcnews-unprecedented-access-to-foxconn-factories-in-china (Accessed 28 December 2012).

Nelson, R.R. and Pack, H. (1999) 'The Asian miracle and modern growth theory', *Economic Journal*, vol. 109, no. 457, pp. 416–36.

Trading Economics (2012) *Chinese Yuan*, [online] www.tradingeconomics.com/china/currency (Accessed 28 December 2012).

Tsui, E. and Rabinovitch, S. (2012) 'China pushes minimum wage rises', *Financial Times*, 4 January, [online] www.ft.com/cms/s/0/847b0990-36a2-11e1-9ca3-00144feabdc0.html#axzz252CKrd1l (Accessed 28 December 2012).

United Nations Conference on Trade and Development (UNCTAD) (2012) *International Trade in Goods and Services*, UNCTADstat database, [online] http://unctadstat.unctad.org/ReportFolders/reportFolders.aspx?sCS_referer=&sCS_ChosenLang=en (Accessed 28 December 2012).

Wright, J., Sahni, M. and Zamora, R. (2011) *Wage Increases in China: Should Multinationals Rethink their Manufacturing and Sourcing Strategies?*, Accenture, [online] www.accenture.com/SiteCollectionDocuments/PDF/Accenture_Wage_Increases_in_China.pdf (Accessed 28 December 2012).

Chapter 12
Market forces

Gary Slater

Contents

1 Introduction

Plunging prices set to trigger tech boom

The tumbling prices of everything from flatscreen TVs to ereaders have become a bane for makers of digital hardware, even as they enjoy soaring interest in their widening range of mobile devices.

Yet falling prices are also set to be a trigger for the long-awaited boom in access to digital media, as a new wave of connected TVs, computers and mobile devices start to change the habits of consumers.

'Access points are becoming so affordable,' said Richard Doherty, an analyst at Envisioneering. Along with simpler ways of finding media online, 'it will reduce consumer indecision and lead to higher sell-through at retail'.

(Waters, 2012)

Why do the prices of goods and services change? How do the decisions of firms and individual consumers impact on market prices, and what impact do these market price changes have, in turn, on producers and consumers? The news story in the quote above provides an example of a dynamic consumer goods market in which technology, costs and prices are all changing rapidly. Consequently, a change in consumer behaviour and market demand is expected to follow from the fall in price. But how are you to try to make sense of the complex interplay of these different forces? This chapter provides an analysis of market forces and the price mechanism with which you can begin to understand fluctuations in prices and their consequences.

You will see that it is market forces – the interaction of **supply** and **demand** – that drive firms to change their production decisions and consumers to change their consumption decisions. Whether there is a relative shortage of supply or a relative shortage of demand, this information is transmitted to producers and consumers by the price mechanism. Shortages of supply relative to demand tend to lead to rising prices, whereas shortages of demand (and hence excesses of supply) tend to push prices down. In turn, these price signals change the behaviour of producers and buyers. Rising prices act as an incentive

Supply
Supply is the quantity of a good or service that sellers wish to sell over a specified period of time.

Demand
Demand is the quantity of a good or service that buyers wish to purchase over a specified period of time.

for producers to increase production to meet demand, while consumers look to reduce their consumption or switch to cheaper alternatives. When there is excess supply and prices fall, producers cut back on output and look for more profitable activities, while falling prices attract more buyers into the market. In both cases, changing prices lead to a realignment of demand and supply. Accordingly, market economics emphasises the role played by the price mechanism in coordinating millions of individual decisions such that the resources of society are allocated and reallocated between competing uses in the best possible way.

The price mechanism, supply and demand are concepts that lie at the heart of economics in the market model. Because of the elegance of the model and the powerful conclusion that it leads to – that the anonymous interactions of millions of individuals simply pursuing their own best interests lead to the best outcome for all – the market model and price mechanism have become increasingly influential as a way of organising social and economic activity.

The chapter begins with the analysis of demand at the level of a market (in contrast to aggregate demand, which, as you saw in Chapter 3, considers the whole economy). Section 2 examines the idea expressed in the extract from Waters (2012) that falling prices lead to the more rapid take-up of new products by consumers. This is an example of the widely observed relation between the quantity of a good demanded and its price: the lower the price, the greater the quantity demanded. However, as you will see, there are also other factors that influence demand. For example, if consumer incomes rise, then so too may demand. Next, Section 3 considers the determinants of supply to a market. Again, I start with the relationship between quantity and price, and consider why firms supply more to the market as the price that they can obtain rises. Section 4 brings the two parts of the analysis together to analyse market forces. Here I consider fluctuations in price and corresponding reactions. I also consider what remedies may be put into place if market forces lead to prices for some goods and services that differ from those needed to achieve certain social goals. Finally, Section 5 considers an alternative perspective on the nature and role of markets. Here the price mechanism and market forces remain central to the analysis but it is argued that rather than simply reflecting given information and preferences, markets are actually highly creative arenas in which new information is revealed and preferences are shaped. Far from undermining the power of market forces, this more radical perspective strengthens the role of the price mechanism and emphasises the dynamic nature of market behaviour.

The learning outcomes for this chapter are:

- to understand the relation between the quantity demanded of a good and its price as represented by the demand curve
- to understand the relation between the quantity supplied of a good and its price as represented by the supply curve
- to understand how demand and supply interact to establish an equilibrium price and quantity in competitive markets
- to understand what determines movement along and shifts of demand and supply curves
- to understand the economic consequences of imposing price ceilings and price floors
- to understand alternative perspectives on how markets work.

2   Market demand

This section focuses on market demand and its determinants. You will see that price is not the only factor that explains the demand for a good or service, but first I must abstract from those other influences and take a step-by-step approach that starts with price alone. By looking at the issue in this way, I will be able to develop an analytical framework that will help me to address the complexity of real-world cases and determine the underlying drivers of the observed outcomes.

Market

Markets are about the sale and purchase of a narrowly defined set of goods or services.

Before we do this, it is worth considering what is meant by a **market**. In considering markets I am focusing on the relations between suppliers (sellers) and buyers of a particular good or service. We take for granted that buyers and sellers are engaged in a voluntary exchange of money for goods. Importantly, we also assume that buyers are able to exercise a choice in the trades that they make. That is, buyers are free to buy or not to buy, or to buy this good rather than that good, or from that seller rather than this seller. In this chapter I also assume that there is no dominant agent on the side of either supply or demand. This situation of many buyers and sellers, each of which is too small to have an impact individually on prices and quantities, is a feature of a model called *perfect competition*. (You will study the model of perfect competition in more depth in the next chapter.) It is not the only possible market structure and, indeed, its conditions are rarely met in full in practice. However, it provides a useful model for analysing the behaviour of many real-world markets, and is an important benchmark against which other types of market structures are compared, as you will see in Chapter 14.

The scope of a market is chiefly determined by the good or service being traded. Beyond that, one may be interested in the geographical spread of the market, or the extent of different groups on the side of buyers. To take an example that is relevant to the quotation at the start of this chapter, there is a private consumer market for tablet computers as well as a business market. One can also consider the UK market for tablet computers, the European market or the global market. Particularly in the case of buyers, it may sometimes not be straightforward to say where one market ends and another begins. While it is important to consider these issues when examining a real-world case and be clear about how the market is defined, these considerations do not alter the fundamental analysis in this chapter.

2.1   Market demand and price

The relationship between demand and price can be represented in a variety of ways: descriptively in words, in a table, in a diagram or algebraically.

I have already described market demand in words: the lower the price, the greater the quantity of a good or service demanded. I can also display the relationship between demand and price in a table that is known as a *demand schedule*. This shows how the quantity demanded of a good or service changes as its price changes during a specific period of time and, importantly, holding constant all other determinants of quantity demanded. I am thus considering demand in relation to price as the only relevant variable. Holding constant all other potential influences on the quantity demanded, and considering only the relationship between demand and price, is part of my step-by-step approach. This procedure is commonly referred to in economics by the Latin phrase *ceteris paribus*, which means 'other things being equal'. It is the method used to abstract from the complexities of the real world in order to concentrate on the one or two key factors that appear to be important. Once I have analysed and understood how a change in one variable affects the other, *ceteris paribus*, it is possible to move on and introduce more variables. In this way, I gradually make the model more complex as I add in more and more aspects that may impact on the variable that I am seeking to explain. Thus economic models provide a systematic analytical framework with which one can think about causal relationships, as discussed in Chapter 1.

So, to help you to understand the relationship between demand and price, consider an example relevant to the quotation at the start of this chapter to illustrate the central ideas: the demand for tablet computers. Total quantity demanded in the market depends on the behaviour of individual consumers at various price points. This individual demand, in turn, depends on each consumer's willingness and ability to pay for a tablet computer. (This concept is examined in more detail in Section 2.3.) So the market demand is the sum of all these individual decisions. How can I present market demand at various prices? Given that there are many other factors that influence demand other than price, as discussed in the next subsection, I cannot simply use real-world price and quantity data; price is only one determinant of the observable quantity. Rather, when I present a table or graph showing market demand, I am depicting what the quantity demanded would be in the market at each and every price, *ceteris paribus*. In effect, I am simply showing what people as a whole would be willing and able to buy at various possible prices, holding constant any influences on demand other than price.

Table 12.1 presents such hypothetical market demand data for the example of tablet computers. In essence, it shows the total market demand as price changes, assuming that no other determinants of demand change.

Table 12.1   Demand schedule for tablet computers

Price per unit (£)	Quantity demanded (thousands per week)	Label in Figure 12.1
400	2	A
375	3	B
350	4	C
325	5	D
300	6	E
275	7	F

From the table, you can see that at a relatively low price of £300, the demand for tablet computers would be 6000 units per week. If prices were to rise, for example to £400 per computer, the demand would drop to 2000 units per week. This demand schedule therefore illustrates the quantity that consumers would demand, depending on the price. This 'quantity demanded' is not necessarily the number of tablet computers needed by people as a whole, but it shows the amount that consumers are willing and able to purchase in total at each different price.

Activity 12.1

Figure 12.1 shows the information in the demand schedule in Table 12.1 in the form of a plot of price (vertical axis) against quantity (horizontal axis). What do you observe about the slope of the line?

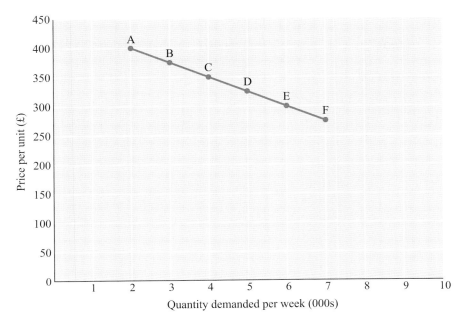

Figure 12.1   A market demand curve for tablet computers

Answer

The line in Figure 12.1 is known as a **demand curve** (by convention in economics always known as a 'curve' even if drawn as a straight line). Each point on the demand curve shows the quantity demanded at a particular price, assuming no changes in other factors that influence demand.

The market demand curve in Figure 12.1 shows the quantity demanded at each and every price by all consumers in the market for tablet computers. As with the demand schedule, in the demand curve you can see clearly the inverse relationship between price and quantity. As before, at a price of £300 demand is relatively high at 6000 units per week (point E), whereas a price of £400 leads to a demand of only 2000 units demanded (point A). This illustrates the general inverse relationship between the quantity of a good or service and its price, and is reflected in the negative slope of the demand curve (sloping downwards and to the right). In economics this negative relationship between quantity demanded and price is known as the 'law of demand'.

Demand curve
The demand curve shows the quantity demanded of a good or service at each price, assuming that all other factors that influence demand are fixed.

Finally, it is possible to represent the model of market demand in algebraic terms. The 'law of demand' – the idea that the quantity demanded depends on the price – can be written as

$$D = f(P), \textit{ceteris paribus}$$

This is read as demand (*D*) is a *function* of price (*P*), all other factors held constant. Both demand and price can vary in this model, but the quantity demanded is the dependent variable because it changes in response to price, which is the *independent* variable. This algebraic statement makes clear the causal relationship proposed by the model, whereas the diagram and the demand schedule show simply that this relationship is a negative one: a higher price results in a lower quantity demanded (*ceteris paribus*).

2.2   Other determinants of market demand

Having set out the law of demand by abstracting from potential influences on demand other than price, I now need to ask what those other factors may be.

The incomes of consumers

A key driver of consumption is the amount of income that consumers have: people with higher incomes tend to purchase more goods and services than those with lower incomes. If on average all people's incomes rise, then consumers will demand more of most goods, even if the price remains the same. A good or service with a positive relationship between consumers' incomes and quantity demanded is called a *normal good*. In industrialised countries where average incomes are relatively high, the majority of goods will be normal goods (for example, tablet computers, music downloads, haircuts and clothes). However, for some goods, fewer may be demanded as the incomes of consumers rise. These are known in economics as *inferior goods*. In industrialised countries, examples include basic foodstuffs or long-distance coach travel. As incomes rise for poorer households, one would expect their demand for these commodities to fall as they switch to better-quality food items or take the car or train for long journeys. In low-income, industrialising and developing economies, as households see incomes rise, they are able to substitute meat and fish for part of the basic diet of rice and grains, which indicates that the latter are inferior goods. Indeed, the World Bank (2011) reports that global demand for grain has stabilised while the demand for meat is continuing to rise faster than population, consistent with rising incomes across the world.

A shift in an entire demand curve indicates that demand has changed at *every* given price. If consumers as a whole have more income to spend, then they will want to buy more of a good or service at every price and the demand curve shifts to the right. If income decreases, then consumers are willing to buy less of the good or service at every price and the demand curve shifts to the left.

You can see the effect of an increase in income in Figure 12.2 (overleaf). The demand curve shifts from D_1 to D_2: at any given price, the quantity demanded has now increased. For example, if a good is sold at a price P_1, then a quantity Q_1 is demanded before the shift. After the shift, keeping price at P_1, the quantity demanded has increased to Q_2.

Figure 12.2, unlike Figure 12.1, does not include numbered scales on the axes. Rather, it is drawn in general with 'Price' (P) against 'Quantity' (Q), where quantity should be understood as 'quantity per period of time', such as a day, week or year. This more general diagram is common in economic analysis where one wishes to examine the direction of change of variables and their implications, rather than measure some exact magnitude.

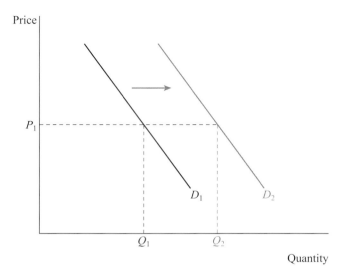

Figure 12.2   The impact of an increase in income on demand: a rightward shift

Activity 12.3

Make a list of the other factors, besides income, that may be modelled as a shift in the market demand for a good or service.

Answer

Besides consumers' income, other factors whose changes shift the demand curve are the price of other goods, consumer preferences, socio-economic factors, and expected future prices.

The price of other goods

In many cases, consumers can choose between alternative goods or services to meet a particular need. A change in the price of one good (x) will then affect the quantity demanded of a substitute good (y). The tablet computer is a close substitute for the traditional laptop computer. As the price of tablet computers has fallen, one would expect the quantity of laptops demanded to fall. Alternatively, two goods x and y are *complements* if the quantity demanded of good x *increases* when the price of good y falls. Here the fall in the price of good y encourages consumers to buy more of it but also of goods that are used with it, such as good x. To stay with this example, a fall in the price of tablet computers would also lead to an increase in the demand for apps to run on those computers. Hence tablet computers and apps are complements.

Consumer preferences

Advertising works by changing the preferences of consumers, hence successful advertising campaigns shift the demand curve for a good or service to the right. Conversely, bad publicity in relation to a product (for example, a connection between use of a product and a negative health effect) would have the opposite effect, shifting demand to the left.

Socio-economic factors

Although now overlooked by economics textbooks, the US economist James Duesenberry (1949) developed an important analysis of consumer behaviour. Duesenberry argued that demand for particular commodities, as well as consumption patterns in general, are affected by a 'demonstration effect' rather than the outcome of individual decisions alone. This means that any one individual's purchasing will be influenced by what others have (particularly those in a slightly higher income bracket), generating social pressures on consumption. Duesenberry also suggested that individuals and households suffering losses in income would try to maintain their previous consumption patterns and hence to maintain their social position. What this implies is that the demand for many goods and services may be less in order to meet a direct need and more to express identity, self-definition or social standing. Hence particular goods and services may see demand shifts because they are 'on trend', adopted by high-profile aspirational figures.

Expected future prices

If people expect that prices will be higher in the future, then in the case of non-perishable goods they will bring forward their purchases, raising demand. This behaviour explains the policy of time-limited cuts in Value Added Tax in the UK economy as a way of raising aggregate demand as an anti-recessionary measure. Conversely, if consumers expect that prices will fall in the future, either for a specific good or service or in general, then they are likely to delay their purchases, leading to a leftward shift in a demand curve. Again, linking to macroeconomics, this is one reason why deflation (a general fall in prices) is bad for an economy: falling aggregate demand intensifies as the price level drops.

Summary

Just as I did with the law of demand, it is possible to summarise the expanded model of demand using some simple algebra. The demand function captures the ideas explored so far as it shows that demand for a good or service depends on its own price and on the other factors discussed in this subsection. So now my demand function for commodity x is

$$D_x = f(P_x, P_r, Y, Z, P_e)$$

This expression states that the market demand for commodity x (denoted D_x) is a function of, or depends on, five variables: its own price P_x; the price of other related goods (both substitutes and complements) P_r; the income Y of all consumers or households together; socioeconomic factors Z; and expected price P_e. As you can see, once I relax the *ceteris paribus* assumption, the model of market demand becomes rather more complex as I do need to consider whether other factors are changing within the period of analysis. However, by examining each variable's relation with demand in turn, I can build up a good analytical understanding of the key drivers of demand.

To summarise, the quantity demanded will respond to both changes in the price of the good or service in question and changes in the other factors, but the way in which the reaction is represented diagrammatically in each case is different:

- A change in the price of a good or service leads to a movement along a given demand curve.
- A change in any other variable that impacts on quantity demanded leads to a shift of the entire curve.

2.3   Individual and market demand

So far I have been considering the market demand curve for a good or service. I have already noted that total demand can be thought of as the sum of many individuals' demand curves for a given commodity, but the question remains: what determines an individual's demand curve? Having earlier recognised that socio-economic influences and interdependencies between consumers are likely to have an impact on an individual's demand for a particular commodity, in order to understand how individuals behave, I need to hold constant those influences (the *ceteris paribus* assumption once more). This allows me to consider each consumer as an independent decision maker.

Consumers are faced with a huge array of options each day about how to allocate their income. How do they decide what to buy and in what quantities? Economists have answered this by developing a theory of consumer choice that starts from the proposition that consumers will spend their income in such a way that they maximise their satisfaction, or **utility** (about which you will learn more in Chapter 17). Consumers are assumed to know what is in their best interests and to make their choices in a way that is consistent with these interests, given the income that they have to spend. To allocate income in such a way that their total utility is maximised, consumers must spend their income so that the last pound's worth of each commodity purchased provides them with equal utility. To see why, consider a situation where this is not so: utility in total could then be increased by reallocating spending from commodities that provide consumers with less utility to a commodity that provides more.

Utility
Utility is a numerical representation of the amount of satisfaction derived from consumption.

Thus in allocating income among competing possible purchases, consumers will adjust their decisions until the ratio of the utility derived from the last unit consumed of a commodity (the 'marginal' unit) to the price paid for that commodity is the same for all commodities purchased. So, for example, if a consumer buys a tablet computer and a short holiday, and the computer costs twice as much as the holiday, then this argument implies that the computer is worth twice as much to the consumer. If the computer was worth less to the consumer, then he should have purchased a cheaper computer and spent more on a holiday in order to maximise his utility.

This analysis rests on two key assumptions. The first is that total utility or satisfaction increases with more consumption, without limit. The second is that the utility of something diminishes the more of it that is consumed. Hence the more you buy, the less the additional – or *marginal* unit – is worth. In other words, the **marginal utility** of a good or service consumed decreases as consumption increases: there is diminishing marginal utility. For example, if you are very thirsty, then you would be willing to pay a high price for a bottle of water to quench your thirst. A second bottle would add to your satisfaction but not by as much as the first since you have reduced your thirst. Accordingly, you would be willing to pay a lower price for a second bottle and, following this logic, less still for a third bottle.

Marginal utility
Marginal utility is the additional utility gained when an additional unit of a good is consumed.

Now, this allows me to think about an individual demand curve in a different way. The demand curve is no longer just a description of how much of a commodity is demanded at each price; for the individual, it represents the consumer's *willingness to pay* for the additional (marginal) unit of each commodity bought. The slope of the demand curve is negative because of diminishing marginal utility: the consumer's marginal utility, and therefore her willingness to pay, decreases as the quantity demanded increases (see Chapter 17 for more on marginal utility).

You can now see why I had to use hypothetical data in my example of the demand schedule and demand curve: these are theoretical concepts, based on notional demands, and are derived holding constant all factors other than price and quantity. If I had used actual data, many of these factors would be changing and influencing the observed price–quantity observations.

Next I need to think about the link between individual and market demand. It turns out that market demand can be easily derived from individual consumers' demand curves. In Figure 12.3, the demand curves of two individuals (person A, whose demand curve is D_A, and person B, whose demand curve is D_B) for the same commodity are shown. On the assumption that they pay no attention to each other's decisions when making their own and are the only two consumers in the market, I can simply add the two individual demand curves D_A and D_B horizontally to derive a market demand curve D_M.

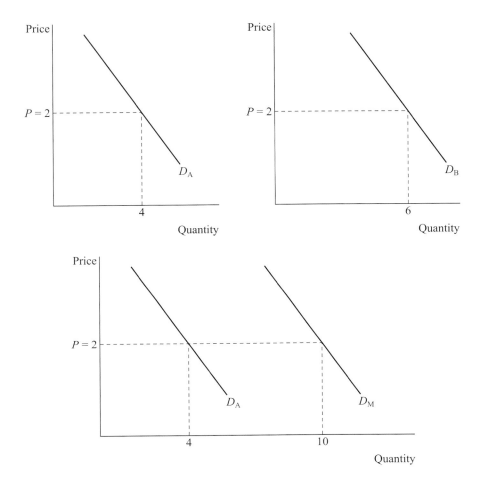

Figure 12.3   Deriving the market demand curve D_M

To see this, I will examine each person's demand at a particular price. If I choose a price of £2, then I can see that person A would demand a quantity of 4 units and person B would demand 6 units. Adding these two quantities gives a total quantity of 10 units at a price of £2, as shown in Figure 12.3, which identifies a point on the market demand curve D_M. Repeating the process for each price gives the market demand curve D_M.

2.4   The price elasticity of demand

I have now derived the market demand curve from individual consumer decisions, and I have already explored the 'law of demand': the inverse relationship between the price of a good or service and the demand for it. But how much might demand change if price varies? This is a

Price elasticity of demand
The price elasticity of demand measures the responsiveness of demand to a change in price.

question that is commonly of importance to governments and firms in thinking about the impact of tax changes on government revenue or of market price changes on a firm's revenue. Economists have developed a measure called *elasticity* that addresses this question. In general, the elasticity of demand measures the response of quantity demanded to a change in one of the determinants of demand. Here I will focus on the **price elasticity of demand**, which indicates how much the quantity demanded in the market changes when the market price changes.

Now this might seem simple: one just needs to divide the change in quantity by the change in price. However, if you think about it, this is not going to give a consistent answer because the value that you get depends on the units used to measure quantity and price (should one use pounds, pence, millions of pounds?). If you want to compare the price elasticity of two different goods, then you need to make sure that the units used do not affect the result. To avoid this happening, you should measure both the change in price and the change in quantity in proportionate terms. This means that whatever the units used to measure the price and quantity demanded, you will be able to calculate a consistent value for the elasticity and hence compare different commodities.

I can represent the price elasticity of demand in the formula

$$\text{price elasticity of demand} = \frac{\text{proportionate change in quantity demanded}}{\text{proportionate change in price}}$$

I can express the proportions as percentages in undertaking any calculation. Given the inverse relation between price and quantity demanded, the overall value will be negative (when price increases, quantity demanded declines; when price declines, quantity demanded increases), although often economists follow the convention of presenting the magnitude of the price elasticity of demand without considering its sign. The value also has an important meaning: if the price elasticity takes a magnitude greater than 1, then the demand is said to be price *elastic*. This is because a magnitude over 1 indicates that the percentage change in quantity is *greater* than the percentage change in price. Conversely, if the magnitude of elasticity is between 0 and 1, then the demand is said to be price *inelastic*.

So far the discussion may appear to be quite abstract. However, price elasticity of demand is very important as it tells you what the impact of a price change will be. Take the example of taxation. If a tax is levied on a good or a service, then the price will increase. However, this will reduce the quantity demanded and this, in turn, will have an impact on the tax revenue generated for the government.

Activity 12.4

Why is it a good idea to tax goods and services with inelastic demand?

Answer

The government's tax revenue partly depends on the price elasticity of demand. If the government's objective is simply to raise tax revenue, then it should target commodities that are price inelastic in demand. If it targets commodities with highly price elastic demand, then tax imposition or tax rises will lead to a large fall in quantity demanded and therefore a low tax yield.

For example, petrol is heavily taxed and a good source of tax revenue because it has a low price elasticity of demand: consumers cannot easily change their demand a great deal when the price goes up. Estimates indicate that the short-run price elasticity of demand for petrol is around −0.3, or 0.3 if we only consider its magnitude (Graham and Glaister, 2002).

By contrast, consider a tax on potatoes. Consumers have many possible alternatives to potatoes (rice, bread, pasta, etc.). A reasonable estimate for the price elasticity of demand for potatoes is −1.0. This means that as the price rose due to the levying of a tax, the quantity demanded would fall in the same proportion. Hence a 10% rise in price due to a tax would reduce the quantity demanded by 10%. Although this would still clearly generate some revenue for the government, at the same time it would cause a greater switch in consumption patterns than would a tax on petrol, and would thereby significantly undermine the basis of the tax.

Government should also consider the timeframe of their decision because the price elasticity of demand usually differs between short and long run. For example, in the long run, consumers can switch to alternative modes of transport or more fuel-efficient vehicles, but in the short run, tax on petrol is an effective source of revenue: a 10% rise in the price following a tax would lead to only a 3% fall in quantity demanded, generating high tax revenue for the government, However, in the long run, the change in consumer behaviour will lead to a greater reduction in the quantity demanded – Graham and Glaister (2002) report estimates of the long-run price elasticity of petrol around −0.7.

3   Supply

So far I have concentrated only on individual and market demand. To understand market forces more fully, I also need to consider market supply. In common with demand, the supply of any good or service is variable and depends on many factors. As with demand, I will begin by considering the relationship between price and supply in isolation. Subsequently, I can consider other factors that may impact on supply and cause a supply curve to shift.

3.1   Supply and price

In general, as price rises, the quantity of a good or service supplied increases – suppliers are willing to sell more. To understand this, it is helpful to consider the concept of **opportunity cost**. In order to supply a good or a service, a business firm needs resources. These include various inputs of labour, machinery and raw materials. Take the example of tablet computers once more. If resources are deployed to produce tablet computers, those same resources cannot be used to produce a different good. So in supplying the firm making the tablet computer, the owners of those resources cannot deploy those resources to other uses. They are, in effect, giving up the income or profit from supplying a different firm. This is precisely the idea of *opportunity cost*: the lost opportunity for earnings in the next best alternative use.

Now, with a given set of resources and a given set of technologies, if the production of a particular good or service rises, then the opportunity cost also rises. This is because more and more resources will be diverted into the production of a particular good. Furthermore, not all resources are equal, and as production increases the firm is forced to start using less productive resources and thus to use increasingly more of them to generate given rises in output. Hence, as the quantity of a good supplied rises, the opportunity cost of producing an additional unit also rises. Thus producers will find it profitable to increase production only if they can sell their product at a higher price, sufficient to cover the additional costs necessary to raise production. A more detailed derivation and discussion of supply follows in the next chapter, but for now I have established that the supply of a good or service to the market has a positive relationship to price: as the price in the market rises, the quantity supplied rises; price falls lead to falls in the quantity supplied.

Opportunity cost
The opportunity cost of producing (or consuming) a unit of good X is the amount of an alternative good Y that could be produced (or consumed) with the same resources.

I can illustrate the relationship between price and quantity supplied in a *supply schedule*. Table 12.2 shows a hypothetical supply schedule for tablet computers. Here you can see how many computers producers are willing and able to supply at a range of possible prices. If this sounds familiar from the earlier discussion of the demand schedule, it should do, since I am again looking at a price–quantity relationship but this time from the perspective of producers in the market. Just as with the earlier analysis of demand, I derive the supply schedule using the *ceteris paribus* assumption, which means for the moment that I ignore the effects of other possible influences on supply.

Table 12.2   Supply schedule for tablet computers

Price per unit (£)	Quantity supplied (thousands per week)	Label in Figure 12.4
400	8	A
375	7	B
350	6	C
325	5	D
300	4	E
275	3	F

As you can see from the supply schedule, a high unit price such as £375 induces a supply of 7000 units per week to the market, whereas a low price such as £275 leads to a total supply of only 3000 units per week.

Supply curve
The supply curve shows the quantity supplied of a good or service at each price, assuming that all other factors that influence supply are fixed.

Graphing these data produces what is known as the **supply curve**, as shown in Figure 12.4. As for the demand curve, along with the supply schedule, the supply curve is drawn holding constant other possible determinants of supply. What might these be? I consider the possible factors and their impact on supply in the next subsection.

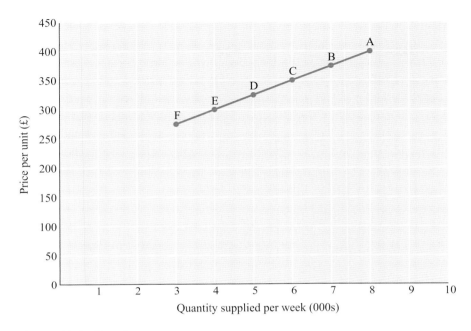

Figure 12.4 Supply curve

3.2 Shifts of the supply curve

Just as I did with the analysis of demand, I can identify the principal determinants of supply, in addition to the price of the good or service.

Activity 12.5

Can you list possible factors, besides price, that would impact on the quantity of a good supplied? How would you represent changes in those factors in a diagram?

Answer

Besides the price of the good or service sold, other factors that influence supply are prices of inputs, technological progress, the number and size of firms, substitutes and goods in joint supply, and unexpected events. Just as in the case of demand, changes in other factors that affect the quantity supplied are represented diagrammatically by shifts of the supply curve.

Prices of inputs

Returning to the example of tablet computer manufacture, production requires inputs of silicon chips, among other components. If the price of these rises, then producers will no longer be able to supply the same number of tablet computers to the market at the existing price, without damaging their profits. Thus supply will fall at the current market price – and all other possible prices – so the supply curve shifts to the left. This result is generalisable: a rise in input prices shifts the supply curve to the left; a fall in input prices shifts the supply curve to the right.

Technological progress

Businesses are very good at finding better ways of organising their production processes. This might entail the invention of new machinery with which to make a firm's products, or it might be an innovation in the way that production is managed and organised, which leads to greater efficiency and productivity using existing labour and capital resources. Examples of these changes were discussed in the previous chapter. In terms of supply, the effect of a technological improvement in production would be that firms could supply a greater quantity of a product at each possible price. In my diagram this would be represented by a rightward shift of the supply curve.

The number and size of firms

The entry and exit of firms to and from a market will have an impact on the supply curve. For example, if more firms enter a particular market, then the quantity supplied will rise at any given price. This is represented by a rightward shift in the supply curve. Conversely, if some firms leave the market, then the supply curve will shift left. Even if there is no entry or exit, the same shifts may arise if existing firms either expand or contract their output.

Substitutes and goods in joint supply

Changes in market prices may mean that it becomes more profitable for firms to switch their production from one commodity to another. In this case it pays the firm to divert its resources to the commodity that is a substitute in supply. This means that the supply of the original commodity will fall, reflected by a leftward shift in the supply curve. Consider, for example, a manufacturer of soft drinks that produces both bottled water and cola. If the price of bottled water increases, then this firm would switch its production focus to water and away from cola, leading to a fall in the market supply of cola.

In some production processes there is joint production, where two or more goods can be made from the same raw material. These are goods in joint supply. If the profitability of one commodity rises, following a rise in demand, then firms will produce more of that commodity and, necessarily, more of the joint product, leading to a rightward shift in the supply curve of the other product. Examples include a rise in the production of beef cattle leading to a rising supply of leather, or a rise in the supply of petrol from crude oil that also allows a rise in the supply of other grades of fuel, such as diesel.

Unexpected events

From time to time, supply may be adversely affected by events outside the control of producers and firms. In agriculture, extreme weather events have an impact on supply. In extractive industries, such as oil and gas production, accidents or damage to pipelines reduce supply at all prices. In a related way, the supply of manufactured goods depends on the reliability of the supply of energy, raw materials and labour, and any unexpected reduction in those inputs adversely affects supply if it is sustained. (Firms may hold stocks of finished goods to cushion themselves from short-term input fluctuations.)

Summary

Just as with demand, I need to distinguish between a movement along a given supply curve and movements of that entire supply curve. A change in the price of a commodity leads to a movement *along* a given supply curve. A change in any other determinant of quantity supplied *shifts* the whole supply curve.

Figure 12.5 (overleaf) shows a shift of supply to the right from S_1 to S_2; at each and every price, the quantity supplied increases after the shift. At price P, the quantity of a good initially supplied is Q_1. After the rightward shift of supply, for the same price, the quantity supplied increases to Q_2.

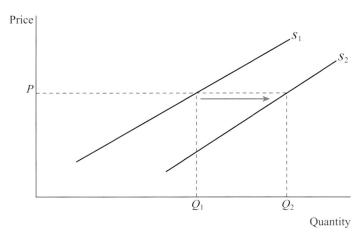

Figure 12.5   Rightward shift of supply

So far I have derived the market supply curve and considered factors that may cause it to shift. Just as in the case of demand, a market supply curve is the result of the decisions of many sellers, as you will see in more detail in Chapter 13.

Price elasticity of supply

The price elasticity of supply measures the responsiveness of supply to a change in price.

Finally, I note that, in parallel to the price elasticity of demand, I can also define and consider the **price elasticity of supply**. This tells you the proportionate response in quantity that sellers are willing and able to supply to a proportionate rise in the price prevailing in the market. Given the positive relationship between price and quantity supplied, the value of price elasticity of supply will be positive. It is also likely to be greater in the long run than in the short run.

Activity 12.6

Can you think why the price elasticity of supply will be greater in the long run?

Answer

In the short run, as price rises firms may only be able to increase the quantity supplied to a limited extent using stocks of goods or spare capacity. At some point, capacity constraints will be hit until new capacity can be installed. In the longer term, therefore, price elasticity of supply will be greater as existing firms expand and new firms enter the market.

---

4   Market interaction

The starting point in this chapter was the role of market forces and the price mechanism in the economy. You have seen how, within a market, demand and supply can be understood. These are the essential building blocks of the *neoclassical* competitive market analysis. Consumers formulate their demands by making choices, on the basis of their income, preferences and the prices of commodities. Firms decide on a level of output given their technology, input prices, and the price at which they can sell their goods. You can see that in both cases, price plays a central role. Price guides individual and firm behaviour, leading to a particular allocation of resources and pattern of consumption in the economy that best meets consumers' desires and fulfils firm's profit-seeking objectives. However, price is, in turn, determined by such behaviour through the forces of supply and demand. How then can one understand the determination of a market price? I will explore this in more detail in this section.

4.1   Market equilibrium

In the analysis of how market forces determine price, I need to bring demand and supply together. This will tell me if the wishes of consumers are consistent with those of producers. In the analysis of a market, recall that the demand curve shows how much consumers are willing to buy in total at each given price. The supply curve shows how much producers as a whole are willing to sell. By bringing together supply and demand, I can determine which price satisfies both consumers and producers.

Table 12.3 returns to the example used previously. It gives the quantity demanded in the market for tablet computers against the supply at each price, holding other factors constant.

Table 12.3   Price determination in the market for tablet computers

Price per unit (£)	Quantity demanded (thousands per week)	Quantity supplied (thousands per week)	Market position	Direction of price response
400	2	8	Surplus	Down
375	3	7	Surplus	Down
350	4	6	Surplus	Down
325	5	5	Equilibrium	No change
300	6	4	Shortage	Up
275	7	3	Shortage	Up

I also plot the supply and demand curves together in Figure 12.6. It is apparent that there is only one price at which the quantity demanded by consumers is exactly equal to the quantity that producers are willing to sell. This is the price of £325, labelled as P_{Eqm} in Figure 12.6. At any price above this level, supply is greater than demand and there is a *surplus* (firms in total produce more than consumers wish to purchase). Consumers are able to buy the quantity that they wish, but producers are not able to sell all that they would like to supply, and find themselves left with stocks of unsold goods. At any price below £325, the opposite is true: quantity demanded exceeds quantity supplied and there is a *shortage* in the market. Producers are able to sell all that they are willing to supply, but consumers are frustrated by their inability to buy all that they are willing to purchase at that price. Examples of different prices are shown in Figure 12.6. At a price of £350 ($P_{Surplus}$), the quantity demanded is less than the quantity supplied. At a price of £300 ($P_{Shortage}$), the quantity demanded is greater than the quantity supplied.

The price at which demand is equal to supply is known as the *equilibrium* price (P_{Eqm}). At this point, the forces of supply and demand are in balance. The price is such that both consumers and firms are meeting their objectives and, all else being equal, there is no tendency for any change in market behaviour. This is the meaning of equilibrium: a situation in which there is no inherent tendency to change (see Chapter 3, Section 2). The only reason for change would be if one or more of the factors being held constant along the supply and demand schedules were to change (the effect of this will be examined in the next subsection).

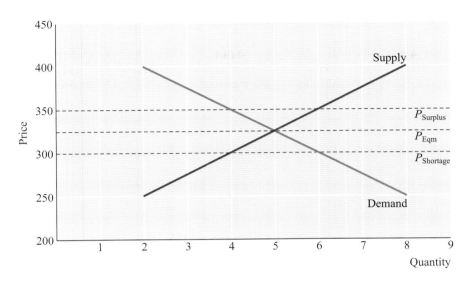

Figure 12.6   Supply and demand curves for tablet computers

But what happens if the market price is not at its equilibrium value? My analysis tells me that market forces will ensure that any deviations of price from equilibrium will be temporary, and that imbalances will drive the price to its equilibrium value. Returning to Table 12.3, I can consider why this might be. If the price is above equilibrium, then there is a surplus of output at that price. This leaves many producers with unsold stock and some will undercut competitors by accepting a lower price. This drives down the price until it reaches equilibrium. By contrast, if demand exceeds supply because the price is below equilibrium, some consumers are unable to carry out all the purchases that they wish. If these consumers offer to pay more, this pushes up the price, encouraging greater supply and a move towards equilibrium.

In summary, in a competitive market, forces of supply and demand ensure that the price is driven to its equilibrium level. At this level, consumers and firms are doing the best that they can given their preferences and constraints (from income and technology, for example).

4.2   Changes in supply, demand and equilibrium

I have identified the equilibrium price for a given supply schedule and a given demand schedule. But what if these schedules change? Put simply, a change in any determinant of supply or demand other than price will lead to a shift of the relevant curve and hence to a change in the equilibrium price in the market and the equilibrium quantity sold. To see this, assume that there is a change in consumers' real disposable incomes (that is, income adjusted for inflation and taxes). In the market for tablet computers, it is reasonable to assume that an increase in real income causes the demand curve to shift to the right as shown in Figure 12.7. If, after a shift in demand from D_1 to D_2, prices remain at the current market price P_1, this will lead to a shortage. At price P_1, the quantity *supplied* is Q_1 but the quantity *demanded* after the shift is Q_2. Quantity demanded is now greater than quantity supplied. Hence, to restore equilibrium, the price must rise. This will lead to firms raising output to meet the greater demand and to a new equilibrium point at a higher price and quantity. Equilibrium is restored when price rises to P_2 because both quantity demanded and quantity supplied are Q_3.

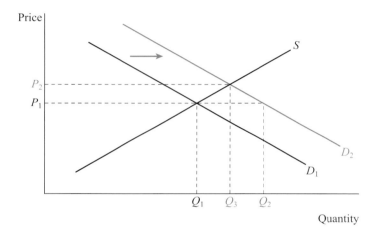

Figure 12.7   Shift in demand curve and new market equilibrium

Now consider a change in supply conditions. Assume that new firms are attracted to enter the market for tablet computers, given their popularity among consumers. This will have the effect of shifting the supply curve to the right (a shift from S_1 to S_2 in Figure 12.8), as total output will rise at all prices. At the existing price P_1 there will now be an excess supply and a surplus. This is not sustainable, and the effect on the equilibrium position is to reduce price and raise quantity sold. Equilibrium is restored when price falls to P_2. Only at price P_2 are the quantity demanded and quantity supplied equal (shown as Q_3).

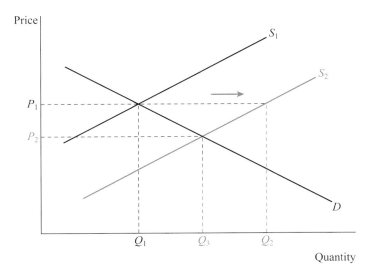

Figure 12.8   Shift in supply curve and new market equilibrium

This analysis is very helpful for thinking about the characteristics of market equilibrium and the effects of changes to supply and demand. However, the analysis tends to focus on identification of equilibrium. It says very little about the process by which a market may move from one equilibrium point to another. This is a limitation of the approach, which is commonly referred to as *comparative static* analysis: the comparison of two equilibrium positions. This is not to say that the approach is without its uses. Indeed, this simple model is incredibly useful for thinking through the effects of policy changes and shocks to markets. It is also incredibly powerful in that it can be applied to a vast range of markets. In the examples in this chapter I have focused on the market for a particular product, the tablet computer. But the basic framework of analysis is deployed in a range of situations by economists, and is very useful for understanding and predicting price movements. For example, the market model can be used to understand, among other things, exchange rate movements (where the exchange rate is the price of a currency), the labour market (where the price is the wage rate) and changes in money market interest rates (via movements in the market for government bonds).

In the next subsection, I consider some particular applications of the market model and examine the implications of policy interventions in markets. In the final section, I consider the limitations of this analysis in more detail, focusing first on the limits to markets and second on the limitations of the comparative static approach to markets that has been my focus.

4.3   The control of prices

From the discussion of the market model so far, you have seen that the price mechanism plays a very powerful role: changes in prices are driven by shifts in supply and demand conditions, and in turn these price changes create incentives for producers and consumers in the economy to change their decisions. You have also seen that the competitive market model indicates that market forces will lead to an equilibrium price being established. But what if society or lawmakers believe that the equilibrium price is not the most desirable or fair price? In this case, government may intervene in the market, taking steps to ensure that the prevailing price is above or below the competitive market equilibrium.

I will consider some examples that illustrate each case in general terms. First, if the government seeks to impose a minimum price (price P_2) that is above the market equilibrium (price P_1), then this will generate a surplus of supply over demand. This is shown in Figure 12.9. Commonly referred to as a *price floor*, under this policy the price level will not be allowed to drop to eliminate the surplus at the chosen minimum price.

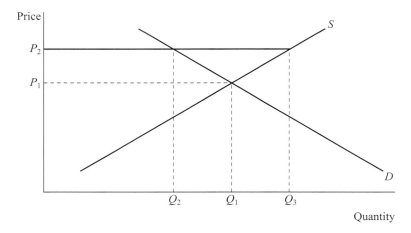

Figure 12.9   Price floor diagram

But why might a government wish to impose such a price floor? One reason might be to reduce fluctuations in producer incomes. A good example of this relates to farmers and the price interventions associated with the EU's Common Agricultural Policy (CAP). The demand for and supply of agricultural products are generally relatively price inelastic (it takes time to change production levels; consumers cannot easily substitute for basic foodstuffs). Hence shifts in supply and demand would lead to large changes in price in the absence of price control. The resulting income fluctuations and uncertainty would then reduce output by damaging investment and driving some farmers out of business. By guaranteeing farm incomes, the price floors established by the CAP provide for greater revenue stability for farmers, sustaining production within the EU. One of the problems is that surplus output will be generated with the introduction of a price floor, as you can see from Figure 12.9. This may be useful if there is the possibility of future shortages, since it allows stocks to be built up (EU cereal stocks were very useful in 2010 following a Russian export ban on grain, for example). However, in other cases it may lead to large unwanted surpluses. In the attempt to reduce these, CAP reforms have included the introduction of maximum guaranteed quantities, but price supports remain a contentious area.

Another area in which a price floor is commonly found is the labour market, with many countries operating a minimum wage system. A minimum wage works in the same way as the price floor in Figure 12.9. However, in considering a market for labour, I need to rethink my supply and demand framework a little. First, in the labour market, the price needs to be replaced by the wage rate (in effect, the price of a unit of labour time). Second, and inverting the normal origins of supply and demand in consumer markets, individuals supply labour services whereas firms provide the demand when considering labour services – this has already been shown in Chapter 1, Figure 1.3 and Chapter 7, Section 3. I also need to define the market clearly as there will be different markets for workers with different skills, with varying supply and demand conditions. With these adjustments, it is possible to use the standard demand and supply apparatus to interpret labour market behaviour and outcomes if I assume that the labour market is competitive and neither workers nor firms can influence outcomes. (Note that the analysis of the labour market and unemployment in Chapter 3, Section 3, does not assume a competitive labour market because of the presence of trade unions and large companies, which can influence market outcomes because of their size relative to the market).

Returning to how a price floor would operate in the labour market, what would prompt such a policy? A key reason for introducing a minimum wage is to alleviate in-work poverty among those in low-skill labour markets, where wages can be very low. The introduction of a national minimum wage to the UK in 1999 was a response to falling wages in the lower part of the wage distribution following a period of prolonged high unemployment and weakened trade unions through the 1980s and 1990s. At the time, critics were quick to seize on the conclusions drawn from the competitive market model: a minimum wage above the competitive market equilibrium will lead to unemployment (a surplus of labour supply over labour demand). This can be seen in Figure 12.10. If the minimum wage W_{MIN} is higher than the equilibrium wage W_E, then the demand for labour will fall to L_2 from L_1, with the size of this drop depending on the elasticity of labour demand.

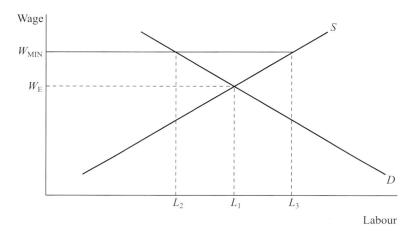

Figure 12.10   Competitive low-skill labour market with minimum wage

The conclusions of this model are stark: a minimum wage will hurt the very group of workers that it is designed to help, by raising unemployment (and hence exacerbating poverty). Indeed, the predictions of this model and attempts to create a free and flexible competitive labour market lay behind the policies of deregulation and weakening of trade unions of the 1980s and early 1990s that arguably created the conditions for the introduction of a minimum wage in the UK. But what was the actual effect? In reality, little or no evidence has been found for reduced employment following the introduction of the UK minimum wage. This could be, of course, because the minimum was set at or below the equilibrium. However, this can be dismissed because wages did in fact rise for many thousands of low-paid workers. Rather, research indicates that the minimum wage was absorbed largely due to accommodation by a combination of rising productivity, lower profits and higher prices for services produced largely by workers paid the minimum wage (Metcalf, 2008). Indeed, in a competitive market, since all firms face the same increase in costs, each individual firm can raise prices in the knowledge that competitors will be doing the same. However, this still does not explain why the level of employment did not fall. So although my model of market processes provides a useful indicator, in some cases I need to consider the extent to which the assumptions of a competitive market actually hold.

There are also times when the government may want to restrict price levels.

Activity 12.7

Can you think of examples where the government might want to stop prices rising? What might be the problems that result?

Answer

A common example is rent control for private housing. Introduced in England in 1915 in response to pressure on housing caused by the lull in new building during the First World War, rent controls imposed a maximum price (a *price ceiling*) on rental values. The aim was to prevent prices rising to such a level that people could not afford to rent, given an excess demand for housing. However, the continuation of what was intended to be a temporary measure led critics to argue that rent control was damaging the rental market by reducing supply as landlords sold properties that generated only a low yield or failed to maintain their stock properly, given the ease of letting in conditions of excess demand.

In Figure 12.11 (overleaf) you can see the effect of a price ceiling. By maintaining the price below the market equilibrium, an excess demand of $Q_3 - Q_2$ is created. In general, price ceilings can create severe problems. Queues of consumers will form, or firms will establish waiting lists that then create incentives for underground markets to develop. In these illegal markets, consumers may be willing to pay a price well in excess of the equilibrium in order to obtain the product. To overcome these problems, governments may introduce a system of rationing in an attempt to generate a fairer allocation. Such price controls and associated rationing are seen particularly at times of war or famine.

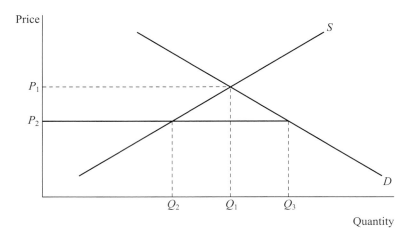

Figure 12.11   A price ceiling

Finally, another area in which a government may wish to intervene is in relation to the price of its own currency, that is, the exchange rate (see Book 1 Chapter 6, Section 4.3). In order to provide stability to exporters or to prevent imported inflation from a falling currency value, a government may want to fix or at least stabilise its exchange rates against other key currencies. Before entering the European Exchange Rate Mechanism, the UK government 'shadowed' the German deutschmark, effectively seeking to control the price of the pound. However, as you have seen already from the above discussion, interventions to control prices in the face of market forces can have counterproductive effects given the excess demands and supplies that can result. Setting the prices of currencies is no different, with supply and demand pressures ultimately leading sooner or later to readjustments in fixed exchange rates. In particular, against an excess supply of its own currency, a central bank must purchase this excess to maintain a given desired exchange rate. However, a limit to this is set by the country's reserves of other currencies that it can use to intervene in the market. In the extreme, these reserves may near exhaustion, leading to an abandonment of the fixed exchange rate in the face of market forces. As the former British Prime Minister Margaret Thatcher observed when discussing her government's policy of shadowing the German deutschmark: 'There is no way in which one can buck the market' (Margaret Thatcher Foundation, 1988).

5   Markets: their limits and alternative perspectives

This analysis of the price mechanism and market forces generates powerful conclusions: the free interplay of millions of individual buyers and producers leads to the efficient allocation of society's resources. Attempts to intervene in the operation of the price mechanism are then said to lead to distortions that are often worse than the problem that they are designed to address. It is on this basis that arguments are made to extend the reach of the private market into the provision of a wide range of goods and services and to minimise or remove altogether government regulations. However, I need to sound a note of caution at this point. There may be limits to market forces. One limitation is that the analysis here is based only on the assumption of price-taking individual firms and consumers. But what if suppliers (or buyers) can exercise market power and influence prices? Should one then seek to extend market forces and allocate resources simply by the price mechanism? The impact of this will be considered in Chapter 14. A further limitation relates to the efficiency of the market in meeting social ends. What if market forces lead to too much harmful activity such as smoking tobacco, or too little desirable activity such as eating healthily? Are the market and the price mechanism always the best ways of directing activity? It may be that incorporating certain activities into market production and sale, and pricing them, crowds out voluntary behaviour, ultimately reducing social welfare. This set of issues is considered in Part 5.

While it might be relatively uncontroversial that there are limits to markets, some economists have argued that the neoclassical competitive model that has been investigated so far is an inappropriate basis on which to understand the nature and role of markets.

The Austrian school of economics, grounded in the works of Friedrich Hayek (1899–1992), Ludwig von Mises (1881–1973) and Joseph Schumpeter (1883–1950) rejects the equilibrium view of markets. The account that I have considered here takes as given the range of commodities available, consumer preferences among them, and the range of techniques available to firms with which to produce them. Individual maximisation of profit and utility then gives rise to the supply and demand schedules that determine equilibrium prices. As you have seen, shortages or surpluses quickly drive the market price to equilibrium in a free market. Should conditions change, then a new equilibrium price can be identified and it is assumed that the market moves to this new point without difficulty. By contrast, Austrian economists argue against this focus on equilibrium and the use of comparative static analysis. Rather, Austrian economists argue that the nature of markets is dynamic: it is the *process* of change, not the point of equilibrium that characterises markets.

The key difference between the Austrian view of markets and the competitive neoclassical model discussed in this chapter is the view of knowledge. The neoclassical model assumes that individuals are well informed. Indeed, for the price mechanism to work in the neoclassical model, individuals need to know the range of prices offered by the full range of suppliers in order to drive the system to an equilibrium price. Thus if you know the preferences of individuals, their resource endowments and the technology available to firms, then you could, in principle, derive a set of equilibrium prices for the whole economy that equates supply and demand in all markets at the same time.

The Austrian perspective does not reject the power of market forces – quite the reverse – but, by contrast, it starts from a position of incomplete knowledge and disequilibrium. The role of the price mechanism and market forces is then to *reveal* knowledge. Despite the different starting points, market forces are still seen as the best method of allocating resources in a way that meets the needs of consumers and the resources of the economy. The difference is that the analysis is *dynamic*. Indeed, Austrian economists argue that the market is very efficient in utilising knowledge as it becomes available. For example, a change in relative (disequilibrium) prices will be sufficient to cause producers and consumers to economise on products using newly scarce resources:

> The marvel is that in a case like that of the scarcity of one raw material, without an order being issued, without more than perhaps a handful of people knowing the cause, tens of thousands of people whose identity could not be ascertained by months of investigation, are made to use the material or its products more sparingly.

> (Hayek, 1945, p. 523)

No time or effort needs to be expended to discover the causes of changing demand or supply conditions, but an appropriate response still follows. On this view, prices are not parameters (a 'given') to which individual consumers and producers respond. They are, instead, the unique reflection of the various fragments of knowledge that individuals across the economy hold and the signals through which decentralised knowledge is coordinated and communicated:

> We are only beginning to understand on how subtle a communication system the functioning of an advanced industrial society is based – a communications system which we call the market and which turns out to be a more efficient mechanism for digesting dispersed information than any that man has deliberately designed.
>
> (Hayek, 1974)

Austrian economists go further. Not only is the market an efficient mechanism for bringing together disparate, existing knowledge as reflected in price movements, it is also a creative process that generates new knowledge. Schumpeter's emphasis on the role of the entrepreneur is central here. Entrepreneurial activity responds to disequilibrium prices in seeking profit, but is itself a major source of disequilibrium. The invention of a new or improved good or service, the introduction of new production techniques, the creation of a new market or capture of a new source of supply or a new organisational structure, are all entrepreneurial activities and causes of instability and change. This is very different from the neoclassical assumption of given technologies. It also is at odds with the view that consumers have given preferences. For Austrian economists, rather than given preference leading to consumer choices, preferences *emerge* in the process of choice as consumers are confronted by the new products and services provided by entrepreneurs. In this sense, the market is a *creative process*.

The contrast between the neoclassical and Austrian approaches could not be more stark. Austrians reject the notion of equilibrium that requires that all relevant facts are known and there is no undiscovered knowledge, but they do not reject the power of the market. Indeed, they argue that the neoclassical model does not go far enough in celebrating the achievements of competitive markets. From scraps of knowledge held by diverse individuals, markets discover new ways of meeting individual need. Further, entrepreneurial activity within markets actively creates new products and services, generating new consumer desires in the process.

6 Conclusion

This chapter has taken a preliminary look at the factors shaping demand and supply in competitive markets. The analysis focused on the interaction of individual consumers and producers in markets who are each seeking to maximise their own well-being (utility for consumers, profit for producers). The key conclusion of this model is that the price mechanism ensures that market demands are met by producers' supply responses. Where there are shortages, prices will rise and a greater supply will be forthcoming. Where there are surpluses, prices drop, indicating that producers need to cut back on production.

Overall, then, this leads to a very positive view of market forces. However, two criticisms have been highlighted. The first is that in some cases, market forces may lead to an outcome that is not socially beneficial. In these cases, it may be preferable to cap prices or set a minimum value. The second criticism comes from the Austrian school of economic thought. This actually strengthens the positive view of market forces but holds a very different view of the nature and role of markets. In place of the tendency to a given equilibrium based on given information and knowledge, Austrians argue that a crucial function of markets is that their operation actually reveals and creates new knowledge and information, which leads to some quite radical conclusions about the need to leave market forces unfettered.

References

Duesenberry, J.S. (1949) *Income, Saving and the Theory of Consumer Behavior*, Cambridge, MA, Harvard University Press.

Graham, D. and Glaister, S. (2002) 'The demand for automobile fuel: a survey of elasticities', *Journal of Transport Economics and Policy*, vol. 36, no. 1, pp. 1–25.

Hayek, F.A. (1945) 'The use of knowledge in society', *American Economic Review*, vol. 35, no. 4, pp. 519–30.

Hayek, F.A. (1974) 'The pretence of knowledge', Lecture to the memory of Alfred Nobel, 11 December, [online] www.nobelprize.org/nobel_prizes/economics/laureates/1974/hayek-lecture.html (Accessed 29 December 2012).

Margaret Thatcher Foundation (1988) *House of Commons PQs*, 10 March, [online] www.margaretthatcher.org/document/107195 (Accessed 29 December 2012).

Metcalf, D. (2008) 'Why has the British national minimum wage had little or no impact on employment?', *Journal of Industrial Relations*, vol. 50, no. 3, pp. 489–512.

Waters, R. (2012) 'Plunging prices set to trigger tech boom', *Financial Times*, 8 January, [online] www.ft.com/cms/s/2/e2ee3706-3a24-11e1-a8dc-00144feabdc0.html#axzz2DVp173Wj (Accessed 29 December 2012).

World Bank (2011) *Global Economic Prospects*, Vol. 3, Washington, DC, World Bank.

Chapter 13
Perfect competition

Roberto Simonetti

Contents

1   Introduction

> When markets work well, firms thrive by providing what
> consumers want better and more cost-effectively than their
> competitors. As such, effective competition provides significant
> benefits for consumers through greater choice, lower prices, and
> better quality goods and services. Competition also provides strong
> incentives for firms to be more efficient and innovative, thereby
> helping raise productivity growth across the economy.
>
> (Office of Fair Trading, 2009, p. 1)

The Office of Fair Trading (OFT), the British agency that promotes
competition and the interests of consumers against unfair practices,
summarises here the economic virtues of competition in the market. In
the previous chapter, you learned about the price mechanism, one of
the key forces that make markets so powerful and widespread in the
world. This chapter and the next turn to the analysis of competition,
which is the other main reason why markets are such a successful way
to organise economic activity.

In this chapter, I start exploring how competition works in markets by
analysing the model of *perfect competition*. This model has been and
remains one of the most influential ways of thinking about competition
both in academic economics and in policy-making. The model of
perfect competition underpins the neoclassical model of the market that
you studied in the previous chapter, and therefore is closely related to
the way the price mechanism works. If markets are not competitive,
then the signals sent by prices in the economy are distorted, and
resources will be allocated inefficiently.

In particular, this chapter mainly focuses on the supply side of markets,
analysing the way a typical firm behaves in a competitive market,
maximising its profits given its costs and the market price. You will see
how it is possible to derive the industry supply curve, which, as you
have seen in the previous chapter, is used to study the market as a
whole.

The chapter also addresses important questions faced by firms and
policymakers, such as the following. What strategy is needed to
maximise profits? In which conditions should firms decide to shut

down production and leave the market? Why are entry into and exit from a market important for economic efficiency? You will see that often to answer questions in economics one needs to think 'at the margin', that is, to look at marginal costs and revenues (or, more generally, benefits) to achieve the best possible outcome.

Section 2 analyses the four key assumptions of the model in detail. Section 3 explains how in perfect competition firms cannot influence market prices. Sections 4 and 5 analyse the decisions taken by firms to maximise profits in the short and the long run. Section 6 draws on Chapter 12 to tie together the analysis of consumers and firms in perfectly competitive markets, and explores the important implications of the results of the model for the way markets are considered by policymakers.

The learning outcomes for this chapter are:

- to be able to analyse the behaviour of firms and industries in the model of perfect competition
- to understand how the assumptions of the model of perfect competition influence the outcome of the model
- to appreciate the significance of the model of perfect competition as a policy benchmark
- to appreciate the importance of marginal analysis in economics.

2   The assumptions of the model of perfect competition

The perfect competition model is based on some simplifying assumptions about the nature of the market:

- all buyers and sellers (for example, consumers and firms) are small relative to the size of the market
- all buyers and sellers are fully informed
- products are homogeneous
- there is free entry into and exit from the market.

The four assumptions that underlie the model are quite extreme conditions, and few actual markets satisfy *all* of them. The term 'perfect' itself suggests that perfectly competitive markets are an ideal to which policymakers aspire, a benchmark against which real economic markets are compared. Precisely because of the influence of the model on economic theory and policy, its assumptions have to be considered and understood in detail.

However, there are real-world markets into which this model can provide useful insights. Local food markets, for example, tend to come close to the ideal case of perfect competition: buyers and sellers are usually too small to influence prices, it is easy for buyers to compare prices, specific food items offered by different sellers differ little from each other, and the costs of setting up selling points (market stalls) are low.

I will now analyse each assumption in detail.

2.1   All firms and consumers are small relative to the size of the market

In a perfectly competitive market, all sellers and buyers are small relative to the size of the market. This is not unusual. Many markets contain large numbers of small firms, such as hairdressers and convenience stores. Industry statistics show that most of the firms in the economy are small. Figure 13.1 (overleaf) shows that nearly 90% of enterprises in the USA in 2007 had fewer than 20 employees, whereas under 2% had more than 500 employees.

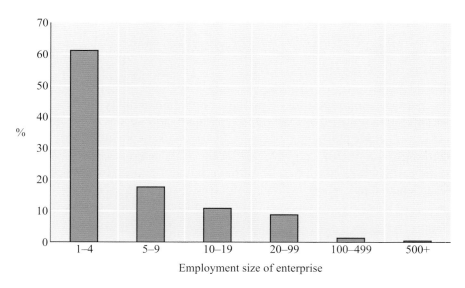

Figure 13.1   The size distribution of firms in the USA, 2007

(Source: US Census Bureau, 2007, Table 2b)

Market share
The market share of a firm is its share of total industry output. It is usually expressed as a percentage.

This assumption is important because it rules out situations in which a seller has a large **market share**, with output a very large proportion of the total industry output so that it could arbitrarily raise its price without losing much of its business. As you will see in the next chapter, authorities are often wary of firms becoming too big and dominating their industry, so they will stop them growing too much, for example by forbidding them to buy other companies.

But when are firms 'small enough' for the market to be competitive? The relation of the size of a firm's output to the total market output (the firm's market share) is crucial: a 'small' firm in this context may have a very large absolute turnover but still count as 'small' if it is unable to influence the market price. For example, a city may support many large general food retailers but only one small seller of exotic foods appealing to specialist tastes. The latter is large relative to the local market for such specialised tastes because consumers will not want to travel far for relatively low-value purchases. Hence the seller influences price and quantity in the local market, while the general food stores compete with each other despite their greater size. By the same token, a large steel firm may be small compared with the world market for the product since the market for steel is global – the proximity of the firm to the buyer is of less importance because of the high value of transactions and the importance to buyers of getting the right kind and quality of steel. Therefore in determining whether a firm counts as 'small', one has to pinpoint the relevant market.

2.2   Buyers and sellers have perfect information

In perfectly competitive markets, both buyers and sellers are fully informed about prices and costs. In the low-cost segment of the clothing industry, for example, producers in the same area face similar costs as they hire cheap labour and equipment from the same known local sources to set up small factories. Local fruit and vegetable markets also fit the information requirement well because of the ease of price comparisons: by wandering around the stalls, buyers can easily discover the different prices and qualities on offer. This example shows how important it is for information to be easily available. If buyers are poorly informed about the range of prices available and are unable to 'shop around', then they have no way of judging whether the price being offered by one particular seller is reasonable, so competition does not work well. A seller who is aware of a customer's lack of knowledge (for example, a vendor located immediately outside a railway station) can exploit the situation by raising his price above the market level. If it is very difficult to find the price that different suppliers might charge (for example, for a non-standard car repair), then gathering information becomes costly, and consumers may not be prepared to pay these 'search costs'.

In recent years, the amount of information available to buyers and sellers has increased because of easier and cheaper access to the internet. Price comparison websites report the product range and prices of many online suppliers. Even inside shops, barcode scanner apps on mobile phones enable shoppers to use their mobile phones to find out if an item is available elsewhere more cheaply.

2.3   Products are homogeneous

You saw in Chapter 12 that the scope of a market is 'chiefly determined by the good or service being traded'. Competition based on price works best if the goods and services exchanged are – or at least are perceived by consumers to be – virtually identical, or 'homogeneous'. For example, shopping around by customers is a more effective discipline on the pricing behaviour of firms when the products of the various firms are homogeneous in the perceptions of buyers so that they can see nothing to differentiate one firm's product – for example, detergent

Price comparisons are made easier by barcode scanners available on mobile devices

– from another's. In this case, individual suppliers of the product have little room to manoeuvre with respect to price because buyers will simply opt for the cheapest product available. Conversely, if it is believed that the detergent produced by firm A gets clothes cleaner than the detergents produced by all the other firms, then firm A will be able to charge more than its competitors, even if its product is manufactured to the same formula as all the others.

Often industry bodies or regulators intervene to agree standards in order to define products clearly so that they are homogeneous for buyers and sellers. Eggs, for example, are easy to standardise (by size and colour), leading buyers to regard one egg of a given grade as the same as another. Eggs of different grades, therefore, can be regarded, in a sense, as belonging to different markets. Standardisation is particularly important when goods and services are traded electronically in commodity exchanges, because traders do not even see the goods that they buy and sell. Traders who buy and sell large quantities of, say, bananas, need to be sure about their quality and appearance without having to check each batch. For this reason, industry bodies value the existence of trading standards and put pressure on governments for the introduction of clear regulations. In a well-known case, when industry organisations asked for standards for the quality of bananas, the

European Commission responded by introducing standards so detailed that the British Eurosceptic press complained about interference from 'power-hungry Eurocrats' who wanted control over the shape of bananas. The standards were ill-specified and were subsequently revised, but the press neglected to report that the European Commission acted on requests from food producers and traders. The absence of standards made it harder for traders to buy good-quality bananas from the cheapest producers because they might receive fruit of lower quality or spend more to ensure that quality is adequate. Without standards that clearly define a homogeneous commodity, consumers may end up paying higher prices or receiving lower-quality goods.

2.4   Freedom of entry and exit

For competition to work properly in the long run, it is necessary for firms to be able to enter and leave the market with ease. The competitive pressures on established firms arising from new entrants is often identified by policymakers as a key ingredient of competition. Competition authorities, who oversee the smooth operation of competition in markets, pay close attention to obstacles that make it harder for new firms to enter a market. ('Barriers to entry' are discussed in Chapter 14, Section 6.) Empirical studies have shown that there are high levels of entry and exit in all industries: industry productivity increases are in great part generated by new, efficient firms gaining market share at the expense of older, less efficient firms, which, if they fail to improve their efficiency, eventually exit the market. In recent years, policymakers around the world have taken steps to support entrepreneurs who want to create a new firm by removing factors that make it harder for new firms to enter a market. An example of such developments is the creation of indicators that measure the 'ease of entry' across countries, such as those used by the World Bank Doing Business database illustrated in Figure 13.2 (overleaf). The figure shows that in most of the countries surveyed, the bureaucratic barriers that delay the entry of new firms decreased between 2003 and 2010, and it has become quicker to set up a new firm to enter a market. Looking at cross-country differences in 2010, entrepreneurs faced more favourable conditions in countries such as New Zealand and Australia, while in Indonesia, Brazil and Spain on average they had to wait over a month to enter a market.

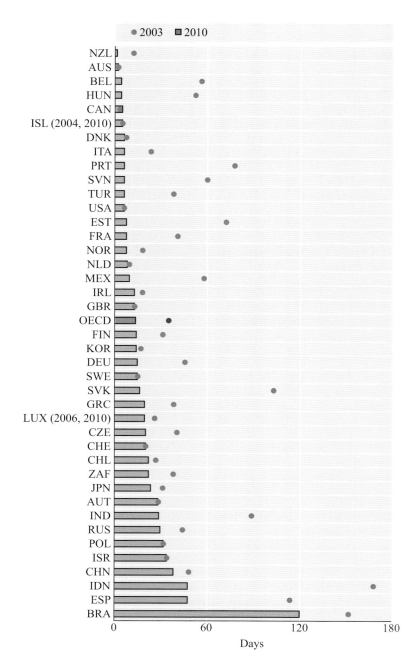

Figure 13.2   Country comparisons of ease of entry: days needed to start a business, 2003 and 2010

(Source: Organisation for Economic Co-operation and Development (OECD), 2010)

In the model of perfect competition, firms can also exit the market at zero cost in the event that production is no longer profitable. In any market, some firms are less efficient than others because they use more

costly production techniques or have less experience (learning) of production. Those firms making a loss because their costs are too high then have an incentive to leave the market rather than continuing to produce. As the analysis in Chapter 12 suggested, as the number of firms falls and total industry output is reduced, price is bid up until the point is reached at which all remaining firms are again profitable and there is no longer any incentive to exit.

Having laid out the main features of perfectly competitive markets, the chapter will now focus on how the firm, modelled in Chapter 11 using the production function and cost curves, behaves in perfectly competitive markets.

3   A competitive firm's demand curve

A key consequence of the assumptions of the perfect competition model is that in perfectly competitive markets, no single firm has any power to influence market price. As you saw in the previous chapter, the market price is set by the aggregate choices of buyers and sellers, which determine the market demand and supply. However, each firm is so small relative to the market that price reductions are unnecessary even to sell additional quantities that seem large by the firm's standards; so the firm can increase output as *much as it wants* and sell it all at the current market price. And if the firm were to try to raise its price above the market level, then it would simply lose all its sales to rivals who continued to sell at the lower price, since consumers are well informed and the products are homogeneous.

Consider, for example, a local market for eggs. Because there are many different suppliers of eggs, if one shop raises the price of eggs of a certain grade while all the others maintain a lower price, then buyers will simply make their purchase at one of the many rival outlets selling identical eggs for less. So the expensive shop will soon find that its customer base has dissolved. It will need to either restore the price of eggs to its original lower level or close down. On the other hand, if the shop increases its supply of eggs, then it will be able to sell them all without lowering its price, because the small size of the shop means that the increase in overall supply is negligible.

Price taker
A price taker is a buyer or seller that has to accept the price set by the market as given.

Firms in perfectly competitive markets, therefore, cannot choose the price that they charge: they are **price takers**. They can choose only how much output to sell at the market price, rather than being able to choose from a range of combinations of quantity and price. On the demand side, buyers are price takers too. As a consumer you are probably aware of what it means to be a price taker in this way; most of us demand quantities that individually are so small relative to the entire market (say, for clothes, phone apps or food) that we are used to taking the market price as given and do not expect to be able to negotiate a lower price. Similarly, many firms are also so small in their market that they must sell what they produce at the 'going rate'. For example, individual operators on the foreign exchanges sell currencies at prices dictated by overall market conditions. The low-cost clothing industry also contains many small producers who can exercise little individual influence on market prices. The model of perfect competition assumes a market composed entirely of such small 'actors' with no dominant operators.

As you saw in Chapter 12 (Figure 12.1), the *market demand curve*, which represents the overall quantity of a good or service demanded per time period at each price, slopes downwards, indicating that a lower price is required to sell a greater quantity of goods and a higher price will result in a lower quantity demanded. However, the demand curve facing an individual firm in a perfectly competitive market will be different from the *market* demand curve because it reflects its position as a price taker.

Figure 13.3 illustrates the demand curve for the firm and its relationship with market demand. Market demand and supply, made up by the aggregate choices of buyers and sellers, determine the market price that is taken as a given by the firm.

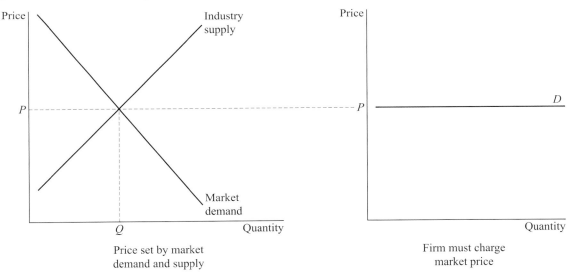

Figure 13.3   The horizontal demand curve facing a firm in perfect competition

The firm faces a horizontal demand curve. This reflects the fact that in perfect competition, the firm is left with no discretion about price at all. If it raises its own price above the market price, then all sales are lost to competitors. At the same time, there is no point in lowering its own price, because it can sell as much as it wants at the market price and need not reduce price to sell more. The firm is constrained to sell at the prevailing market price but decides how much to produce. This quantity decision will depend on the firm's costs, as will be discussed below. But remember that the horizontal demand curve is the demand curve facing the *price-taking firm*, whereas the *market* demand curve will be downward-sloping, as you saw in Chapter 12.

Activity 13.1

What is the price elasticity of demand of a point on the horizontal demand curve?

Answer

Recall that the price elasticity of demand is equal to the proportionate change in quantity demanded divided by the proportionate change in price. At a determinate price and quantity, as the demand curve gets flatter and flatter, the proportionate change in quantity demanded becomes very large for a small proportionate change in price. In the limiting case of a horizontal demand curve, the price elasticity of demand becomes infinitely large for all points on the demand curve, and the firm's horizontal demand curve is said to be infinitely elastic.

---

4   Profit-maximisation in the short run

You have seen that a competitive firm has to sell its output at a price determined by the market (i.e. it is a price taker) and can sell all the output that it decides to produce at this price. But how much should the firm produce? To answer this question, I need to define the objectives of the firm. In modelling perfect competition, I assume that firms choose their actions so as to maximise their total profits, which are calculated as the difference between the total revenue of the firm and its total costs:

   total profits = total revenue − total costs

So firms need to find out which level of output maximises profits at the given market price.

A key insight from economic analysis is the importance of considering decisions at the margin, which in this case means decisions that relate to an additional unit of output produced. Chapter 11 introduced the notion of marginal cost, i.e. the cost of an additional unit produced. In order to understand how firms maximise their profits, I also need to consider the **marginal revenue**, which is the revenue brought in by each additional unit sold, that is, the change in total revenue as a result of the sale of an additional unit of output.

The firm will keep producing more output as long as the extra revenue from doing so exceeds the extra costs. At any given level of output, the firm will produce an extra unit only if this is profitable, that is, the marginal revenue is higher than the marginal cost. So long as the extra output produced adds to its total profits, the firm will keep expanding its output. Assuming that marginal cost rises with output (as you saw in Chapter 11), the firm will expand output until the point where marginal revenue becomes equal to marginal cost. Conversely, if marginal revenue is below marginal cost, the firm can increase its profits by reducing output since it is selling the marginal unit at a loss. So the firm will maximise its profit at the level of output where marginal revenue is equal to marginal cost. This is the **profit-maximising rule**.

Note that this rule applies for all models of markets, not only perfect competition, as you will see in the next chapter.

Marginal revenue
The marginal revenue is the change in total revenue resulting from the sale of an additional unit of output.

Profit-maximising rule
A firm maximises its profit when marginal revenue is equal to marginal cost.

4.1   A firm's profit-maximising output in perfect competition

I now explore the profit-maximising decision of a firm in a perfectly competitive market in more depth, with the help of diagrams. The first step is to revisit Figure 13.3 in which I showed the firm's horizontal demand curve, and to add to it by representing the firm's costs.

With a horizontal demand curve, the firm's price is dictated by the market and is the same for any quantity sold. Therefore the addition to total revenue from selling one more unit is simply the price for that unit. For the perfectly competitive firm, therefore, marginal revenue equals price and does not change as output expands. As Figure 13.4 shows, in perfect competition a single horizontal line represents both the demand (D) and marginal revenue (MR) curves.

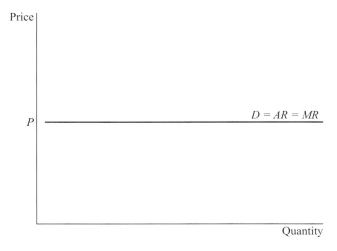

Figure 13.4   Demand, average revenue and marginal revenue for a firm in perfect competition

The demand curve also traces the firm's average revenue (AR), that is, the revenue that the firm would receive on average for each unit sold, at each level of output. Since all units are sold at the market price P, this price is also the firm's average revenue, which is constant for all levels of output.

So, since the firm faces a given market price, and marginal revenue and average revenue both equal price, in perfect competition

$$AR = MR = P$$

Having modelled the demand conditions faced by the firm, which are needed to determine the firm's revenue, I need to add the cost curves that you met in Chapter 11 in order to analyse the firm's costs. Remember that Chapter 11 introduced a distinction between short run and long run in the analysis of costs. Reversing the order used in Chapter 11, this time I begin with the output decision of the firm in the short run, holding market conditions constant, and then move on to discuss events taking place in the long run as market conditions change. In the perfect competition model, the short run means not only that the firm is modelled using short-run cost curves, but also that the market price is fixed, and entry and exit do not occur. This constraint is relaxed in the long run since, as Section 2 showed, in perfect competition there is free entry and exit in the long run.

Activity 13.2

Before you proceed, revise the analysis of costs from Chapter 11. Make sure that you understand the short-run average and marginal cost curves in Figure 13.5, which you have already seen in Chapter 11, Section 7.

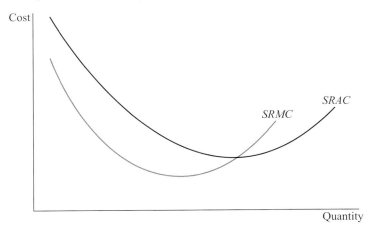

Figure 13.5   Short-run marginal cost (SRMC) curve with a U-shaped short-run average cost (SRAC) curve

I can now put together the firm's revenue and costs to identify the level of output that will maximise profits for the firm. As you saw above, in order to maximise profits, the firm should produce the quantity of output at which the marginal cost of production is equal to marginal revenue for a given market price ($MC = MR$).

You also saw above that for a competitive price-taking firm, marginal revenue is equal to the market price ($MR = P$) at all levels of output. So for the competitive firm, the condition for profit-maximising reduces to

$$MC = P$$

This condition is illustrated in Figure 13.6. The difference between this diagram and Figure 13.4 is the introduction of the firm's short-run marginal cost (SRMC) curve, which you will recognise from Chapter 11, Section 7 and Figure 13.5. Q is the profit-maximising output. At Q, the firm has no incentive to change its output. To see this, compare Q with Q_1 and with Q_2. At Q_1, marginal revenue P is above marginal cost MC_1, so increasing output by one unit will increase profits. Conversely, at Q_2, marginal revenue P is below marginal cost MC_2, so output should be reduced. There is only one profit-maximising level of output, namely Q, which is where $MC = MR = P$, represented by the intersection of the two curves.

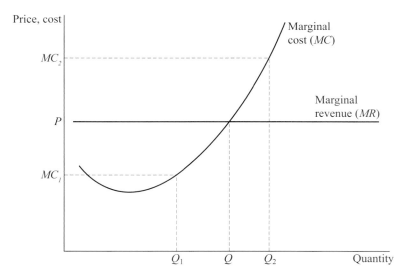

Figure 13.6   Profit-maximising output of a firm in perfect competition

In reality, firms might not think in terms of marginal revenue and marginal cost curves when deciding on the amount of output to produce. Terms like 'marginal revenue' and 'marginal cost' are parts of the economist's apparatus for modelling decisions, but they may not be part of the vocabulary of a firm. Perhaps it is helpful to imagine a discussion at a board meeting between the marketing director and the production controller along the following lines. If the marketing director believes that the revenue from increased sales will be more than the extra costs that the production manager says would be incurred, then the firm will decide to produce more output; conversely, if the revenue from increased sales would be less than the extra costs, then the firm will decide not to increase output. The discussion taking place between these individuals is the same as the decision process described by economists, but the argument is framed without using the term 'marginal' explicitly.

4.2   A firm's profits in the short run

You have just seen what level of output a firm has to produce in order to maximise its total profits, but how much profit will it earn? Even more importantly, will it make a profit at all?

To answer this question I need to know total revenue and total costs of the firm at the profit-maximising level of output. I can discover these by adding the average revenue and average cost curves to the diagram in Figure 13.6. In fact, it is not necessary to draw a separate average revenue curve because, as you saw in Figure 13.4, in perfect competition the same horizontal line shows demand, average and marginal revenue.

But what about the average cost curve? The firm faces three separate situations according to the position of the average cost curve in the diagram, that is, whether the minimum point of the average cost curve lies *above*, *below* or *tangential* to the market price (the demand curve).

Normal and supernormal profits

Figure 13.7 (overleaf) shows the situation when the minimum point of the average cost curve lies *below* the market price. As you saw above, the firm will produce the profit-maximising output Q at the ruling market price P. In this case, the firm's total revenue – that is, the number of units of output (Q) multiplied by the market price (P) – is shown in the figure as the sum of the areas of the blue and pink rectangles. Total costs at output Q are shown as the area of the pink rectangle, and they equal the units of output (Q) multiplied by the average cost at that output (AC).

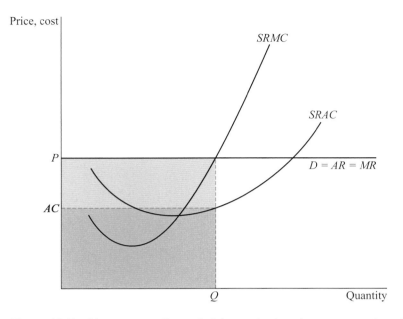

Figure 13.7   Short-run profit-maximising output and supernormal profits of a firm in perfect competition

Since, at output Q, revenue is greater than cost, the firm is making profits equivalent to the blue rectangular area, which is equal to the quantity Q multiplied by the difference between the price P and average cost AC:

$$\text{Total profit} = Q \times (P - AC)$$

An interesting point to remember is that the profits that I have identified are not the same as accounting profits. They are called 'supernormal' profits to distinguish them from 'normal' profits, which are the remuneration of the entrepreneurs, the firm owners who have invested in the capital equipment necessary to run the firm. This 'normal' profit is modelled in economics as a cost for the firm because it is the remuneration of a factor of production, i.e. capital, just like the employees' labour hours or the raw material inputs. So the cost curves already include the 'normal' profits of the entrepreneurs, and any extra profit made by the firm is called 'supernormal'.

Activity 13.3

How much profit will the firm earn if the minimum point of the average cost curve is tangential to the market price (the demand curve)?

Answer

It was given at the start of this section that

total profit = total revenue − total costs

When market price is equal to the firm's minimum average cost, total revenue and total costs are the same. Figure 13.8 shows the firm's total revenue, which is the quantity of output Q multiplied by the price P, as the rectangular blue area below the market price (demand curve). Total costs are equal to the units of output Q multiplied by the average cost (at output Q). In this case total costs are also represented by the same blue rectangular area. This means that the firm has zero supernormal profits, although it still earns normal profits.

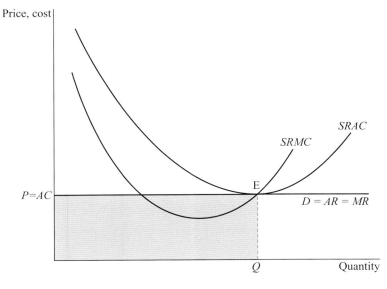

Figure 13.8   Short-run profit-maximising output and normal profits of a firm in perfect competition

The loss-making firm

One in four companies in the UK label industry is making a loss as economic conditions continue to take their toll, according to a new study by industry analyst Plimsoll.

[…]

David Pattison … [says:] '57 companies are making a loss for the second, even third year running and are simply selling at prices their business cannot sustain. … carrying on regardless is now unviable. They can no longer bury their heads in the sand.'

(Labels & labeling, 2012)

As the above quote illustrates, some firms are not profitable – their costs are higher than their revenue. This is illustrated in Figure 13.9, which shows a firm making a loss in the short run. This is the case when the minimum point of the average cost curve lies *above* the market price.

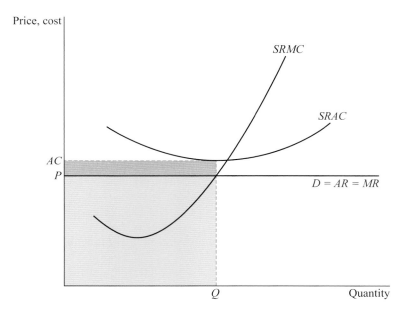

Figure 13.9   Short-run losses of a firm in perfect competition

In Figure 13.9, the revenue of the firm (the blue rectangular area obtained by multiplying Q by P) is less than its costs (the quantity Q

multiplied by average cost AC), which is represented by the sum of the blue and pink rectangles. So the firm incurs a loss (the pink area) which is equal to the quantity Q multiplied by the difference between the average cost AC and price P.

The firm still does the best it can by producing output Q, where marginal revenue and marginal cost are equal. However, this time a more precise description for Q would be the 'loss-minimising' rather than profit-maximising output.

In hard economic times it is common for many firms to operate at a loss, but this does not necessarily mean that they should stop trading. Even the computing giant Microsoft incurred a loss in 2012, but nobody expected it to shut down. However, as the above quotation suggests, firms cannot go on indefinitely operating at a loss. The extent of a firm's losses is also an important factor.

Economic theory can be used to derive a rule that helps firms to decide if they can keep 'burying their heads in the sand' and keep operating a loss, as the label making companies in the extract do, or should call it a day, stop producing and disappear. In order to find this rule, I need to use the distinction between fixed and variable costs introduced in Chapter 11.

Activity 13.4

Before you proceed, revise the distinction between fixed and variable costs from Chapter 11.

Answer

In the short run, a firm's total costs comprise both fixed and variable costs. Fixed costs are those costs that do not vary with the level of output in the short run; they include things such as the rent on factory buildings. Variable costs are the costs of those factors of production that vary with the level of output, such as raw materials and labour hours.

The shut-down rule

Figure 13.10 (overleaf) shows the cost curves of a perfectly competitive firm in the short run. I have distinguished between short-run average variable cost (SRAVC) and short-run average (total) cost (SRAC), since this distinction is important to the firm's short-run decision about whether or not to continue supplying the market. The difference between the two curves represents the average fixed cost of the firm. The average fixed cost decreases as the total fixed cost is spread over a larger number of units as output rises, so the two curves converge as output increases.

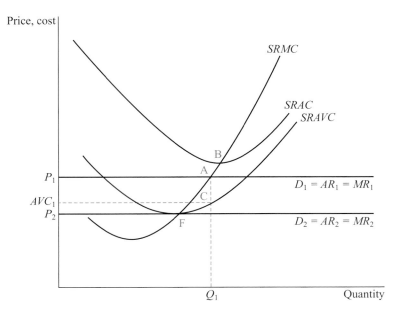

Figure 13.10   The short-run cost curves and supply curve of a perfectly competitive firm

At a market price of P_1, the output level at which marginal cost equals price is Q_1.

Activity 13.5

Look again at Figure 13.10. At price P_1, $MC = MR$ at point A, with output Q_1. Is the firm better off producing Q_1 or not producing at all?

Answer

The firm's decision to produce or not to produce depends on the relation between costs and revenues. At Q_1 in Figure 13.10, the price P_1 that the firm receives for its goods is high enough to cover its average variable cost AVC_1 at that output (point C). But P_1 is not high enough to also cover its average cost since the short-run average cost curve $SRAC$ lies above the firm's demand curve (D_1). The firm is therefore making a loss at Q_1: it is not covering total costs. However, each unit sold is making a contribution towards its fixed costs of a size represented by the difference between P_1 and AVC_1 in Figure 13.10.

The firm's fixed costs are unavoidable in the short run. So if the firm did not produce anything, its loss would be equal to its fixed costs. Thus in the short run, as long as price is above average variable cost, the firm is better off continuing to produce rather than ceasing production altogether because it will lose less money. At price P_1, Q_1 is the loss-minimising output and the best the firm can do in the short run. The excess of price over variable costs at least makes some contribution to fixed costs.

In general, if the market price crosses the marginal cost curve at any point between F and B (where B is the point of minimum average total cost and F is the point of minimum average variable cost), then the firm will continue to produce in the short run despite an overall loss, because if it shut down, its loss would be greater. At any point above B, price is above average total cost and the firm will produce and earn supernormal profits – this is the case you have seen earlier.

If market price falls below price P_2, however, the firm is not covering even its average variable cost. This creates a loss that can be avoided if the firm stops producing altogether. The **shut-down rule** for the firm, therefore, is that the firm will close down production when the price is below the minimum average variable cost.

The firm will therefore keep producing in the short run if the market price is above its minimum average variable cost.

Shut-down rule
A firm will close down production when the price is below the minimum average variable cost.

4.3   A firm's short-run supply curve

I can now derive a supply curve for the firm, which provides information about how much product the firm will supply at each price. This is the same notion as the market supply curve that you saw in Chapter 12, with the difference that this supply curve refers to a single firm in perfect competition and not to the whole market.

You have seen in Figures 13.6 to 13.10 that, under perfect competition, a firm chooses to produce the quantity of output at which marginal cost is equal to price in order to maximise profits. So the marginal cost curve tells you how much the firm will supply at each market price – which is exactly what the supply curve tells you. However, you saw above that the firm will not supply anything if the price is below its minimum average variable cost. This is point F in Figure 13.10, where the short-run marginal cost curve cuts the short-run average variable cost curve at its minimum point.

It follows that the firm's supply curve is only the part of its short-run marginal cost curve that lies above the short-run average variable cost curve. In Figure 13.10, therefore, the **short-run supply curve** of the firm is the part of the firm's short-run marginal cost curve that is above point F.

Short-run supply curve
The short-run supply curve of a firm in a perfectly competitive market is that part of the short-run marginal cost curve above the short-run average variable cost curve. It represents the quantity of output that the firm is willing to supply at each market price in the short run.

5   Profit-maximisation and supply in the long run

So far, the analysis has identified the outcome of the supply decision in the short run when a firm's fixed costs are unavoidable. In the long run, the firm has more options available to it because it is able to vary all its inputs because there are no fixed factors of production. Chapter 11 showed that the long-run average cost (LRAC) curve varies in shape depending on the technology being used by the firm. In perfect competition, the existence of many small firms in an industry suggests that the minimum efficient scale (MES) is small relative to the size of the market and that economies of scale are limited – otherwise a dominant firm would emerge. In these circumstances the firm will face a U-shaped LRAC curve, the upward-turning portion showing that diseconomies of scale set in at a scale that is small relative to the size of the market.

In parallel with the short-run case that you saw in Chapter 11, Section 7, which showed the relationship between short-run marginal and average costs, it is also possible to identify the firm's long-run marginal cost (LRMC) curve and its relationship to the LRAC curve. Both of these curves are illustrated in Figure 13.11, where the LRMC crosses the LRAC curve at its minimum (point A in the figure) just as in the short run.

Note, however, that there are two important differences between the long-run and short-run cost curves of the firm. First, since in the long run there are no fixed factors of production, the rising part of the U-shape of the LRAC curve is due to diseconomies of scale (a long-run concept – see Chapter 11, Section 5) rather than diminishing returns to a factor. Second, because of the flexibility of all factors of production in the long run, the LRMC curve, and hence the LRAC curve, is flatter than the short-run curves. The reason is that costs can be reduced in the long run by adjusting the quantity of the factors that are fixed in the short run as output rises or falls towards the lowest point on the average cost curve (point A in Figure 13.11, overleaf). Point A represents the MES – the level of output at which long-run costs are minimised.

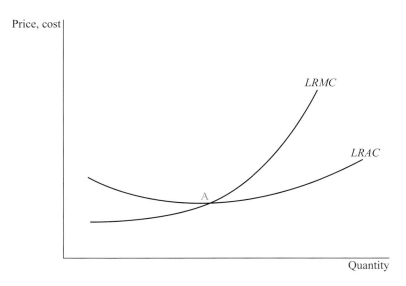

Figure 13.11   The long-run average and marginal cost curves (LRAC and LRMC), and the supply curve of the firm in perfect competition

Activity 13.6

Look back at the derivation of the short-run supply curve in the previous section. By applying the same reasoning to Figure 13.11, can you identify the long-run supply curve of a firm in perfect competition? Remember the difference between short and long run.

Answer

I can derive the **long-run supply curve** of a perfectly competitive firm by applying the same reasoning as for the short run. Similarly to the short run, the firm will produce where price equals marginal cost, so the supply curve will trace the LRMC curve, but not all of it. Remember that in the short run, it is in the firm's interest to supply only when price is above the minimum average variable cost. In the long run, however, there are no fixed costs: all costs can be considered as variable and are represented by the LRAC curve. So the firm will supply whenever price is not below the minimum long-run average cost. Thus the firm's long-run supply curve is traced by the part of the LRMC curve that is above the minimum LRAC, that is, the part of the LRMC curve that is above point A in Figure 13.11.

Long-run supply curve

The long-run supply curve of a perfectly competitive firm is that part of the long-run marginal cost curve above the long-run average cost curve. It represents the quantity of output that the firm is willing to supply at each market price in the long run.

5.1   A firm's output decision and profit in the long-run equilibrium

In 2011, the solar industry saw global oversupply drive [polysilicon] prices to record lows.

[…]

For most of the past decade … growth in solar-end market demand allowed the incumbents to earn healthy and consistent [profit] margins greater than 40 percent. In 2008, a shortage of polysilicon pushed prices to outrageously high levels (greater than $400 per kilogram in the spot market), and with those high prices came eye-popping 70 percent margins that enticed existing players as well as new entrants to embark on plant construction/expansion plans. These massive new plants and expansions made their presence felt in 2011, with a supply/demand imbalance pushing silicon prices to record-low levels, below even the cash costs of many manufacturers.

[According to] Research Senior Analyst, Brett Prior[:] 'After a half-decade of silicon demand outstripping supply, the aggressive expansion plans finally overshot. This supply/demand imbalance will push producers to lower contract prices closer to the level of manufacturing costs at $20 per kilogram, and will force higher-cost manufacturers to exit the industry. … The end result is that the current roster of over 170 polysilicon manufacturers and startups will likely be winnowed down to a dozen survivors by the end of decade.'

(Greentech Media, 2012)

You have seen that in the short run, market conditions, and therefore market price, are fixed. A firm can earn supernormal profit or make a loss depending on the level of the market price. In the long run, however, markets adjust: existing (incumbent) firms change their output in response to price changes, including ceasing production if they make losses, and new firms can enter and compete for a share of the market. Births and deaths of firms are a common feature of economic activity, as the extract above illustrates. When I turn my attention from competitive firms to the perfectly competitive industry as a whole in the long run, I therefore have to add to the model the entry and exit of firms.

Activity 13.7

Based on the extract above, what factors induce new firms to enter a market or exit from it?

Answer

The extract suggests that before 2011, supernormal ('eye-popping') profits stimulated the expansion of existing firms and the entry of new ones in the US polysilicon industry. This is the situation illustrated in Figure 13.7. After 2011, however, the extract predicts that most firms will exit the polysilicon industry because low prices will generate losses for inefficient firms that produce at high costs. The model predicts that this is when prices are so low that they do not cover fixed costs (see Figure 13.10).

So, in the model of perfect competition, the entry (exit) of firms is explained as a response to the existence of supernormal profits (losses), building on the assumption that you saw earlier that firms have a single goal, to maximise profits. In everyday language, this translates to 'seeing a good idea and deciding to do the same'.

Supply by a perfectly competitive industry is determined by two variables: the supply decisions of each firm within the industry, and whether there are new entries or exits. In the short run there is a fixed number of firms in the industry, each deciding on a short-term basis how much to produce according to their marginal costs and the market price. At each market price, I can deduce how much each firm will produce and sell, and I can add up these outputs to find the total supplied. The firms' marginal cost curves, and therefore the industry short-run supply curve, will be relatively steep (as you will see in the next subsection), since some of the factors of production are fixed for example, firms can increase output only by more intensive use of existing capital equipment).

In the long run, however, existing firms can change the scale of their operation, moving along their LRAC curve, and firms may enter or leave the industry – you saw in Section 2.4 the fourth assumption of no barriers to new entry and exit.

Activity 13.8

What will happen to market price as new firms enter the industry?

Answer

As the extract suggests, when new firms come in, output increases and prices are likely to be bid downwards by the increased competition for sales. The supernormal profits depicted in Figure 13.7 will be competed away by new entrants. (This mechanism was already described in Figure 12.8, in Chapter 12, Section 4.2, where a rightward shift of the supply curve leads to an equilibrium with higher output and lower price.) If it is assumed that firms continue to enter the industry until there are no more supernormal profits to be made, then prices will fall until firms are in the situation depicted in Figure 13.12. At price P, a firm maximises its profits by choosing the output for which price is equal to the LRMC, but it earns only normal profits. A representative firm (and therefore the whole industry) achieves productive efficiency, that is, produces at the minimum LRAC, which is the minimum possible cost for the firm. So there is no waste of resources in production.

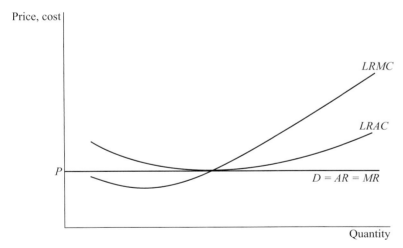

Figure 13.12   A perfectly competitive firm in long-run equilibrium

You can observe here the importance of the assumption of free entry and exit. The competition brought into the industry by the new entrants is necessary to drive the price down to the point of long-run minimum average cost, which is the minimum price that firms can accept without going out of business. So consumers will do as well as they can – that is, pay a price as low as possible – given the firms' costs. At the long-run equilibrium price, a firm will not earn any supernormal profit but will still earn normal profits.

It is possible for falling prices to have dramatic effects on the industry. If eager entrants find that they have together driven prices below average variable costs, as happened in the polysilicon industry in 2011, many firms will fail. This will allow prices to rise again until the remaining firms can cover costs.

The model of perfect competition illustrated in Figure 13.12 supposes that the firm shown is representative of the whole industry. In practice, however, if all the firms in the industry were exactly identical, using the same technology of production and hence having the same cost curves, then there would be an 'all or nothing' situation in which all firms would leave the industry when price was below the minimum average cost, or all would enter for prices above this cost level. This does not seem realistic. It is perhaps more reasonable to think of this firm as the marginal firm in the industry, where its normal profits represent the best that it can expect. Some more efficient firms may be doing rather better, for example as a result of using a more efficient technology or having better access to some factors of production, or perhaps because of the external economies of scale that you saw in Chapter 11, Section 8.

5.2   The market supply curve

As mentioned in the previous subsection, I can derive the market supply curve (the supply curve for the industry) by summing the supply curves of all firms horizontally, just as was done in Chapter 12, Section 2.3 for the demand curve. In the short run, the market supply curve is derived by adding together the firms' short-run supply curves. Similarly, the long-run supply curve is derived by adding together the firms' long-run supply curves.

Activity 13.9

Figure 13.13 shows the short-run and long-run supply curves of a perfectly competitive industry. Why are they different?

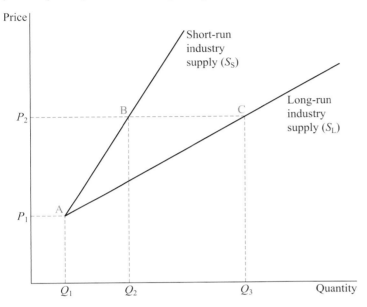

Figure 13.13   Short-run and long-run supply curves of a perfectly competitive industry

Answer

Market supply is likely to be more price elastic in the long run than in the short run. (Price elasticity of supply is explained in Chapter 12.) This is illustrated in Figure 13.13 for point A. If price rises from P_1 to P_2, then supply increases in the short run to Q_2. In the long run it will rise further, from Q_2 to Q_3, as new firms come in and existing firms expand production by employing more of the factors that were fixed in the short run.

Notice that the long-run supply curve (S_L) is likely to be upward-sloping as the industry as a whole may experience cost constraints on expansion. For example, the labour needed by firms entering an expanding industry may not be attracted away from other industries except at increased wages. The industry supply curve then slopes upward, showing the higher price needed to coax in additional factor inputs, and hence the rise in costs as total industry output increases.

The model of perfect competition thus allows one to construct the supply curves for a perfectly competitive industry. These industry supply curves are the supply curves for a product in a perfectly competitive market, as you saw in Chapter 12.

This completes the analysis of supply under perfect competition. In the next section, I will bring into the analysis the insights from Chapter 12 before drawing some conclusions about the significance of the model of perfect competition in Section 7.

6   Putting it all together: the importance of the model of perfect competition

Section 1 stated that the model of perfect competition is very influential among policymakers, who often use it as an ideal benchmark when they design policies that promote competition, as you will see in more depth in the next chapter. This section draws together the main features of the model that make it so powerful in representing how markets should work. In particular, you will see in more detail how the price mechanism coordinates the actions of firms and individuals to allocate the available resources efficiently.

Chapter 12 started to introduce the model of perfect competition by looking at the market demand and supply curves, which are the aggregation of the demand and supply curves of individual consumers and firms. It also briefly introduced the analysis of consumer behaviour, showing how a single consumer aims to maximise utility through her consumption decisions. This chapter has extended the analysis of the supply side of the market by analysing the production decisions of an individual firm that aims to maximise its profit. The model therefore assumes that all consumers and firms are self-interested – they are concerned only with their own satisfaction (utility) or profit – and rational – they make decisions that aim to maximise their interest.

The individual firm, the individual consumer and the market can be brought together in a three-part diagram, as shown in Figure 13.14 (overleaf). Figure 13.14b shows how the aggregated decisions of self-interested consumers and producers interact in the market to determine the equilibrium price P. As you saw in Chapter 12, the intersection of the market demand and supply curves identifies the point at which the market is in equilibrium, that is, the price at which quantity supplied equals quantity demanded. By following the dashed line across to the vertical axis, you can read off the equilibrium price P; and by following the line down to the horizontal axis, you can read off the equilibrium quantity Q_M. At the market equilibrium there is no pressure for change from within the market: given the market price P, no consumer is willing to purchase any more or less, and no producer is willing to supply any more or less.

Figures 13.14a and 13.14c represent the equilibrium for each price-taking consumer and producer, that is, the best position that they can achieve given the market price. The market price that each consumer

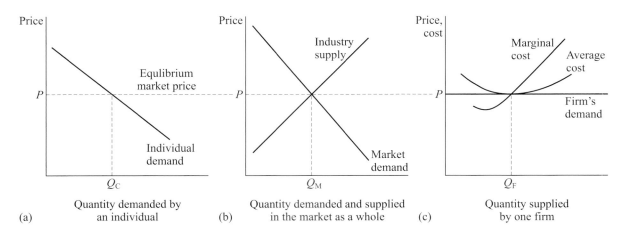

Figure 13.14   (a) Consumer demand; (b) market equilibrium; (c) firm supply

observes determines the amount that they choose to buy (represented by their individual demand curves); by the same token, the market price also determines both the quantities supplied by individual producers and how many producers choose to be in the market. (Notice that the units of measurement of output on the horizontal axis of Figure 13.14b must be much larger than those in Figures 13.14a and 13.14c, because the quantity refers to the whole market.)

Figure 13.14c shows long-run equilibrium for a price-taking firm in perfect competition, which you already saw in Figure 13.12. By producing the quantity of output Q_F where price is equal to marginal cost, the firm maximises its profits, although it earns only normal profits. The firm achieves productive efficiency, that is, produces at the minimum long-run average cost, which is its minimum possible cost. So there is no waste of resources in production.

Figure 13.14a shows a typical price-taking consumer, with a downward-sloping demand curve that models how much of the good this individual will buy at each price, as you saw in Chapter 12, Section 2.3. At the equilibrium price P, the consumer buys quantity Q_C. In equilibrium, the consumer maximises her utility. Just as a firm maximises its profits by setting the quantity supplied so that marginal cost is equal to the market price ($MC = P$), people maximise their satisfaction (utility) by choosing to buy the quantity of the good for which the satisfaction they get from the additional unit consumed is equal to the price paid (the market price) – or, in economic jargon, they maximise utility by choosing the quantity for which their *marginal utility* (MU) is equal to the market price ($MU = P$).

The reasoning behind the consumer's utility-maximisation is parallel to that of profit-maximisation for the firm. If the satisfaction that a consumer gets from consuming an additional quantity of the good (marginal utility) is greater than the price paid – that is, $MU > P$ – then the consumer is better off consuming more. Assuming that marginal utility decreases as more of the good is consumed (Chapter 12, Section 2.3), eventually the price will reflect the marginal satisfaction of the consumer. If, however, the price paid is greater than the satisfaction gained from an additional quantity of the good (marginal utility) – that is, $MU < P$ – then the consumer is better off reducing her consumption of the good until price and marginal utility are equal. Her utility is therefore maximised when marginal utility is equal to price:

$$MU = P$$

This is the **utility maximising rule in perfect competition**.

6.1   The price mechanism and the invisible hand

You can now see that the price mechanism coordinates the actions of consumers and firms so that the marginal utility of a good or service is equal to its marginal cost. You have seen that the market price is equal to both the consumer's marginal utility ($MU = P$) and the firm's marginal cost ($MC = P$). Hence marginal utility and marginal cost will be the same:

$$MU = P = MC$$

This result has important implications for the way in which modern market societies are organised, because it means that if resources are allocated through competitive markets, then waste is avoided and therefore the resulting allocation cannot be improved: the market achieves allocative efficiency. If the marginal utility of a good is higher than its marginal cost, then there is room for improvement: the overall utility can be increased by producing more of that good. Conversely, if the marginal utility of a good is less than its marginal cost, then too much of that good is produced and society is better off producing less of it. When marginal utility is equal to marginal cost, however, no economic agent (consumer or firm) has an incentive to move away from equilibrium.

The remarkable feature of this result is that it is achieved through the actions of self-interested firms and consumers who only think and act rationally to fulfil their goals – to maximise their own profit and utility.

Utility maximising rule in perfect competition
In perfect competition, the consumer maximises her utility when marginal utility is equal to the price paid: $MU = P$.

All this is possible because their actions are guided by market prices. In perfect competition, the price mechanism provides the incentives to consumers and firms to act in such a way that their self-interest leads to market outcomes that are beneficial to society as a whole.

This model therefore illustrates the famous dictum of the Scottish economist Adam Smith on the virtues of free markets:

> Every individual … neither intends to promote the public interest, nor knows how much he is promoting it … he intends only his own security; and by directing that industry in such a manner as its produce may be of the greatest value, he intends only his own gain, and he is in this, as in many other cases, led by an invisible hand to promote an end which was no part of his intention. … By pursuing his own interest, he frequently promotes that of the society more effectually than when he really intends to promote it.
>
> (Smith, 1843, p. 184)

7 Conclusion

This chapter has completed the analysis of the model of perfect competition started in Chapter 12, by focusing mainly on the supply side of markets. In particular, you have seen how, given the assumptions of the model, price-taking firms maximise profits, or minimise losses, by setting output so that marginal cost is equal to price, which is their marginal revenue. You have also seen how supernormal profits and losses motivate firms to enter and exit an industry and therefore lead the market to equilibrium in the long run. Such equilibrium is efficient because firms achieve productive efficiency – they produce at minimum average costs – and resources are allocated without waste.

Remarkably, the model of perfect competition shows that such efficient results are reached because prices coordinate the actions of self-interested rational firms and consumers who aim only to maximise their own profits and utility. The model can therefore be considered a rigorous illustration of Adam Smith's famous metaphor of the invisible hand that guides self-interested people to promote the interest of society.

In spite of the power of the perfect competition model, you might have wondered about the extreme nature of its assumptions. In real markets one can observe firms that are larger than whole countries, and are both sellers and buyers in many important markets. Moreover, information is far from perfectly distributed, and often firms try to avoid the constraints of being a price taker by claiming that their products are of higher quality than those of their competitors, or by innovating. In order to analyse how other types of markets work, other models of competition will be needed, as you will see in the next chapter.

References

Greentech Media (2012) 'Polysilicon prices hit record low in 2011; will head even lower, enabling $0.70/W PV in 2012', 10 February, [online] www.greentechmedia.com/articles/read/polysilicon-prices-hit-record-lows-in-2011-will-head-even-lower-enabling-0 (Accessed 30 December 2012).

Labels & labeling (2012) 'One in four UK label companies "making a loss"', 25 June, [online] www.labelsandlabeling.com/news/latest-news/one-in-four-uk-label-companies-%E2%80%98making-a-loss%E2%80%99 (Accessed 30 December 2012).

Organisation for Economic Co-operation and Development (OECD) (2010) *Measuring Innovation: A New Perspective*, Paris, OECD.

Office of Fair Trading (2009) *Government in Markets: Why Competition Matters – a Guide for Policy Makers*, [online] www.oft.gov.uk/shared_oft/business_leaflets/general/OFT1113.pdf (Accessed 30 December 2012).

Smith, A. (1843) *An Inquiry into the Nature and Causes of the Wealth of Nations*, Edinburgh, Thomas Nelson.

US Census Bureau (2007) *Employers and Nonemployers*, [online] www.census.gov/econ/smallbus.html (Accessed 29 December 2012).

Chapter 14

Industrial structure, competition and regulation

Merlin Stone

Contents

1 Introduction

Information and communication technologies (ICTs) have revolutionised various aspects of the way society works since the invention of the telegraph in the nineteenth century. Nowadays we take for granted that we can access information and services instantly at the touch of a button from our phones, and we live in an increasingly connected world.

Looking at the development of telecommunications (often abbreviated to telecoms), you can see that the industry has been shaped by the activities of very large firms, such as AT&T Technologies, which already in the 1960s was among the top ten largest industrial corporations in the USA with over 150 000 employees, and British Telecom (now BT), which was a UK government-owned monopoly until its privatisation in 1984. Still in 2012 various telecoms firms featured among the top 100 largest firms in Fortune's Global 500 Firms.

The full Fortune's Global 500 list of 2012 shows that other industries – such as oil production, car making, banking, computing, retailing and insurance – also have very large firms. Some of these giants also dominate their industry, such as Microsoft (119th) in the operating system segment of the PC industry with Windows, and Apple (55th) in the tablet business.

Large firms are very important actors in national economies. You saw in the previous chapter that the majority of firms are small. Figure 14.1a (overleaf) repeats Figure 13.1 from the previous chapter, which shows the distribution of firms by employment size in the USA, but adds next to it the distribution of revenue by firm size (Figure 14.1b). The charts show that firms with over 100 employees, which constitute less than 2% of firms (Figure 14.1a), account for nearly three-quarters of total revenue in industry (Figure 14.1b).

The markets in which these large firms operate do not fit the perfectly competitive model, in which small firms minimise costs to remain competitive and sell homogeneous goods at a price determined by the market. In markets that cannot be usefully modelled using perfect competition, firms still compete, sometimes vigorously, with business rivals using a variety of strategies, related to pricing, marketing and innovation. This chapter shows how economists model different types of competition and market structures (i.e. the features that influence the nature of competition and trading in a market), and discusses what

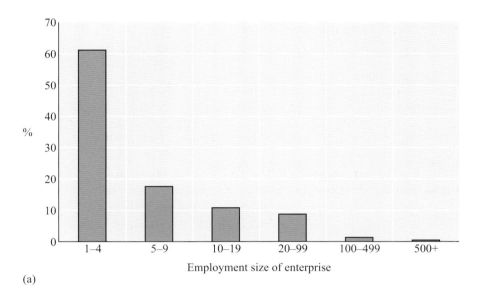

(a)

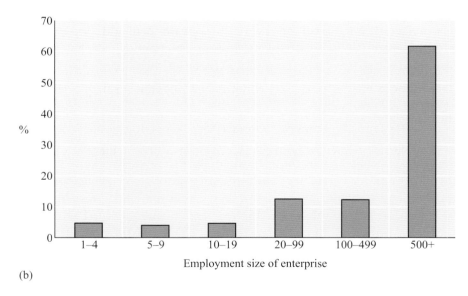

(b)

Figure 14.1   Distribution of (a) number of firms and (b) revenue by
employment size class in the USA, 2007

(Source: US Census Bureau, 2007, Table 2b)

these models explain and predict in terms of prices and benefits to
consumers and firms.

Section 2 introduces the analysis of a pure monopoly using the telecommunications industry as a case study, before monopoly and perfect competition are compared in Section 3. Section 4 introduces another market structure, monopolistic competition, in which small firms gain market power from differentiating their products. Section 5 returns to the telecommunications industry to analyse how governments regulate natural monopolies. Section 6 introduces the importance of strategic competition in oligopolies – markets with only a few sellers whose decisions are interdependent. The chapter concludes by looking at how economists model competition in innovative industries.

The learning outcomes for this chapter are:

- to understand models of pure monopoly and imperfect competition, such as monopolistic competition and oligopoly, and how they compare with the model of perfect competition
- to identify natural monopolies and understand why they need to be regulated
- to understand the implications of a downward-sloping demand curve and market power for the firm and for customers
- to explain why firms enter markets and how entry can lead to changes in market structure by increasing or reducing the degree of monopoly in a market
- to understand the economic rationale for competition policy
- to understand how economists model competition in innovative industries.

2 The early years of the telecoms industry: exploring monopoly

Natural monopoly
A natural monopoly exists if, as a result of economies of scale, a single firm can supply the market at a lower average cost than can be achieved by a number of smaller firms.

Because of its massive benefits to consumers and businesses, the telecommunications industry is of high interest for economists, governments and the citizens whom governments aim to protect from the effects of restricted competition, which is endemic in the industry. When telecommunications networks were first created, they were generally monopolies, often government-owned. They were considered **natural monopolies**, like power and water utilities – other industries in which the investment in extensive physical networks generates economies of scale that are large relative to the market. In telecoms, the most cost-effective way of providing for customers was to have one firm providing the cable networks, the handsets and the exchanges of switches that routed calls. Laying down more than one network of cables was considered wasteful, although in some countries separate regional companies evolved. Once a country-wide network was established, calls could be made within one exchange or between nearby exchanges, or might need routing over long-distance wires, possibly into the territory or even country of another company.

Chapter 11 introduced one of the most important sources of monopoly: economies of scale. If there are economies of scale in an industry, then firms' long-run average cost (LRAC) curves are downward sloping: average cost falls as output rises, as shown in Figure 14.2. The market demand curve is labelled D. If a firm expands ahead of its rivals, it can take advantage of these economies of scale in such a way that it can dominate the industry. You can see that the lowest unit cost possible, given the market demand, is AC_1, which is achieved at quantity equal to or greater than the minimum efficient scale (MES) Q_1. Any quantity lower than Q_1, such as Q_2, is produced at a higher unit cost: AC_2 is greater than AC_1. This cost structure means that the established or existing 'incumbent' firm can sell at a price that no other firm wishing to enter the market can match without incurring losses because of its higher costs.

Pure monopoly
A pure monopoly exists when a single firm is the sole supplier in a market.

If the industry is a natural monopoly, it is cost-efficient to have a single firm supplying the market. When there is only one supplier, the market is called **pure monopoly**.

Note that not all pure monopolies are 'natural', that is, arising because of cost conditions. Some firms are innovators, discovering and selling

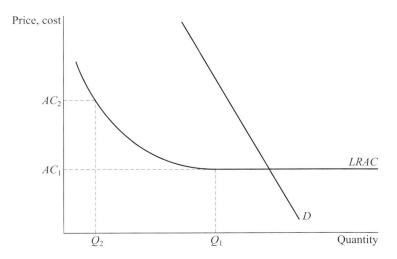

Figure 14.2   A natural monopoly

new products that create new markets, and therefore they are the only sellers, at least until imitators enter the market, without necessarily having economies of scale (the iPad is a good example of this – in the early years of the tablet market, analysts used to say that there was no market for tablets, but only the iPad). Innovators can also use **patents**, which grant them a temporary legal right to exclude others from using the technology they have invented, in order to extend their monopoly for a fixed period of time. In other cases, monopolies are established by law because the goods or services produced are of special national interest. Indeed, a telecommunications network is a key infrastructure for a country, and national interest is often considered when decisions are taken about telecommunications policy.

A key question that economists are asked, for example by government, by consumer groups or even by competing firms, is what happens when an industry is dominated by one firm: what are the pricing and output decisions of a monopolist? In order to analyse this issue, it is necessary to model the behaviour of a typical monopolist.

2.1   The monopolist's demand curve, revenue and market power

As in the previous chapter, a firm is assumed to have a sole objective: to maximise its profit, which is the difference between its total revenue and its total cost.

Patent
A patent is the legal right of an inventor to exclude others from using a particular invention for a fixed period in time.

Costs can be analysed using the cost curves that you met in Chapters 11 and 13. The analysis of a firm's revenue starts from its demand curve. Here, there is an important difference between perfect competition and monopoly. In perfect competition, firms are price takers but can expand output as much as they wish without having to lower their price: their demand curve is horizontal so marginal revenue is equal to market price (Chapter 13, Section 3). For a monopolist, however, marginal revenue is not equal to the market price because the demand curve for the output of a pure monopolist is the market demand curve, since the firm is the only supplier in the market. So the monopolist's demand curve is *not* horizontal but downward-sloping, and the price charged by the monopolist will vary depending on the quantity produced — by producing less, the monopolist can sell at a higher price. The monopolist has **market power** (or monopoly power), that is, the power to influence market price.

Market power

A firm has market power (also referred to as monopoly power) if it has some choice in setting the price of its product, and its decision about how much to supply influences the price that it can charge.

Total and average revenue

In order to find out more about a monopolist's total and marginal revenue, it is worth exploring its demand curve in more detail. The demand for a monopolist's output can be illustrated by a 'curve' such as D in Figure 14.3. A pure monopolist has no competition, so market demand is its only constraint. It can choose either the price at which it sells its output or the quantity of output to produce. If it chooses a selling price, then the demand curve will determine the quantity that it can sell at that price. Alternatively, if it chooses a level of output to offer to the market, then the demand curve will determine the price that can be charged to sell that quantity. Its aim is to achieve the combination of price and quantity that maximises profits.

The total revenue of the firm is given by the price of a good sold multiplied by the number of units sold. In Figure 14.3, if the price is P_1, then the revenue is equal to $P_1 \times Q_1$. Another way to think of the total revenue is as the area of the rectangle AQ_1OP_1.

Activity 14.1

What is the total revenue if the price is set at P_2?

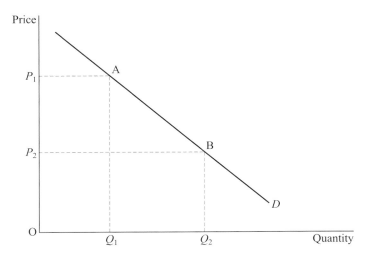

Figure 14.3   Demand curve for a monopolist

Answer

The firm's total revenue is given by the market price P_2 multiplied by the quantity demanded Q_2, which is represented in the figure by the area of the rectangle BQ_2OP_2.

As you saw in Chapter 13, a firm's total revenue is the quantity of its goods demanded times price:

total revenue = quantity sold × price

or

$$TR = P \times Q$$

It follows that the demand curve (D) of the firm is also its average revenue (AR) curve. The average revenue is the revenue per unit sold, i.e. total revenue divided by quantity demanded, and is equal to the price per unit sold. That is,

$$AR = \frac{TR}{Q} = P$$

Each point on the demand curve therefore shows the average revenue (equals price) for each quantity demanded. This is true of all demand curves, including the horizontal firm's demand curve in perfect competition, which you saw in Chapter 13.

Marginal revenue

What about marginal revenue? Chapter 13 showed that for the individual firm in perfect competition, price and average revenue are also equal to marginal revenue because the demand curve is horizontal – the firm in perfection competition is a price taker.

Activity 14.2

Look again at Figure 14.3. Suppose that demand is currently Q_1 at price P_1. Now the firm wants to sell an extra unit. How will price and total revenue change for the monopolist, who faces a downward-sloping demand curve?

Answer

The change in total revenue that the firm receives from selling an extra unit (the marginal revenue) is subject to two opposite effects. The extra unit of output sold generates additional revenue. However, if the firm wants to increase demand by one unit, then it will have to reduce its price because of the downward-sloping demand curve. That means that it will receive a lower price for *all* the units that it sells, not just the additional one – the decrease in price lowers the revenue from each unit sold. So marginal revenue falls as output increases – that is the snag about a downward-sloping demand curve. Marginal revenue is positive if the extra revenue from selling one more unit outweighs the drop in revenue from reducing the price of all the other units.

The relationship between average and marginal revenue is shown in Figure 14.4. As quantity demanded rises, the downward slope of the demand curve means that price (average revenue) falls, so marginal revenue falls. Furthermore, if you compare marginal with average revenue, you will see that marginal revenue is less than average revenue at each quantity demanded. This relationship between marginal and average revenue is implied by the downward slope of the demand curve. Average revenue declines as quantity rises. Marginal revenue must therefore (arithmetically) be *less* than average revenue for the reason explained above in Activity 14.2: the marginal revenue is the price (average revenue) of the additional unit *less* the revenue lost by reducing the prices of *all* the others in order to raise demand.

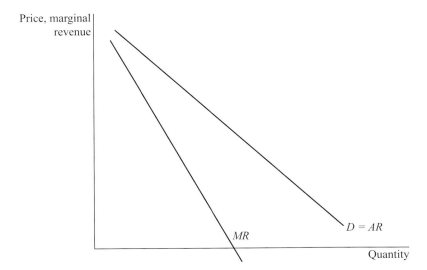

Figure 14.4   Average revenue and marginal revenue curves of a monopolist

A marginal revenue (MR) curve traces the marginal revenue received by the firm at each possible price and each possible quantity demanded. Since marginal revenue is less than average revenue for all quantities, a downward-sloping demand curve is always associated with a marginal revenue curve that lies below it, as in Figure 14.4. Note that the marginal revenue curve can eventually intersect with the horizontal axis (where MR = 0), indicating that at high levels of output, when the marginal revenue curve is below the horizontal axis, marginal revenue is negative, so total revenue starts to fall as the firm expands.

2.2   Profit-maximisation for the monopolist

In order to study how a monopolist maximises profits, both revenues and costs need to be considered.

Activity 14.3

Revise the profit-maximising rule that you met in Chapter 13, Section 4. Will the same rule apply to a monopolist?

Answer

You saw in Chapter 13 that the general condition for profit-maximisation is that marginal revenue is equal to marginal cost. This condition holds for a monopolist as well as for a firm in perfect competition. Each additional (marginal) unit produced and sold increases total revenue (unless marginal revenue is negative) but also adds to total cost. If the marginal revenue is higher than the marginal cost, then the addition to total revenue is larger than the addition to total cost, and profit rises. Conversely, if marginal cost is larger than marginal revenue, then producing and selling the additional unit reduces total profit. Where marginal revenue and marginal cost are equal, profit is maximised. This condition for profit-maximisation applies to firms in all market structures.

Now I will apply this condition to a monopolist. Figure 14.5 shows the firm's cost and revenue curves together on a single diagram. What output will the monopolist choose in order to maximise profits? In Figure 14.5, the marginal revenue curve MR crosses the marginal cost curve MC at point A with output Q_1. At output Q_1, marginal revenue is equal to marginal cost, so Q_1 is the profit-maximising output. At output levels below Q_1, the marginal revenue curve MR is above the marginal cost curve MC. So increasing output towards Q_1 will add to profits. At output levels above Q_1, marginal revenue is below marginal cost, so reducing output will reduce costs more than it reduces revenue, hence profits will rise. It follows that Q_1 is the profit-maximising output. Once it is producing Q_1, the firm has no incentive to change its output.

Activity 14.4

What price will the monopolist have to charge to sell the whole output Q_1?

Answer

The monopolist's demand curve (average revenue curve) is D (= AR). If the firm wishes to sell Q_1, then it must charge P_1. A higher price will leave it with unsold goods, while a profit-maximising firm will not charge a lower price, since that would reduce revenue.

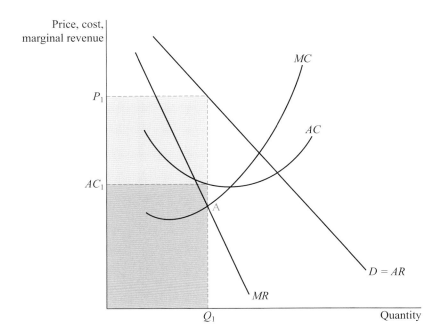

Figure 14.5   Profit-maximisation by a pure monopolist

In pure monopoly there is only one firm in the market. The output Q_1 is therefore the market equilibrium output in Figure 14.5, and P_1 is the equilibrium price.

Activity 14.5

What is the total revenue and total cost of the monopolist producing at Q_1?

Answer

As you saw above, if the price is P_1, then the revenue is equal to $P_1 \times Q_1$, which is represented by the area which is the sum of the pink and blue rectangles. Total cost is calculated by multiplying the average cost (AC) by the number of units (Q). Again this can be represented as an area in Figure 14.5. When output is Q_1, average cost is AC_1. So the area of the pink rectangle represents the total cost of producing Q_1 units.

Activity 14.6

How much profit does a monopolist make when producing Q_1 units?

Answer

Total profit includes both normal and supernormal profit earned by the firm. Under conditions of monopoly, supernormal (or excess) profit is earned if the monopolist receives a price (average revenue) that is any higher than average cost. Supernormal profit is represented by the blue area in Figure 14.5. This is the area left after you subtract total costs (the pink rectangle) from total revenue (the sum of the blue and pink rectangles). Another way to see this is that the supernormal profit per unit is the difference between the price P_1 (average revenue) and average cost AC_1. By multiplying the supernormal profit per unit by the quantity sold (Q_1) we have the total supernormal profit.

The normal profit of an entrepreneur is included in the economic definition of a firm's costs. As you saw in the previous chapter, normal profit is defined as the return to the entrepreneur's time and money that he or she considers necessary to make running the business worthwhile – it is the entrepreneur's remuneration (Chapter 13, Section 4.2). It is an opportunity cost, equal to what could be earned with that time and money elsewhere. That is why it is included in cost.

You saw that under conditions of perfect competition, in the long run, normal profit is all that is earned by the entrepreneur, and it is the profit that would be just sufficient to keep the firm in the industry. In monopoly, however, the firm can earn supernormal profit in the long run if it prevents entry.

3   Monopoly and perfect competition compared

The next step in this analysis of how markets work is to compare the outcome of monopoly with that of perfect competition for a particular industry. The only difference under consideration here is a difference in the number of firms between just one and 'very many'.

All the components of the analysis will be familiar to you; I need simply to bring them together.

Figure 14.6 (overleaf) shows a firm – a monopolist – producing for a market that is potentially perfectly competitive – so, not a natural monopoly. Imagine that government regulations have protected the industry from new entry. Curve D is the market demand curve; because the firm is a monopolist, D is also the demand curve facing the firm. MR is the monopolist's marginal revenue curve. As in Figures 14.4 and 14.5, MR is downward-sloping and lies below the demand curve at every point. This indicates that, in contrast to the perfectly competitive firm, the monopolist must reduce price in order to sell more output (and must reduce output in order to set a higher price). As a consequence, marginal revenue falls as output increases.

To simplify the example, I assume that there are constant returns to scale across the output range so that the average cost (AC) curve is horizontal and average cost is therefore always equal to marginal cost (MC). Constant returns to scale occur if a change of the quantity of inputs results in the same proportionate change in output; for instance, a doubling of inputs results in a doubling of output. Assuming the prices of inputs do not vary, if a firm has constant returns to scale, then as output increases, average cost is constant and is represented by a horizontal cost curve – you saw constant unit (average) cost in Figure 11.6, Chapter 11, Section 5.2. When average cost is constant, it follows that marginal cost will also be constant, because each additional unit of output must cost the same to produce as the previous one. Figure 14.6 shows that the curves for average cost and marginal cost are horizontal and identical as output increases.

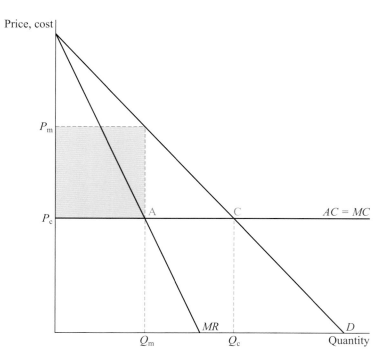

Figure 14.6   Monopoly and perfect competition compared

Activity 14.7

What is the profit-maximising price and quantity for the monopolist? How much supernormal profit does the profit-maximising monopolist make? Think back to Section 2.2.

Answer

The profit-maximising level of output for any firm, whether in monopoly or in perfect competition, is found where marginal cost is equal to marginal revenue. For the monopolist, this is Q_m in Figure 14.6 (follow the dashed line down from point A). The market demand curve shows that at output Q_m, the price is P_m (follow the dashed line up from Q_m, through point A, to where it just meets the demand curve). The monopolist's supernormal profit is represented by the shaded rectangle in the diagram. The area of this rectangle is measured by the excess of price over average cost ($P_m - AC$), multiplied by the quantity sold, Q_m.

Imagine that this firm is a pure monopolist producing a pharmaceutical drug that generates billions of dollars of revenue. The drug can be sold by only one firm because it is protected by a patent, which prevents other firms from selling the product for a finite period of time (normally around 20 years). Suppose that the patent expires, but the *market* demand curve for the drug remains the same. What would you expect to happen?

You might expect other pharmaceutical firms to enter the market, attracted by the opportunity to share some of the revenue and profit from this product. If many firms enter the market, producing the same product as the incumbent, then you can apply the model of perfect competition. Eventually, the market will be supplied by a large number of broadly similar price-taking firms. The cost conditions in the industry are being held constant, so the constant returns to scale experienced under monopoly are carried over into perfect competition. The line $AC = MC$ in Figure 14.6 is therefore the industry supply curve in the long run as industry output expands. You can think of the industry as composed of many small firms, all operating at minimum long-run average cost as in Figure 13.12 of Chapter 13. In Figure 14.6, industry output expands at price P_c through the entry of new firms operating at the same cost. The effect is a horizontal industry supply curve.

The intersection of that supply curve and the market demand curve D at point C gives the equilibrium level of output in the market under perfect competition. This is Q_c at the equilibrium price P_c. Since price equals average cost, the firms in the industry are making only normal profit.

Activity 14.8

Compare the two market equilibria in Figure 14.6. What can you say about consumer satisfaction under monopoly and perfect competition?

Answer

The monopolist charges a higher price and produces a lower quantity than the market price and quantity under perfect competition. Consumers are therefore worse off under monopoly than under perfect competition. Not only do they face higher prices under monopoly, they are not able to buy the quantity of output given by $Q_c - Q_m$. The introduction of competition therefore benefits consumers in these two important respects.

Another negative feature of the market equilibrium under monopoly is that price is greater than marginal cost, which, as you saw in Chapter 13, Section 6, means that resources are not allocated efficiently by the market. There is scope for increasing well-being by producing more output because consumers would be willing to pay more than marginal cost – the cost of producing an additional unit. The market power of the monopolist leads to an inefficient allocation of resources.

The result of the comparison of the models of monopoly and perfect competition is an important one. It is often called on to justify the use of perfect competition as a benchmark for industrial policy. In this example the benefit to patients is the low price of pharmaceutical drugs, although in this particular case the high prices during the period of patent exclusivity are necessary to repay not only the cost of research and development (R&D) for the drug in question, but also the cost of other investment in research that does not result in successful drug products. The supernormal profit is also an important incentive for undertaking very risky R&D investment, without which new drugs would not be discovered. These issues are explored in more depth in Section 7.

Activity 14.9

Can you think of another reason why a monopoly might be more desirable for consumers than a perfectly competitive market structure? Look back at Section 2 for a hint.

Answer

The example illustrated in Figure 14.6 assumes constant returns to scale, but you saw in Section 2 that when there are strong economies of scale, as in the case of natural monopoly, small firms incur a much higher average cost than a large monopolist because they cannot operate at minimum efficient scale. Therefore the competitive market price might be higher than the price charged by a monopolist in spite of the monopolist's supernormal profit because the monopolist is much more cost-efficient.

---

4   Monopolistic competition

The previous section compared two extreme situations. In perfect competition, the numerous small firms in the industry have no power: they are price takers. In monopoly, the one and only seller has full power to set price above marginal cost and earn supernormal profit. In practice, however, most industries fall between these two extremes. Going back to the previous example of drug manufacturers, firms attempt to gain market power by differentiating their product from rivals. Even when a pharmaceutical drug has lost its patent protection, this does not usually result in perfect competition. Some manufacturers of the same pharmaceutical drug will command higher prices for their product than those charged by rivals. Some customers will be prepared to pay high prices if they perceive greater reliability, safety or higher quality in health care products.

For instance, consider the different suppliers of paracetamol or flu relief products at your local supermarket or chemist. The active ingredients on the labels are very similar – sometimes exactly the same – but the prices of particular branded goods vary. Often the supermarket own-branded goods are much cheaper compared to brands advertised in the media. In a perfectly competitive market, these goods would have the same price because the firms supplying them would be price takers and the product homogeneous in every element. But the market for flu relief products is not perfectly competitive; it would appear some firms have market power, yet the appearance of many different suppliers also suggests freedom to enter.

This is a situation where the market is modelled using monopolistic competition. Here, the market has many producers and consumers. No business has total control over the market price. Firms take prices charged by competitors as given and ignore the impact of their own prices on the prices of others – there are just too many competitors to take into account. However, the assumption of homogeneous goods and services that held in perfect competition does not apply: there is product differentiation. There are non-price differences between firms' products, which perform the same basic functions but differ in type, style, quality, reputation, appearance and location. Firms may also advertise and create branding, although the effects of these are not strong enough to prevent entry in the long run. There are few barriers to entry and exit. There are many firms interested in entering, each with slightly different products. Firms that exit do not suffer abnormal liquidation costs – there are low start-up costs and no exit costs.

Product differentiation is characteristic of markets where the products are broadly similar and a firm wants to make sure that its own product is easily recognised by consumers. Markets generally considered to be monopolistically competitive include small retail and personal service outlets (restaurants, hairdressing), but also manufacturing industries such as shoes and clothing (though strong branding has increased the monopolistic element). Shops and personal service outlets are differentiated by their quality of service, the services they supply or the products they stock, and of course by their location. A poor location will mean not enough custom and possible losses. For retailers, choosing the location with the right amount of 'retail traffic' is critical. In all of these markets the products are seen by consumers as quite close substitutes, but not identical.

A key consequence of product differentiation is that firms have a certain degree of market power. For example, if Kellogg's increased the price of its cereals by 20%, some consumers would still buy the Kellogg's brand. One of the Kellogg's advertising slogans has been 'If it doesn't say Kellogg's on the box, it isn't Kellogg's in the box'; the implication is that its products are superior in some way. This means that the firm in monopolistic competition is not a price taker, and its demand curve is downward-sloping, just as in the case of pure monopoly. However, there is an important difference. In the pure monopoly, the demand curve facing the firm is the market demand curve. In monopolistic competition, there is more than one firm, but each firm has its own downward-sloping demand curve, reflecting the demand for the goods that it supplies. The firm's demand curve lies to the left of the market demand curve, since only part of the market demand is now demand for its product.

In the short run, profit-maximisation in monopolistic competition is very similar to pure monopoly, which you saw in Figure 14.5, with the difference that the firm's profit-maximising quantity is only a small fraction of the market's output, and the firm's price is only one of the prices set by the many suppliers, who have their own distinctive downward-sloping demand curve. So the situation is like monopoly in the short term. A firm can raise its prices without losing all its sales, but of course a higher price will attract more competitors in the long run.

In the long run, as new firms enter the market, the original firm's demand curve is likely to shift to the left, as some customers switch consumption to new entrant products – there is less demand for the original firm's product at each price. How far left will the incumbent 'monopolist' demand curve shift? Firms will continue to enter the industry so long as there are supernormal profits being made, since supernormal profits mean, by definition, profits higher than the return available elsewhere. Figure 14.7 shows the point of long-run profit-maximising equilibrium of a firm in a monopolistically competitive industry after entry has ceased.

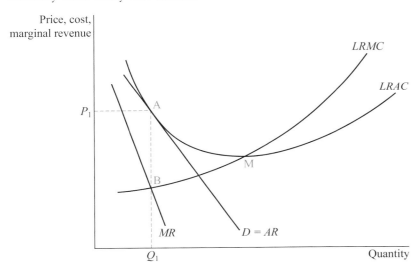

Figure 14.7   Long-run equilibrium of a firm in monopolistic competition

The firm's LRAC curve is U-shaped but flatter than its short-run cost curve. The demand curve $D = AR$ is the firm's individual demand curve in the long run. As other firms have entered the market, the demand curve has shifted left. As a result, the firm will reduce output, and move leftwards along its LRAC curve: it may have disinvested as demand has shifted; demand for the firm's product has decreased at each price. In the long-run equilibrium, the firm is at the point where there are no longer any supernormal profits to be made. This happens at point A in Figure 14.7, where the demand curve is a tangent to the average cost curve; that is, it just touches it without crossing it. At this point $LRMC = MR$ (point B) and the firm maximises profit by setting output to Q_1. Supernormal profits have fallen to zero because price equals average cost. There is therefore no longer any incentive for new firms to move into the industry. The final number of firms serving a given market depends on the market size, economies of scale and the degree of product differentiation.

This model is relevant only to cases where the MES of firms is such that there is room for a number of firms in the market. Notice, however, that at output Q_1 and price P_1 the firm is not operating at the MES point M. Average cost is higher than it would be if the firm was supplying a larger part of the market. So monopolistic competition can drive up costs above their minimum level, and although there are no supernormal profits, consumers may not be getting the best possible deal. Another disadvantage is that consumers must process information on many different brands in order to select the best. The cost of gathering information can exceed the benefit of having the best product rather than another. However, competition has brought product diversity to the market that may be beneficial to consumers, with the benefits of product variety outweighing the disadvantages of inefficiency.

In the model of monopolistic competition, entry plays a key role in increasing choice, and reducing prices and supernormal profits in the long run. Section 2, however, showed that strong economies of scale prevent entry in natural monopolies, so government has felt the need to introduce regulation to prevent the abuse of market power. In extreme cases, government can intervene to break up a monopoly firm into several smaller firms to both reduce their market power and encourage greater entry and competition.

5   Regulating natural monopolies

One way of controlling monopoly power, particularly in the case of natural monopoly, has historically been through the creation of public enterprises. Public enterprises, either wholly or partly owned by national governments, were created to ensure that goods and services provided by natural monopolists would not be overpriced or of low quality.

Public enterprises are usually assumed to produce goods and services that are sold in the marketplace. Their revenue, therefore, derives from sales rather than from government grants, but they may have motivations other than profit-maximisation. Public corporations in areas of natural monopoly, for example, should not attempt to maximise profit since that would imply too low an output at too high a price, but should produce an output and sell at a price that is in the public interest. Often this meant that prices of public enterprises should be set equal to marginal costs so that resource allocation would be efficient (see Chapter 13, Section 6).

During the period 1945–80, the public enterprise sector grew in most countries. In the UK an initial programme of nationalisation after 1945 took into public ownership the public utilities, such as electricity, water and gas, along with rail and air transport, the postal and telephone services, and industries such as coal and steel. This immediate post-war period established public enterprise in areas thought at the time to be characterised by natural monopoly.

In some industries, such as telecommunications, the regulatory approach needed more complex arrangements. As mentioned earlier, British Telecom was a public enterprise, having a natural monopoly of the UK-wide telephone network. By making British Telecom a public enterprise, and so a nationalised industry, the UK government could try to remove the risk of consumers being exploited by being offered high prices or poor service; also, having a UK-wide telecommunications network was considered essential to national interests. A private company might, for instance, concentrate investment to develop a network targeted to urban areas, as these connections are highly profitable, with a large number of customers making frequent calls. In contrast, rural connections are less profitable, requiring connections to users who use the network very infrequently, dispersed over large areas of countryside. To avoid firms focusing investment in urban areas only, obligations were laid on telecommunications companies, such as connecting remote areas.

5.1   Privatisations in the UK

By the late 1970s, alternative policies, such as privatisation, were proposed for dealing with natural monopoly. Privatisation is when government sells public enterprises to private investors. It also aims to stimulate competition by allowing other firms to enter the industry. If a natural monopoly were privatised and entry encouraged such that more than one firm were involved in production, the duplication of facilities would in theory raise the combined costs above the minimum technically achievable. However, this approach to natural monopoly is open to objections. A single producer may not have the incentive to be technically efficient because it lacks the discipline imposed by market competition. If the wasteful use of resources is a serious problem, then the losses in scale economies from having new entrants competing in the industry may be outweighed by gains in technical efficiency. The promotion of competition through privatisation may therefore be in the public interest even where the duplication of facilities raises the minimum potential average cost achievable for the industry.

In the UK, the privatisation of state-held assets became a centrepiece of policy in the years following the 1979 election when Margaret Thatcher's Conservative governments gained power. Since then the number of privatisations has continued even under the Labour governments in the UK and in many European countries. However, state-owned firms still occupy a significant place in the world economy as they play important roles in the economies of emerging countries (*The Economist*, 2012).

Once a natural monopoly is privatised, responsibility for the framework of rules and incentives that seeks to prevent the monopolist from exercising market power against the public interest passes to a regulator. In the UK, the privatised utilities, such as British Telecom (privatised in stages between 1984 and 1992), operate within a regulatory framework established by government. These regulators, some of whom have a high public profile, are supported by offices, such as Ofcom for the telecommunications industry, that are often also referred to as 'regulators'. UK regulators have considerable discretion in pursuit of their duties, which vary between industries but include the promotion of competition, the promotion of efficiency, the protection of consumers, and ensuring that the utilities can finance their functions (Helm, 1994).

The promotion of competition is often achieved by isolating the component of natural monopoly in the value chain and encouraging competition in other areas. Regulators recognise that only part of the activities of public utilities as traditionally conceived is naturally monopolistic. In the case of telecommunications, the equipment that is used on the network and the services that are sold on that network are potentially competitive even if the operation of the telephone wires is a natural monopoly.

The fragmentation of the telecommunications industry structure was facilitated by technological change. In the later part of the twentieth century (generally in the 1980s), advances in telecoms technology, due to the introduction of digital rather than analogue communication signalling, greatly increased the technical efficiency of the network. Greater amounts of data could be sent on a digital network, involving less labour compared to an analogue network. Once digital technology arrived, every call could be accurately metered, and its usage of particular parts of the network tracked, so it was possible to have several firms operating in a single network. Regulators obliged the companies that owned any particular section of the network to lease part of its capacity at attractive prices to other firms. Later this presented opportunity for new entrants in the provision of internet services, such as broadband, with British Telecom (now BT) providing network infrastructure, while other providers such as TalkTalk, Orange and Sky used combinations of their own equipment in BT exchanges.

The arrival of digital transmission was followed closely by mobile telephony. From the late 1980s onwards, mobile telephony expanded rapidly. At the time of writing the bulk of voice traffic is now through mobile telephony, as well as a significant proportion of data. (Two mobile operators, EE and O2, are included in the top six UK broadband providers by number of subscribers.) In most countries, regulators soon took a very competitive approach to mobile telephony. Initially, the incumbent 'plain old telephone company' might provide the service, but soon competition was introduced, with firms generating their own networks of masts, but also allowing other firms to share their infrastructure.

The privatisation of British Telecom and the subsequent entry of rival providers of fixed call services, broadband and mobile communication shows how natural monopoly can be replaced by a market supplied by several firms, competing for customers, but also on occasion sharing resources such as a telephone network. This type of market structure, with a few firms, is no longer a monopoly, but neither does it have the characteristics of perfect competition or monopolistic competition with many firms. A market with only a small number of suppliers is known as an *oligopoly*; a feature of oligopoly is interdependence between producers, which offers the potential for fierce competition, but also the opportunity for collaboration between firms.

6   Oligopoly

Competitive behaviour between firms is sometimes described in the language of 'war'. We read in the newspapers of a 'price war' among firms when prices are reduced aggressively to try to boost market share by taking sales away from rival firms. This happens from time to time in many sectors of the economy, including the major retailing sectors and the markets for specific consumer goods or services. Rival supermarket chains keep a close watch on their market shares and periodically battle for customers by slashing prices. A classic example is competition between the major supermarket chains in the UK. In 2012, the big four (Tesco, Asda, Morrisons, Sainsbury's) accounted for approximately 76% of the UK grocery market (Lawson, 2012), with each firm using price cutting as a key 'weapon' in their competition to attract more customers than their rivals. In price wars of this sort, firms seem to have opposing interests.

At other times, relations between firms competing in the same market seem to go to the opposite extreme; instead of the language of 'war', it is now the language of 'alliance' and 'partnership' that provides the keywords. For example, in June 2012, telecoms giants Vodafone and Telefonica UK (more commonly known as O2 in the UK) 'unveiled a plan to share their network infrastructure, with the promise that this will deliver next-generation 4G services to UK consumers in double-quick time' (Cellan-Jones, 2012). This strategic move by O2 and Vodafone positioned both firms to speed up preparations for the release of a 4G network service. By working together, sharing communication masts across the UK, these two firms were able to offer services to customers two years earlier than if they had worked independently. However, this alliance was also partly in response to an earlier but similar agreement between Orange, T-Mobile and Three to share 4G infrastructure. Here, the costs for an individual firm to enter a market for 4G communications are reduced through the formation of an alliance with a rival firm, rather than by attempting to wage war against it. But an alliance between Vodafone and O2 also helped both firms to avoid falling behind a competing alliance. (Orange and T-Mobile even ended up merging together to form Everything Everywhere, also known as EE.) In cases of this sort, groups of firms can seem to have mutual interests.

Although these two types of firms' behaviour – waging war and forming alliances – are so different, they have one thing in common:

firms are interdependent, in that each firm's actions will affect rival firms, whose reactions will in turn affect their rivals. A firm in this situation will have to take into account the expected reactions from rivals in making its own plans, and if a firm is really smart, it will prompt rivals into reacting in ways that are beneficial to it. In such cases the simple contrast between opposing interests and mutual interests seems to break down, and what we see are various mixes of conflict and cooperation. Competition between firms that is characterised by interdependence is known as **strategic competition**.

Strategic competition
Strategic competition means that firms need to take account of expected reactions from rivals when making their plans.

Strategic competition is different from both perfect competition and monopolistic competition. In the perfect competition model, which you studied in Chapter 13, firms take the market price and technology as given and set their output without considering the behaviour of other firms. In the monopolistic competition model, that is, competition between firms with monopoly power, firms typically compete through product differentiation. But in neither of these types of models do firms take into account the expected reactions of rivals when deciding what to do. So these models miss a key feature of many important markets, including the grocery sector, the motor industry, the airline industry, commercial banks and the markets for many basic household items, including foods, soft drinks, cigarettes – the list goes on and on.

Firms in many markets certainly find it profitable to cut prices, or to innovate, or to advertise. In so doing, however, they may well take into account their interdependence with rivals. Sometimes firms compete globally, as in the case of airlines, which compete for international travellers, but they could be competing for a national market, as in the case of supermarket chains, or even a local market, as in the case of two restaurants facing each other across a town square.

Oligopolistic markets typically display strategic competition. Strategic competition is less likely if the number of firms is large, but the number of firms that may compete strategically depends on the characteristics of specific markets. A useful rule of thumb used in industry analysis is to define an oligopoly when the largest five firms account for more than 50% of the industry or market. In this definition there may be many firms supplying the market, but the top five hold significant market power.

The structure of an oligopoly market can be influenced by the level of competition between firms in the market. Competition between oligopolists in some cases can be extreme, for instance in the case when firms maintain low prices and attempt to sell high output, such as with supermarkets that may aggressively cut prices on staple goods such as bread and milk, forcing competitors to follow suit. In such an example the outcome can approach that of perfect competition, with only normal profits available, in that market. In extreme cases, prices may fall below costs, as firms attempt to woo customers into their stores. As such aggressive competitive warfare between a few companies in the long run can result in reduced profit, an alternative strategy is to attempt to restrict competition. I have already mentioned that firms may use strategic alliances to benefit or share infrastructure, capabilities or know-how to mutual advantage. A stronger attempt to reduce or even remove competition can be achieved via collusion, which is an illegal practice in many cases and countries. Oligopolists may restrict competition by colluding on prices (by agreeing a price for goods with competitors), market shares (agreeing to keep within predetermined shares of a market for a good or service), advertising (by agreeing on levels of advertising expenditure, or types and timings of advertisements), distribution (by avoiding competing in geographical markets) or indeed in any area of business where firms' profits are improved if they work closely together. The key difference between strategic alliances and collusive behaviour is that alliances tend to take place in business activities far from the market, such as R&D, and therefore do not restrict competition. Firms might collaborate, say, on the development of a new technology or the deployment of new infrastructure, such as new phone masts as you saw above in the case of 4G mobile services, but their products that embody such technology will compete in the market.

Formal agreements to collude are known as **cartels**, which can refer to groups of firms or even countries. Ideally a cartel can function as a monopolist in trying to maximise combined total profits for its members (although this is worse for consumers!). For instance, if by forming a cartel firms can manipulate the industry supply such that price is greater than marginal costs (as in the monopoly case), then total industry profits will be greater. In practice, cartels are unlikely to control all the output in an industry and thus cannot aspire to a pure monopoly; the question is whether they can control sufficient output to restrict the total industry output to some extent so that they earn some supernormal profit. In practice, colluding in an oligopoly market can be difficult to maintain over time as each firm faces an incentive to increase output. Each oligopolist must decide between maximising the total profits of the cartel versus the temptation to increase its own

Cartel
A cartel is a group (of firms or countries) that makes joint decisions with a view to increasing the combined profits of its members by suppressing competition between them. This behaviour is also known as (explicit) collusion.

profits, for instance by expanding output in the hope of stealing market share from their rivals. The balance between the willingness of firms to collude or compete may depend on the nature of the agreement and the ability of each firm to negotiate a better deal.

Colluding and cartels are illegal in most countries. To succeed in colluding, firms do not necessarily use formal agreements, and instead can rely on informal agreements. For instance, there may be an acknowledged practice of following or responding to the market leader in setting prices – a process known as price leadership. In fact, in a process known as **implicit collusion**, firms can select strategies independently that lead to the same outcomes as if a joint (collusive) agreement had been made.

Implicit collusion
Implicit collusion occurs when firms behave as if they are colluding but there is no agreement to do so.

One example of implicit collusion might be if a large firm, with significant market share, acted as price 'enforcer' in a market with smaller competitors. If a competing firm attempted to reduce prices, then the enforcer might punish this firm by flooding the market and letting prices fall, thereby reducing the profits of all firms in the market. This would send a strong signal to firms to avoid competing on price in the future. While small defaults from implicit collusion may be tolerated, if they become widespread, then the enforcing firm punishes the others by itself defaulting. The larger firm may thus periodically have to reinforce the point that future profits will be severely reduced if other firms attempt to compete on price. Such a punishment strategy works by making default less profitable to firms over time.

An oligopoly exists because there are few firms, and persists because other firms find it hard to enter, even though the higher profits which might be achieved by oligopolists make this attractive. This is because the market is likely to be protected by barriers to entry.

6.1 Barriers to entry

The examples of monopolistic competition in the previous section and perfect competition in Chapter 13 illustrate the importance of free entry and exit for firms and market outcomes. Firms can earn supernormal profits in the long run only if they can stop other firms from entering their market, as is the case in natural monopolies. If a market is **contestable** – that is, there is freedom to enter and exit – then new entrants will be drawn towards profit-making opportunities.

Contestable market
A market is perfectly contestable if entry and exit are costless.

Oligopolistic firms often try to resist competition from new entrants by creating new barriers to entry, or reinforcing existing ones. Barriers to entry can take many forms. They may be natural (intrinsic to the type of industry or market, such as high economies of scale or high investments required to enter) or artificial (deliberately established to prevent entry, for example, predatory pricing).

Incumbent firms can set *advertising* levels that new entrants cannot afford but need in order to achieve the 'share of voice' required to get customers to pay attention. This is a particularly effective barrier for what are called 'fast-moving consumer goods' (for example, grocery products), partly because retailers (mainly for reasons of efficient use of shelf space) will stock only two or three brands in any one category. Creating a new brand requires a very large advertising spend, to get enough consumers to try and then buy the product. In the age of the internet, this barrier is less effective with some products, as many consumers use the internet for information on new products, while some products succeed by getting consumers to recommend them via social networking or other sites, rather than by advertising. Still, many consumers may be loyal to incumbent brands and require much persuasion to switch. This persuasion might be financial incentives (for example, discounts), which add to barriers to entry.

Distributor agreements may also act as a barrier. Distributors of existing products may not want to add a new product, and may have exclusive distribution agreements with a supplier (though this is forbidden in some countries and/or industries). A special case of this is restrictive agreements allowed to ensure 'orderly' business, for example, control of landing slots at airports. Suppliers may also have restrictive practices, being unwilling to supply competitors to their existing customers. In some cases, *vertical integration* of the supply chain, where a company extends ownership or control to suppliers and customers, can prevent entry, although this can create cost disadvantages for the incumbent caused by involvement in activities in which they are not specialists.

If the product demands *large investments* (for example, research and development, manufacturing), then new entrants may need deep pockets (i.e. access to substantial financial resources). Sometimes the resources required may be controlled by the monopolist, for example, diamond mines. The incumbent may also benefit from a favourable *location*, or simply a scale advantage from very large production facilities with lower costs, or being far along the *learning curve*. The incumbent may possess important (possibly patent protected) *intellectual property*, without which it is impossible to compete.

In *predatory pricing*, the incumbent sells at a loss (for example, temporarily, or to particular customers or markets) to make entry difficult. This is illegal but sometimes difficult to prove. Other approaches include increasing *switching costs* for consumers (which used to be common in the UK telecommunications and utilities industries, but regulators have forbidden it), or creating *discount structures* that make it unattractive for industrial customers to order from several suppliers (illegal in many countries).

Another important barrier to entry is *network effects*. The example of a telephone service shows that the utility people get from consuming such goods depends on the extent to which other people also use these goods. There is little point in having a telephone installed if other people or businesses do not subscribe to the network. Network effects thus 'arise when the attractiveness of a product to customers increases with the use of that product by others' (Fisher and Rubinfeld, 2000, p. 13). The more people who subscribe to the same standardised system, the more services and people the user can access, and so the greater the value of that system to each individual user. The more users of the network there are in an area, and the more they use it, the less it costs the network provider to serve an additional user (in terms of carrying overheads), and so the lower the price it needs to charge to cover costs. The firm with the largest network can achieve economies of scale. The cost advantages are particularly dramatic for a firm that can establish its own network, or a technical component essential to the functioning of a network, as the industry standard.

Network industries have in common a number of characteristics, including complementarity, compatibility and standards (Shy, 2001, pp. 1–3). A network industry produces complements, such as trains and railway tracks, computers and software, mobile phones and mobile applications (apps), and cars and fuel. These complementary products must be compatible with one another. Trains are no use unless they fit tracks; applications are no use unless they run on their target devices. Without standards, product standardisation cannot take place and economies of scale are unobtainable. Establishing an industry standard may involve a struggle between competing would-be standards. At the time of writing, the battle for standards for mobile phones seems to have been won by Google with its Android operating system (strongly supported by Samsung, the dominant supplier of smartphones), and

Apple with its iPhone. Where proprietary standards may give great monopoly power, regulators may intervene to ensure open standards. The implication is that firms that can establish their network face huge rewards from establishing an early lead for their product, and in extreme cases result in a monopoly structure. Even if competing products have more useful features, the product with the largest network will be difficult to dislodge simply because the number of its subscribers makes it the most attractive option for new subscribers.

Finally, in some cases, the barriers to entry that maintain an oligopoly may exist because of *regulation*, such as in mobile telecommunications networks.

6.2   Competition policy

In order to check that oligopolists do not take advantage of their market power either by colluding or creating or maintaining artificial barriers to entry, governments have set up specialised competition authorities whose task is to promote fair competition. The antitrust prosecutors in the USA, like the competition authorities in Europe, including the UK's Competition Commission, have as their objective the prevention of the abuse of monopoly power to the detriment of consumers. The theory in this chapter helps to identify some central dilemmas faced by policymakers, especially when dealing with firms in highly innovative and rapidly changing industries.

Government authorities that are considering acting against a firm for abuse of monopoly power will investigate both market structure – the extent of monopoly power enjoyed by the firm – and market conduct – the behaviour of a firm with monopoly power. Gilbert and Katz (2001) list the methods used by the US courts to assess the extent of market power. They first define the relevant markets affected by the firm's conduct. (A market is a set of products that consumers consider to be reasonably close substitutes for each other.) Then the assessment of market power moves on to the calculation of market share, examination of competitive interactions, determination of the conditions of entry and analysis of other pertinent structural features of the market (Gilbert and Katz, 2001, pp. 29–30).

The 'structural' features of the market that determine the assessment of monopoly power cover a broad range, including the level of sellers' concentration, barriers to entry and the pattern of interaction with actual and potential competitors. In many cases, a pertinent issue is the

Concentration ratio
A concentration ratio measures the share of industry output produced by the top few (usually three, four or five) firms.

size of the relevant market: an industry dominated by a single firm in one country may none the less operate and face competition in integrated international markets. The degree of sellers' concentration, a key indicator of market structure, is often measured using concentration ratios. A **concentration ratio** measures the share of industry output produced by the top few (usually three, four or five) firms. Competition authorities monitor market concentration particularly carefully because a high concentration makes it easier for the largest firms to restrict competition by colluding. Merger proposals between large firms are also scrutinised by competition authorities if they increase the level of concentration significantly, especially if the market has high barriers to entry, since the resulting firm might dominate the industry and behave like a monopolist.

After the assessment of market structure, the analysis moves on to the market conduct of the firm. Here, the behaviour of the firm is scrutinised either for collusive behaviour or, if the industry is dominated by a single firm, for abuse of monopoly power, such as monopoly pricing and deliberate blocking of competition by 'predatory' behaviour against the interests of consumers. EU legislation bans the abuse of a 'dominant position' in a market by a monopolist, and that wording was brought into UK law by the Competition Act 1998. In the USA, similarly, the courts need to be convinced *both* that the firm held monopoly power *and* that it had abused it to the long-term detriment of consumers. The possession of monopoly power alone is not an offence; as Gilbert and Katz (2001, p. 30) put it: 'Indeed it would not make economic sense to punish a firm that possesses market power solely as a consequence of its having developed a superior product, because doing so would erode the incentives for innovation.'

The structure/conduct distinction is a fuzzy one: evidence of conduct can be and is used to assess the competitiveness of a market structure. But the distinction between the extent of monopoly power and its abuse is central to policy options. However, finding reliable evidence of anticompetitive behaviour is not easy, so competition authorities have resorted to offering legal immunity to individuals and firms who cooperate with them by providing evidence to challenge collusive or predatory conduct in courts.

Competition authorities, whether in the USA or Europe, once convinced that a firm is abusing monopoly power, can seek to remedy the situation by structural remedies, that is, reducing the extent of market power by, for example, breaking up a dominant firm into two or more smaller ones. Alternatively, they can seek to impose remedies that seek to change market conduct by directly prohibiting or penalising particular forms of conduct, for example, ordering price reductions and changes in pricing structure.

7   Competition through innovation

In the models presented so far, firms mainly compete on price and by product differentiation. However, as the Austrian economist Joseph Schumpeter pointed out, firms also compete by creating radically new products and markets, changing consumers' lives in the process (see Chapter 12). This section analyses competition through innovation and takes a perspective on market power that is different from that in the previous sections. The models that you have seen in the previous sections showed that market power is associated with higher prices, less output and possibly inefficiency and worse quality of services. Those models, however, analysed market outcomes from a *static* perspective, without considering the introduction of technological change. The analysis of high technology industries requires instead a *dynamic* approach because innovation is at the heart of competition: particular firms can build up a dominant market position with new products and processes – or disappear.

Building on the work of Schumpeter, evolutionary economists such as Richard Nelson and Sydney Winter (1982) have developed a series of models that are more suited to the analysis of industries in which firms mainly compete through innovation – a process that they call 'Schumpeterian competition'. Like Schumpeter, evolutionary economists argue that models based on price and quantity, where all firms have the same technology, lack a sense of past and future. An evolutionary model overcomes that: it analyses how particular firms build on their past to create scope for future success – or drive the firm to bankruptcy by being unable to change. Schumpeterian competition is therefore a process of 'creative destruction', where new technology and successful innovators thrive while older technologies and firms that cannot innovate successfully exit the market. This approach assumes that firms may pursue a range of objectives, among which are a dominant market share and monopoly profits. Such profits, however, are only temporary, as in the long run competitors erode them through successful imitation. Firms like Apple can be seen as typical Schumpeterian companies, which earn very high profits because of their successful innovative and high-quality products and services. In 2010, Apple's iPhone was so technologically superior to its rivals that it could be sold at such a high price that it earned over half of the mobile phone industry profits with a market share of less than 5% (see Figure 14.8). In order to keep earning high profits, however, successful firms need to keep innovating by increasing quality, offering new products and improving productive efficiency. For example, in 2013, Apple's profits fell and commentators associated this fall (though still to a very high level) with lack of radical new products.

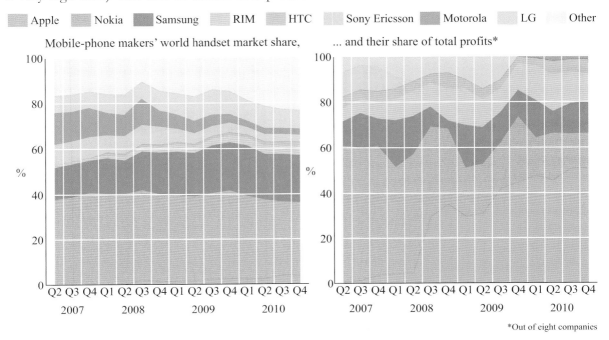

Figure 14.8   Apple's monopoly profits from the iPhone. A small market share generates half of the industry's profits.

(Source: The Economist, 2011)

Schumpeter's view went even further concerning the way in which monopoly should be seen in dynamic industries. He argued in the 1940s that large firms with monopoly power may be particularly likely to pursue innovation compared with firms with little market power, because they can obtain financial backing from banks for risky innovation, and they may have a flow of supernormal profits to be reinvested (Schumpeter, 1975 [1942]). Furthermore, large firms with monopoly power have incentives to innovate since they can hope to benefit from their innovations by reaping further monopoly profits, hence monopoly power can drive industrial growth and create cheaper products for consumers.

Schumpeter argued that these benefits of innovation may even be threatened by contestability. In highly contestable markets, there is little incentive for a firm to innovate, if imitators will quickly compete away the market advantage gained by the innovator. Moreover, the lack of supernormal profits makes it more difficult to invest in risky activities, such as R&D, which generate returns only over a long timeframe. Thus for policy purposes contestability has to be tempered with the opportunity for innovative firms to make adequate returns. This is the key argument for allowing firms to take out patents on inventions that are the basis for innovation, allowing them to protect and exploit for profit the intellectual property rights in their ideas for a limited period.

So, from a Schumpeterian, evolutionary perspective, competition in innovative industry is best served by firms chasing temporary monopolies and high profits through the introduction of innovation. The presence of monopoly is a small price to pay for the rapid improvement of technology so long as it is temporary or constantly renewed through successful innovation.

The Schumpeterian perspective therefore introduces a *trade-off* between the static perspective, which focuses on the allocative inefficiency caused by the supernormal profits of dominant firms, and the dynamic perspective that emphasises the improvements in productive efficiency generated by the introduction of new technology by innovating dominant firms.

Figure 14.9 illustrates this trade-off by showing the effects of the introduction of cost-cutting process innovation by a profit-maximising monopolist. Process innovation involves producing existing products more efficiently, and is therefore represented by a shift of the firm's long-run average cost curve downwards (Chapter 11, Section 6). For simplicity, the firm's LRAC curve displays constant unit costs, as in Section 3, so $LRAC = LRMC$. The monopolist's profits are maximised initially where $LRMC_1 = MR$ at point A. Output is Q_1, with average cost per unit AC_1 and price P_1. Supernormal profits are initially shown by the blue rectangle. The process innovation shifts the long-run cost curve downwards to $LRAC_2$ and therefore improves productive efficiency.

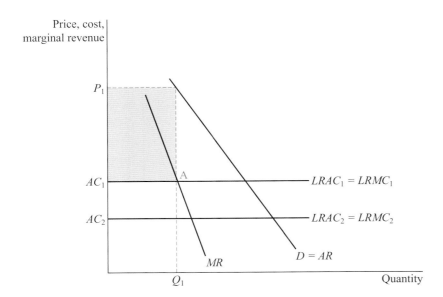

Figure 14.9   The effect of a monopolist's innovation on price and costs

---

Activity 14.10

Indicate on Figure 14.9 the monopolist's new profit-maximising price and quantity after the innovation. What has been the effect on price?

Answer

Figure 14.10 (overleaf) shows that even a pure monopolist will charge a lower price (P_2) and produce more (Q_2) after the innovation than before; the innovation benefits consumers. If technological change is rapid and shifts cost down enough, consumers will be better off with a profit-maximising monopolist that drives costs down through the introduction of new technology even though it gains high profits in the short run.

7.1   Innovation and competition policy

The Schumpeterian perspective raises an important issue in competition policy because successful innovators gain market power and often dominate their industry by virtue of their superior innovative performance. Competition policy does not stop successful innovators from becoming dominant, but aims to stop the abuse of dominance to prevent competitors from catching up successfully. So competition authorities have to scrutinise large dominant firms, such as Microsoft,

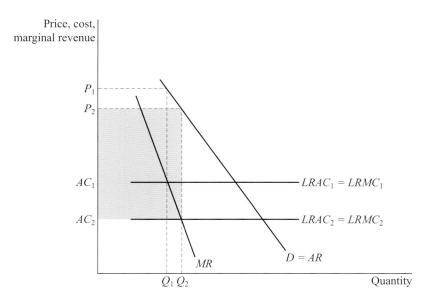

Figure 14.10   A monopolist's profit-maximising price and quantity after a process innovation

Google and Apple, to answer the following question: is this dominant firm constantly searching for improvement, responding to competitive threat with better products, or, as it gained monopoly power, has it stopped innovating and gone over to defensiveness, trying to prevent competitors from innovating rather than winning through innovating?

The answer to this question is not always easy to find, as a famous lawsuit brought against Microsoft for the dominance of its Windows operating system shows. In defence of Microsoft, the industrial economist Schmalensee argued that whatever the arguments about the extent of the threat from competitors, Microsoft's behaviour was consistent with that of a firm facing intense dynamic competition, and presented evidence of 'relentless innovation' to improve its operating system (Greene, 1999). Schmalensee contrasted the evidence relevant to the standard static pure monopoly model with evidence relevant to the dynamic evolutionary model. However, the government used company emails to support their argument that Microsoft displayed the opposite behavioural tendency: an organisational focus on suppressing potential competition to the detriment of product improvement and consumer choice.

So there is no single answer to the question of whether firms with monopoly power continue to innovate. Even Apple has faced some criticism for focusing too much on preserving its high profits through lawsuits against Android phone makers rather than introducing new groundbreaking products. A firm's behaviour will depend on its history and its current competitive challenges. Firms with monopoly power may continue to face competition through product innovation. In that case, a highly concentrated industry – one containing very few firms – may continue to behave competitively in a dynamic sense: the incumbent firms innovate constantly, since they perceive barriers to entry through product innovation as low, and entry always as a potential threat. Competition authorities are increasingly concerned to get the policy framework right to promote and sustain competition through innovation.

8   Conclusion

This chapter concludes the study of firms and industries that is the topic of Part 4. It has considered some of the main approaches to analysing markets where competition is not perfect. It used the telecommunications industry to demonstrate how evolving industry structure – driven by innovation – requires a constantly changing regulatory approach to ensure that consumers get the full benefits of developments. It examined different ways of modelling different competitive situations – such as monopoly, monopolistic competition and oligopoly – and analysing their benefits and costs. Markets can vary widely, so the theories covered in this chapter do not cover the analysis of other market structures, such as monopsony or oligopsony (where there is only one or few buyers, respectively), and situations where market outcomes are the result of bargaining between a few sellers and buyers – this is sometimes the case in some labour markets where large firms bargain with trade unions. However, the theories you have studied provide the basis for the analysis of competition in a wide variety of markets. In Part 5, you will also learn about game theory, a modelling technique that analyses interdependence and is therefore often used to analyse competition in oligopolistic markets.

References

Cellan-Jones, R. (2012) 'O2 , Vodafone, and a 4G promise', BBC News, Technology, 7 June, [online] www.bbc.co.uk/news/technology-18355569 (Accessed 16 February 2013).

The Economist (2011) 'Blazing platforms', 10 February, [online] www.economist.com/node/18114689?story_id=18114689 (Accessed 16 February 2013).

The Economist (2012) 'The visible hand', 21 January, [online] www.economist.com/node/21542931 (Accessed 17 January 2013)

Fisher, F. and Rubinfeld, D. (2000) 'United States v. Microsoft: an economic analysis', Public Law and Legal Theory Working Paper no. 30, University of California, Berkeley School of Law.

Gilbert, R. and Katz, M. (2001) 'An economist's guide to US v. Microsoft', *Journal of Economic Perspectives*, vol. 15, no. 2, pp. 25–44.

Greene, J. (1999) 'Economist challenges colleague's testimony', *Seattle Times*, 21 January, [online] http://community.seattletimes.nwsource.com/archive/?date=19990121&slug=2939925 (Accessed 2 April 2013).

Helm, D. (1994) 'British utility regulation: theory, practice and reform', *Oxford Review of Economic Policy*, vol. 10, no. 3, pp. 17–39.

Lawson, A. (2012) 'Tesco and Morrisons lose share in competitive market', Retail Week, 22 May, [online] www.retail-week.com/sectors/food/tesco-and-morrisons-lose-share-in-competitive-market/5036938.article (Accessed 16 February 2013).

Nelson, R.R. and Winter, S.G. (1982) *An Evolutionary Theory of Economic Change*, Cambridge, MA, Belknap Press.

Schumpeter, J.A. (1975 [1942]) *Capitalism, Socialism and Democracy*, New York, Harper.

Shy, O. (2001) *The Economics of Network Industries*, Cambridge, Cambridge University Press.

US Census Bureau (2007) *Employers and Nonemployers*, [online] www.census.gov/econ/smallbus.html (Accessed 16 February 2013).

Part 5   Global inequality in human well-being: what can governments do?

Chapter 15
Trade and inequality

Maureen Mackintosh

Contents

1 Introduction

International trade can bring huge benefits to an economy. It has a major impact on employment and economic growth, increases the range of goods and services available to buy, and can lead to lower prices for consumers. It also affects patterns of inequality both between and within countries, creating winners and losers.

Big shifts in global economic leadership have often been associated with export success, from Britain's early role in the Industrial Revolution as 'workshop of the world', to the dramatic rise in manufacturing exports that has led China's rapid economic growth since the 1980s. Rising economic interdependence among countries since the end of the Second World War has been driven by growth in merchandise exports (that is, exports of goods, not services), measured in real terms that has far outstripped total global production (Figure 15.1).

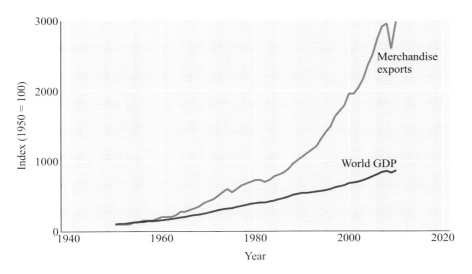

Figure 15.1   Real total world merchandise exports and real world GDP: indices for 1950–2010 (index 100 in 1950)

(Source: calculated from data in World Trade Organization (WTO), 2012, Table A1)

This chapter analyses some key interactions between trade, growth and inequality. There are four strands to this analysis.

The first strand begins with the theory of comparative advantage. This is one of the founding propositions of the discipline of economics: the argument that specialisation and trade can produce economic benefits for all, even when those participating are profoundly unequal in economic strength (Section 2). However, international trade typically distributes its benefits very unequally. Changes in international market prices are a powerful mechanism for redistributing the gains from trade between countries, influencing, for example, who has gained from the rise of China as a manufacturing power (Section 3).

Second, the trade policies adopted by a government will affect their country's prosperity and that of others. Observing a historical link between export success and growth, a large economic literature promotes policies of 'openness' to trade as a route to economic development (Sachs and Warner, 1995). Trade policies include tariffs (taxes on trade) that strongly influence the extent and pattern of trade. However, a country's influence over outcomes of trade policy depends on its economic weight in international markets, and some countries may lose out absolutely (Sections 4 and 5).

Third, trade influences inequality *within* as well as between countries. In some circumstances, trade may impoverish sections of a population. A country's resources and skill levels, and the productivity with which they are used, strongly shape the domestic impact of international trade (Section 6).

Finally, I argue that to understand trade and its effects, it is necessary to incorporate analysis of firms and industries from Part 4, and to consider international market structure. Many international markets are imperfectly competitive, and both countries and firms can exercise market power. International market power influences the distribution of gains from trade liberalisation, and opens up more scope for strategic trade policy to benefit national economies (Section 7).

The learning outcomes for this chapter are:

- to understand and apply the concepts of comparative advantage and the terms of trade
- to define trade liberalisation, and analyse the economic impact of tariffs
- to explain and discuss some ways in which trade influences inequality in and between countries
- to outline the Heckscher–Ohlin model of the sources of comparative advantage

- to discuss some implications of imperfect competition in international markets for trade policy and the gains from trade

- to understand the relevance of the concept of purchasing power parity to debates on trade policy.

2   The gains from trade

The theory of comparative advantage is one of the founding concepts of economics, and remains one of its most influential. The form in which I describe it here can be traced back to David Ricardo, writing in his *Principles of Political Economy and Taxation* in 1817. Ricardo used his theoretical arguments to attack trade protectionism in the form of tariffs (taxes) on grain imports. Writing in a period of poor harvests and high prices, he argued that these tariffs, known as the Corn Laws, protected the interests of landowners, undermined industrial investment and growth, and impoverished wage earners. These arguments, linking theory and policy, retain strong resonance today.

The theory of comparative advantage demonstrates that specialisation and trade can benefit two trading parties *even* if one producer is less efficient than the other at producing all the traded goods. Ricardo's argument concerned international trade between countries, and this is how I describe it here. But the proposition in itself is more general: it can be applied to specialisation and trade among individuals and firms as well as countries. In this form, 'gains from trade' is one of the founding arguments of economics.

2.1   Comparative advantage

Absolute advantage
A country has an absolute advantage in the production of good X if production of a unit of X requires fewer resources in that country than it does abroad.

To understand comparative advantage, think of countries as having different amounts of resources such as mineral resources and labour, and also differing in the productivity that they achieve from their resources. Then a country that can produce a particular good using fewer resources than its trading partners is said to have an **absolute advantage** in the production of that good. It is the most efficient producer.

Comparative advantage
A country has a comparative advantage in the production of good X if the opportunity cost of producing a unit of X is lower in that country than it is abroad.

Comparative advantage is a more subtle concept, and to understand it one needs the idea of opportunity cost. As you saw in Chapter 12, the opportunity cost of a good is determined by the best alternative use of the resources required to produce it – that is, what might have been produced instead. A country has a **comparative advantage** in the production of a good when the opportunity cost of producing a unit of that good, in terms of other goods forgone, is lower in that country than it is abroad. Even if a country is absolutely less efficient in producing everything, it will still have a comparative advantage in some goods.

To see how this works, consider the following example, which is quite similar to Ricardo's nineteenth century demonstration. (Ricardo used the examples of Portugal and England, and trade in wine and cloth.)

Suppose that there are two countries: a low-income country and a high-income country. Each country's only resource is working people. Each country can produce two goods: food (tons of grain) and a manufactured good, mobile phones. In each country, consumers want to consume both goods. In the absence of trade, each country will therefore produce both goods. Figure 15.2 shows the production possibilities of each country.

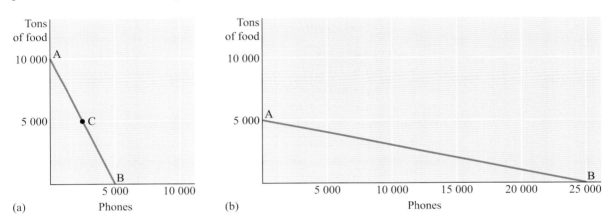

Figure 15.2   Production possibility frontiers for two countries: (a) low-income country, 10 000 people; (b) high-income country, 1000 people

Look first at Figure 15.2(a). It shows the production possibilities of the low-income country. This is a much larger country, with a working population of 10 000 people. Line AB shows this country's **production possibility frontier (PPF)**. Line AB tells you that if no food is produced, then the country can produce 5000 phones at point B. If no phones are produced, then it can produce 10 000 tons of food at point A.

Alternatively, the low-income country can produce food and phones in any mix represented by a point along AB: for example, 5000 tons of food and 2500 phones at point C. Since members of the population want to consume both food and phones, in the absence of trade the country would produce a mix of the two goods. So it will produce at some point along AB, the exact production mix being determined by the population's needs and preferences for food and phones.

Production possibility frontier (PPF)
A PPF shows a country's maximum output mixes: that is, at each point along the PPF, more of one good cannot be produced without producing less of another.

Now look at Figure 15.2(b). It shows the production possibility frontier AB of the high-income country. This is a smaller country, with 1000 working people. Its PPF shows that its maximum production of food is 5000 tons (and no phones); alternatively, it can produce 25 000 phones and no food. In the absence of trade, it would be likely to produce both goods, in a mix located at some point on AB, again depending on the population's preferences and requirements.

Each country has just one factor of production: labour. So absolute advantage is determined by the productivity of labour: output per working person.

Activity 15.1

Which country has the absolute advantage in the production of food? Which country has the absolute advantage in phone production? Take a moment to work it out for yourself.

Answer

The high-income country has the absolute advantage in the production of both goods. To see this, calculate the productivity of labour in each country. In the high-income country, 1000 workers can produce 5000 tons of food, i.e. five tons per worker. Alternatively, they can produce 25 000/ 1000 = 25 phones per worker.

In the low-income country, 10 000 working people can produce 10 000 tons of food (i.e. one ton per worker) or 5000 phones (i.e. half (0.5) of a phone each). So the high-income country is more efficient at producing both goods.

In this case, why should the high-income country trade at all? Surely it can do better on its own using its highly productive resources? It was Ricardo's argument that trade can still be beneficial to both countries. To see why, one must first establish which country has the comparative advantage in which good.

Start by calculating the opportunity cost of a ton of food in each country. The low-income country can produce 5000 phones or 10 000 tons of food. So the opportunity cost of each ton of food in the low-income country is 5000/10 000 = 0.5 of a phone.

The opportunity cost of a ton of food is therefore *lower* in the low-income country: 0.5 of a phone rather than 5 phones. The low-income country has a comparative advantage in food production.

2.2   The gains from trade

Suppose now that each country specialises fully in the good in which it has the comparative advantage. The high-income country produces only phones, and the low-income country produces only food. Trade then opens, and food is traded for phones so each country can consume a mix of goods.

International prices are discussed further below. Initially, suppose that the international price at which the two countries trade is set at two phones per ton of food. The gains from trade are shown in Figure 15.3.

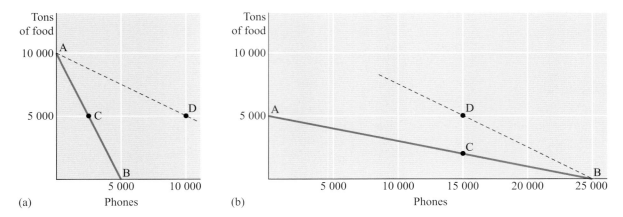

Figure 15.3   The gains from trade: (a) low-income country, 10 000 people; (b) high-income country, 1000 people

The gains to the low-income country from trade are shown in Figure 15.3(a). The dashed line is a trading line, showing the country's trading possibilities. The slope is determined by the price of food in terms of phones. Starting from point A, the country can trade out along the dashed line, exchanging food for phones. At a price of two phones per ton of food, the low-income country could trade, for example, 5000 tons of food for 10 000 phones, to take it to point D.

Figure 15.3(b) shows the high-income country's trading possibilities. Starting at point B with 25 000 phones, it can trade out, for example, to point D, buying the 5000 tons of food offered by the low-income country in return for 10 000 phones.

In Figure 15.3, each country's new consumption point, D, is *outside* its production possibility frontier, as are all the consumption points along the trading line. Each country can consume more in total, through specialisation and trade, than it can consume using its own resources in production of both goods. These are the economic gains from trade.

Table 15.1 *illustrates* these gains by comparing total world output and consumption if each country were to consume at point C in Figure 15.3 using its own resources, to the total when trade takes each country to point D. Many different production mixes are possible, but trade allows higher total production and consumption of both goods. This holds even when, as in this example, one country is absolutely more efficient than the other in producing both goods.

Table 15.1   Illustration of the gains from trade

	Output at C without trade		Output at D after specialisation and trade	
	Food	Phones	Food	Phones
Low-income country	5 000	2 500	5 000	10 000
High-income country	2 000	15 000	5 000	15 000
Total world output	7 000	17 500	10 000	25 000

2.3   The gains from trade and inequality

So where does the opening of trade leave inequality between the two countries? I started by characterising one country as low-income and one as high-income. Table 15.2 again compares points C and D in Figure 15.3, this time in terms of consumption per head before and after trade. The first two columns show the number of people needed in each country to produce one ton of food or one phone: fewer in the high-income country, with the absolute advantage in production. The next two columns show the implication – the amount of food and phones that each person can consume at point C without trade – this is much lower in the low-income country. The final column shows average consumption at point D in each country after trade.

Table 15.2   Inequality before and after trade

Country	People to produce 1 unit		Consumption per person without trade (C)		Consumption per person with trade (D)	
	Food	Phones	Food	Phones	Food	Phones
Low-income	1.0	2.0	0.5	0.25	0.5	1.0
High-income	0.2	0.04	2.0	15.0	5.0	15.0

Both countries have benefited, but people in the high-income country can still consume far more food and phones than people in the low-income country. Inequality remains after trade – inequality that is rooted in the lower productivity of labour in the low-income country.

3   The terms of trade

So what determines how inequality between countries is changed by trade? One major influence on the distribution of the gains from trade comes from the international prices at which the goods are traded, that is, the **terms of trade**.

In Section 2, I simply chose an international price ratio to illustrate the gains from trade. Now I look at the terms of trade more closely.

Terms of trade

A country's terms of trade are calculated as the ratio of its export prices to its import prices.

Activity 15.4

What is the lowest price of a ton of food in terms of phones that the low-income country in Figure 15.3 would accept before refusing to specialise and trade?

Answer

Look back at Figure 15.3. In the absence of trade – a condition called *autarky* – the low-income country can obtain a ton of food by ceasing to produce half a phone (the opportunity cost). Trade will therefore be worthwhile so long as the price of food in terms of phones is above that level. If a ton of food can buy more than half a phone on the international market, then the trading line in Figure 15.3(a) will be above AB, and trade will be worthwhile.

The higher the price of food (in phones per ton), the further away from AB is the dashed line along which the country will trade, and the greater the gain from trade for the low-income country.

Conversely, the high-income country aims to export phones. It will want the price of phones in terms of food to be as high as possible. The more food it can buy per phone, the better for the high-income exporter. There is thus a conflict of interest between trading partners over the terms of trade.

A country's terms of trade determine the amount of imports that can be bought with its exports. A shift in the terms of trade redistributes the gains from trade between trading partners.

3.1   Trends in the terms of trade

Out in the real world, countries import and export a mix of products. To measure changes over time in a country's terms of trade requires calculation of a ratio between price indices for baskets of goods. (Chapter 1 explains price indices.)

A country's terms of trade are calculated as

$$\text{terms of trade} = \frac{\text{index of export prices}}{\text{index of import prices}} \times 100$$

Trends in the terms of trade are of major political significance, since they strongly influence the distribution of the gains from trade between countries. An economic debate about industrialisation in developing countries was triggered in the 1950s by the Prebisch–Singer hypothesis of a long-term decline in the terms of trade between primary and manufactured exports. Raúl Prebisch (1901–1986) has been called the 'Latin American Keynes'. With Hans Singer, a British development economist, Prebisch argued that the continuing dependence of developing countries on primary exports from mining and agricultural production would damage their economic prospects. Declining terms of trade would redistribute the gains from trade towards the high-income countries importing the primary products. Prebisch used the argument to promote industrialisation in Latin America.

In subsequent decades, some developing countries such as China have moved successfully into manufacturing. Others, such as Nigeria and Angola, have relied on oil exports, while some developing countries have remained dependent on other primary exports. These groups of developing countries have experienced very different trends in their terms of trade.

As Figure 15.4 (overleaf) shows, the terms of trade of developing country oil exporters have fluctuated wildly since 1960. The terms of trade turned greatly in their favour as the oil price rose in the mid-1970s, then turned against them from the mid-1980s to 2000. After 2000, oil and gas price increases sharply improved the terms of trade once again.

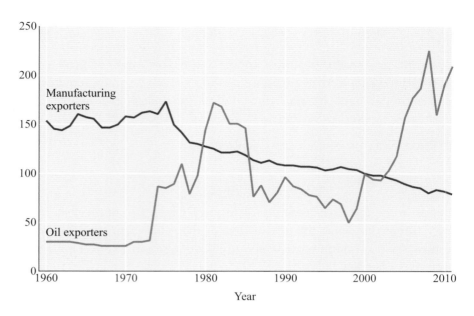

Figure 15.4   Terms of trade of developing countries: major oil exporters and major exporters of manufactured goods, 1960–2011 (index 100 in 2000)

(Sources: 1960–2006 based on data supplied by Bilge Erten, from UNCTAD data (Erten, 2011); 2000–11 data from UNCTADstat, 2012)

The developing countries that are major exporters of manufactures have had a very different experience, as Figure 15.4 shows. Since the mid-1970s they have faced a long decline in their terms of trade.

Activity 15.5

What does this terms of trade decline tell you about who has benefited from the rise of China and of other developing country manufacturing exporters?

Answer

Some of the benefits of Asian export manufacturing have been redistributed to the high-income countries importing those manufactures, in the form of falling prices. This helped to hold down inflation in the UK during the 'great moderation' from the mid-1990s to 2008 (Chapter 1, Section 6).

The implications for China are considered in the next section.

The remaining developing countries – not major exporters of oil or manufactures – have had a mixed experience. As a group they experienced a terms of trade decline from the mid-1970s to the early 2000s (Erten, 2011); however, after 2000, those countries exporting agricultural commodities (food and tropical beverages) and minerals experienced a price boom and improving terms of trade.

4   Trade policy: liberalisation and tariff protection

> Openness to international trade accelerates development: this is one of the most widely held beliefs in the economics profession.
>
> (Dollar and Kraay, 2004, p. F22)

'Trade liberalisation', 'freeing trade', increasing 'openness to trade': these phrases all refer to the reduction or removal of a wide range of impediments to trading goods and services across national boundaries. Arguments for free trade are rooted in the theory of comparative advantage and its demonstration of the mutual gains from trade.

Since 1945, the world has moved, though unevenly, to a much more liberalised trade regime. The General Agreement on Tariffs and Trade (GATT) and its successor body the World Trade Organization (WTO) have negotiated eight completed general 'rounds' of trade liberalisation. A ninth, the 'Doha Round', collapsed. The previous 'Uruguay Round' (1986–94) cut tariffs of participating members by a weighted average of 38% (weighted by import values) (WTO, 2007, Table 5).

From the 1980s onwards, international institutions such as the World Bank and International Monetary Fund required recipients of their funding to open up to trade, by lowering tariffs (taxes) on imported or exported goods and allowing markets to determine exchange rates. Economic integration between countries, as in the EU, has reduced restrictions on cross-border trade, as has harmonisation of regulations for the international trading of particular goods and services. Bilateral (country to country) and multilateral free trade treaties, such as the North American Free Trade Agreement (NAFTA) or the ASEAN[1] Free Trade Area (AFTA), have reinforced international integration.

Finally, 'openness to trade' is also widely defined in economic analysis as including a capitalist economy with widespread private ownership and no state monopoly of trade (Sachs and Warner, 1995; Lucas, 2009). Trade liberalisation is thus a highly political topic.

---

[1] Association of South East Asian Nations

4.1   The economic impact of tariffs

To assess trade liberalisation, one first needs to study the effects of **tariffs**, that is, taxes on imports, which are a key trade policy tool.

Tariffs influence both the pattern of trade – that is, who trades in what with whom – and the effects on the welfare of consumers in different countries. The impact of a tariff on an internationally traded good can be analysed using supply and demand diagrams. You will use this type of technique again in Chapter 17 to analyse the effect of taxes in a national economy. Economic analysis for trade policy must distinguish carefully between the effects of tariffs in the domestic market of the country imposing the tariff, and the effects in international markets.

The model of comparative advantage in Section 2 assumed that countries specialise completely in a single good. Here we move closer to the real world, by recognising that internationally traded goods are produced in many competing countries.

Suppose that the price at which a good is sold on the world market (the 'world price') is much lower than the price at which it would be sold by domestic firms in a country's domestic market in the absence of trade (the 'domestic price'). This may well be the case if domestic firms lack economies of scale or have less good technology than overseas producers. Now trade is opened.

Figure 15.5 (overleaf) shows what will happen in the domestic market for the good. D is the domestic market demand for the good. S is the domestic supply curve: that is, it shows the amount that firms producing within the country are willing to supply at each price. If there were no trade, P_D would be the domestic price.

The world price for the good is P_W. Once free trade is opened, the price of the good sold by domestic producers cannot be above P_W, otherwise consumers will simply purchase imports. So the price in the domestic economy will drop from P_D to P_W. The world price sets the domestic price.

Tariff
A tariff is a tax imposed on the import of goods and services.

Activity 15.6

At price P_W, how much will be produced domestically?

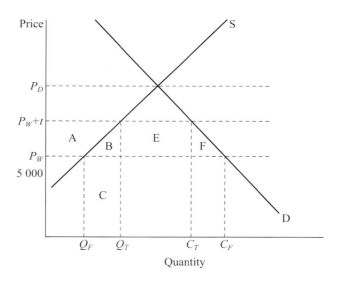

Figure 15.5   The domestic impact of a tariff

Answer

At price P_W, the domestic firms' supply curve S shows that the firms will offer to sell only Q_F of the good. Beyond Q_F, domestic firms would require a price higher than P_W.

However, domestic consumers want to consume C_F of this now modestly priced good. The difference is $C_F - Q_F$, and under free trade this demand will be met by imports from overseas firms willing to sell at the lower price.

Now suppose that domestic producers organise lobbying of government, arguing that more employment in domestic industry is needed. The government imposes a tariff on imports at level t per unit of the good. As a result, the price in the domestic economy rises to the world price plus the tariff, $P_W + t$.

At that price, the supply curve S shows that domestic producers are willing to supply more, increasing output to Q_T. Domestic consumers, however, economise on the higher priced good, buying only C_T. Imports, filling the gap between domestic consumption and production, fall to $C_T - Q_T$.

This economic impact is called *industrial protection*, since it protects domestic firms from overseas competition.

However, not everyone wins. Figure 15.5 also helps to identify the redistributive effects.

Tariffs generate revenue that goes to government. This revenue is measured by the volume of imports $(C_T - Q_T)$ multiplied by the tariff t. In Figure 15.5 this is the area labelled E.

The chief losers are domestic consumers, who pay more and consume less. Consumers' additional payment for the good is t times the amount that they now consume, C_T. This is the area A + B + E in Figure 15.5. The consumers no longer pay for the goods they no longer consume. However they lose area F, which shows the additional price that they would have been willing to pay for each of those units above the price P_W. (Chapter 12 Section 2.3 discusses demand curves and willingness to pay.) So consumers *lose* A + B + E + F.

The winners are domestic firms. They produce more (Q_T rather than Q_F) and receive a higher price for all their production. Their gains are measured by their additional revenue, area A + B + C. However, they also have additional production costs, measured by area B + C, which shows the additional marginal cost of each extra unit supplied. (Chapter 13 explains that the supply curve in a competitive market traces the marginal cost of each unit supplied.) So the net benefit to the domestic firms is (A + B + C) − (B + C) = A. Some of the consumers' loss is the firms' gain.

As Figure 15.5 shows, therefore, the losses to consumers in the domestic economy from the imposition of a tariff outweigh the gains to firms and government. Adding the gains and losses together shows a net loss of areas B + F:

$$E - (A + B + E + F) + A = -(B + F)$$

4.2   Tariff policies and trade liberalisation

> In most cases, trade liberalisation is welfare increasing, but it also brings about large income redistribution.
>
> (Bussolo et al., 2011, p. 2019)

Together with the comparative advantage model of gains from trade, this demonstration of the net costs of tariff protection makes a powerful case for trade liberalisation, that is, tariff reduction, based on the benefits to consumers. However, the models examined so far are based on some specific assumptions.

First, they are models of perfect competition. They assume that resources are fully employed, so that the price changes reallocate resources rather than leaving some unused.

Second, the market analysed in Figure 15.5 is a market of a 'small' country in the same sense that perfectly competitive firms are 'small': that is, the country is a *price taker* in the international market for this good. The changes in imports as a result of the tariff shown in Figure 15.5 do not affect the world price for the good, which the country can take as given.

Third, the comparative advantage model in Figure 15.3 assumed that resources are fixed. In Figures 15.2 and 15.3, the only resource was a population of a given size.

The rest of chapter gives a flavour of the implications for trade policy of relaxing some of these assumptions.

5   Trade policy and countries with market power

Just as firms can exercise market power, so can countries. A country that is a major trader of a good or service on the international market will be able to influence world prices by the scale of its trade.

For example, a country may be a major world producer of an export commodity. In primary products this is quite common: big coffee producers such as Brazil and Colombia; Saudi Arabia's dominance in oil; China's domination of the rare earth minerals extraction needed for electronics, 'green' technologies and military hardware manufacture; Zanzibar's once-dominant world market position in cloves. In manufactures, individual countries may also dominate particular global markets: China, for example, dominates toy manufacturing at the time of writing. In these circumstances, countries have market power: changes in their export volumes influence their export price.

Conversely, a country or group of countries such as the EU may not be price-taking importers in particular markets. Examples of importers with market power include China's demand for certain raw materials and food imports, and US demand for consumer electronics imports. In these cases, changes in import demand can influence world prices. These forms of market power bring both opportunities and dangers for trade policy.

5.1   The optimal tariff

If a country has market power in a market for a major *import*, then imposing a tariff can turn the terms of trade in the country's favour. To see intuitively why this may be so, recall from Section 4.1 that a tariff reduces a country's demand for imports. If a country is a large importer, than the tariff will sharply reduce world demand, potentially pulling down world prices. For the importing country, this is a terms of trade improvement. It brings a gain to the country, that may offset the net losses described in Section 4.1. The tariff that brings the maximum benefit to the country in this way is called the *optimal tariff.*

To see how this can work, look at Figure 15.6 (overleaf), which is based on Figure 15.5. As in Figure 15.5, S is the domestic supply curve of the good, and D is domestic consumer demand. The free trade world price is P_W as before, with total consumption C_F and domestic supply Q_F.

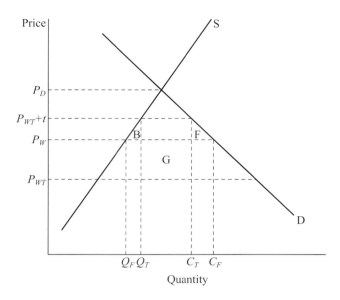

Figure 15.6   An optimal tariff

Now, what happens when a tariff is imposed? The world market price falls; the influences on how much it falls are discussed further below. Suppose that it drops to P_{WT}. The country now imports the good more cheaply than before, and the government collects the tariff at the border. Consumers pay the new lower world price *plus* the tariff. Suppose that this takes the domestic consumer price up to $P_{WT} + t$.

As in Figure 15.5, therefore, consumers are paying more than the previous free trade price, inclusive of the tariff. Domestic producers receive the higher price $P_{WT} + t$, so they expand production from Q_F to Q_T. Consumption of the good falls from C_F to C_T, and imports fall to $C_T - Q_T$. As in Figure 15.5, there is a net loss to the country, when gains to firms and government are balanced against losses to consumers. In Figure 15.6, to keep the diagram uncluttered, just the net loss is labelled as before as areas B + F.

However, there is now an offsetting gain to the importing country. Although domestic consumers are paying more, the country as a whole is paying less for its imports at the border, because the world price has fallen to P_{WT}. The additional benefit to the importing country is the import price decline $(P_W - P_{WT})$ multiplied by the imports $(C_T - Q_T)$. This is area G.

As drawn, G is larger than B + F: the gains outweigh the losses from the tariff. The *optimal tariff* is the tariff rate that maximises the net gain, i.e. maximises G − (B + F).

In what market circumstances will governments be able to exploit this opportunity to benefit from trade policy? The extent to which a country can influence its terms of trade in this way will depend on the international supply curve for the import. If a country is a large importer of a good in fairly inelastic world supply (with a steep international supply curve), then a reduction in its demand will tend to reduce prices substantially. (Elasticity is explained in Chapter 12.) If the supply curve for the imported good is more elastic (flatter), then the price reduction will be smaller. So, for example, were China to reduce sharply its demand for minerals by imposing a tariff, the world prices of minerals might well fall. A reduction in demand by European countries for an imported good in more elastic supply, such as clothing, might not have such an impact on international prices.

Research shows that governments do exploit these trade policy opportunities. Countries not constrained in their trade policy by WTO membership have been found to set import tariffs 9 percentage points higher on inelastically supplied imports than on those in elastic supply. Similarly, US trade restrictions not covered by the WTO were found to be significantly higher on goods where the USA has more market power (Broda et al., 2008).

Who loses from an optimal tariff on an import? The answer is the exporting countries, since the terms of trade are turned against them. While trade policy offers scope for strategic behaviour to benefit the domestic economy, the danger arises of mutual harm through competitive tariff retaliation and rising protectionism. Preventing such cumulative mutual harm is a major argument in favour of organisations such as the WTO.

5.2   Export market power and immiserising growth

While buyer power can turn terms of trade in your favour, unfortunately seller (exporter) power can have the opposite effect. A country that is dominant in its export markets will tend to drive down world prices if it expands its exports. Picture a low-income country relying for foreign exchange primarily on one primary export – perhaps a mineral, or coffee or cocoa. Producers invest, and production expands. When the larger production is put onto the world market, total global supply expands sharply. The global supply curve shifts to the right.

Activity 15.7

How will the response of the world price be affected by the elasticity of global demand for the good?

Answer

So long as the global demand curve is downward-sloping, the export supply expansion will reduce the world price for the export and turn the terms of trade against the exporting country. The extent of the impact depends on the response of global demand. The less elastic the global demand curve, the greater the decline in world prices when the country expands its supply.

Can trade policy respond? Just as restricting imports can drive down prices, so reducing exports can support prices. A tax on an exported good reduces the supply of that good for export, and can raise world prices. For example, in 2012 the WTO ruled that China's taxes on exports of nine minerals widely used in industrial production – along with quotas that limited export quantities – were in breach of WTO trade rules. The USA, the EU and Mexico had complained that China's policies had led to higher prices of the raw materials and put their industries at a disadvantage.

In extreme cases, a country's terms of trade decline as a result of export expansion may be so severe that the volume of imports that can be bought with the country's exports actually falls. This grim effect is called 'immiserising growth' (Bhagwati, 1958): expansion of export production actually lowers total domestic consumption.

To what extent has this actually occurred? Yasuyuki Sawada (2009) found 26 episodes between 1945 and 1985 that fit the definition, a large majority of these in Africa (Table 15.3). The countries are mainly exporters of primary commodities other than oil.

Table 15.3   Episodes of immiserising growth

Region	1970–5	1975–80	1980–5
Africa	Burkina Faso	Congo	Benin
	Burundi	Ghana	Gabon
	Guinea	Guinea	Rwanda
	Liberia	Somalia	Zaire
	Senegal	Swaziland	Zimbabwe
	Togo	Tanzania	
		Zimbabwe	
Asia	Afghanistan	Nepal	
Europe			Netherlands
			Portugal
Caribbean	Jamaica	Barbados	
South America	Suriname		
Oceania		Fiji	

(Source: Sawada, 2009, p. 1615)

Activity 15.8

Look back at Figure 15.4. The dominant manufacturing exporter among developing countries is China. Does Figure 15.4 suggest that China has experienced immiserising growth?

Answer

China has certainly faced a major decline in its terms of trade as it has expanded manufactured exports. This is likely to be in good part the result of its own success in exporting. However, you know from Chapter 2 that total domestic consumption has expanded rapidly in China despite high saving rates. It seems that export growth has been far from immiserising in China.

The reason why China's growth has not been immiserising can be found in the discussion above. We expect international demand for manufactured goods to be elastic: people will buy many more manufactured goods such as clothes and toys as prices fall. Therefore export expansion does drive a terms of trade decline, but the total purchasing power of exports in terms of imports has increased for

China. Some of the benefit of the export expansion has been transferred to consumers purchasing the imports in Europe, North America and elsewhere, but some of the benefits have also remained with Chinese consumers.

6   Trade and inequality within countries

The efficiency consequences of trade reform pale in comparison with its redistributive effects.

(Rodrik, 1998, p. 19)

The justification for trade liberalisation concerns economic efficiency: that free trade encourages resources to be reallocated to more efficient uses. The previous section explored the extent to which trade also redistributes benefits and losses between countries. Trade also, however, influences inequality within countries, often causing a political backlash against liberalisation. The internal impacts of trade depend on the pattern of exports and imports, which depend in turn on the resources and productivity of resource use in each country.

6.1   Sources of comparative advantage

Section 2 identified two sources of comparative advantage: endowments of labour (working people) in each country, and differences in productivity of that labour, which you can think of as differences in skills and technology. More generally, the comparative advantage model of trade assumes that at a given moment, a country has a stock of factors of production, such as land, labour with different levels of skill, capital goods such as machinery and installed software systems, and mineral resources. This stock can change over time, as investment increases the capital stock, training raises skills, exploration discovers new mineral deposits, and technology identifies new methods of extraction. Together with technological and organisational capabilities, these factors determine an economy's productive capacity.

These factors of production vary between countries. Some countries have abundant unskilled labour and land, but relatively little skilled labour and installed capital; others have relatively more skilled labour, capital and technological capability.

So how do these differences influence the pattern of trade? One of the key models in trade theory, called the Heckscher–Ohlin model, was developed to try to answer this question. The model is named after Eli Heckscher and Bertil Ohlin, Swedish economists writing in the early twentieth century. They predicted that countries will have a comparative advantage in those goods and services that use relatively intensively the factors of production with which they are relatively well endowed. So countries with abundant low-skilled labour should export goods that use this factor intensively in production, such as clothing. Countries with abundant skills and installed capital should export goods requiring intensive use of those inputs, such as machine tools.

While this model seems plausible, early attempts to test it produced what came to be called the 'Leontief paradox'. The economist Wassily Leontief found that in 1947, contrary to expectations, the exports of the USA appeared to be less capital-intensive than its imports. Leontief assumed that in 1947 the USA was relatively abundant in capital compared to the rest of the world, so this result appeared to contradict the Heckscher–Ohlin predictions.

Since then, these predictions have been further tested, in particular by disaggregating labour into skilled and unskilled (which Leontief did not do), adding in land as a factor of production (abundant in the USA and omitted by Leontief), and including technological knowledge and capabilities by adding, for example, extent of research and development (R&D). Empirical estimates based on models that allow for different technologies show that technological differences between countries are an important determinant of trade patterns (Baldwin, 2008).

6.2   Skills, trade and internal inequality

The dependence of trade patterns on skill differences creates winners and losers from trade within countries. Suppose that one country, say Bangladesh, is relatively well endowed with low-skilled labour, while another, say Germany, is relatively abundant in more highly skilled labour.

Suppose now that trade is opened along the lines predicted by Heckscher–Ohlin. Bangladesh specialises in and exports low skill-intensive clothing; Germany specialises in and exports high skill-intensive machinery.

Activity 15.9

Which groups of workers – high- and low-skilled – gain, and which lose in each country from opening of trade?

Answer

In Bangladesh, demand for low-skilled labour in clothing production rises, pushing up wages of lower skilled workers relative to wage rates of those with higher skills. In Germany, conversely, demand for highly skilled labour rises, while demand for low-skilled workers drops, widening the wage differential.

Lower skilled workers in high-income countries are likely to oppose trade liberalisation and the associated outsourcing of products and services that are intensive in the use of lower skilled labour. It would be expected that wage inequality in high-income countries would increase as a result of competition from lower income exporters.

Figure 15.7 (overleaf) shows what happened to male wage inequality in some high-income countries during a period of major trade expansion (see Figure 15.1). Figure 15.7 uses a measure of inequality that you saw in Chapter 1: the ratio of the 90th percentile wage to the 10th percentile wage of the distribution. The UK and the USA stand out in displaying a rapid rise in wage inequality in the 1980s. However, over the period 1990–2008, many other countries – including Germany, but not France – have seen wage inequality rise.

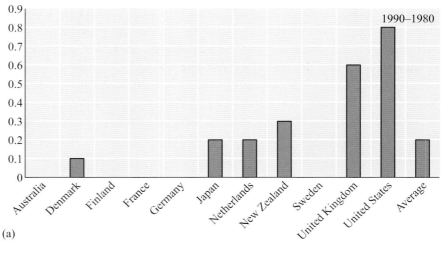

(a)

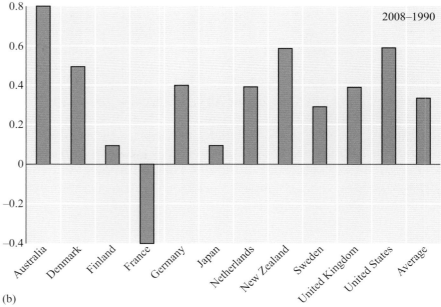

(b)

Figure 15.7   Change in male wage inequality (change in ratio of 90th to 10th percentiles) in OECD countries: (a) 1990 compared to 1980, (b) 2008 compared to 1990

(Source: Van Reenen, 2011)

Explanations of this widening inequality identify the interaction of two major influences: technological change and trade. Technological change has squeezed 'middle' jobs, while expanding 'lousy' and 'lovely' jobs at the two ends of the wage spectrum (Van Reenen, 2011). Trade has shifted low-skill-using production offshore, and in the process, competition from China and other lower-income manufacturers has stimulated technical change in high-income countries, pushing production techniques 'up' the skill ladder. The net effect has been wage polarisation in the UK, the USA and more widely. The social consequences of this wage polarisation are large, and there are many losers, causing political resistance to freer trade.

Proponents of trade liberalisation argue that if trade liberalisation brings aggregate national benefits, then it is justified, since the winners can compensate the losers. However, there are two problems with this argument.

First, the compensation may not occur. Second, and worse, compensation may not effectively be possible. According to Dani Rodrik, a US economist specialising in trade and industrial policy issues, this is the case for many African countries (Rodrik, 1998). He argues that the efficiency gains from trade liberalisation can be small in many African countries relative to the redistributive effects. The gains to farmers exporting agricultural output may well outweigh the losses incurred by urban residents and the government. But the scale of additional taxation (in countries that find it difficult to raise taxation) required to transfer a large part of those benefits to the losers is infeasible and would generate its own efficiency losses. Resistance to trade liberalisation in these circumstances is both explicable and intractable.

7   Market structure and strategic trade policy

So far, this chapter has analysed trade mainly as if 'countries' do the trading. But in practice, of course, it is mainly private firms that trade goods and services across national boundaries. So this final section applies some analysis from Part 4 to international trade, and considers further aspects of strategic trade policy.

7.1   Intra-industry trade

In the comparative advantage model in Section 2, countries specialise in different goods and then trade: that is, all trade is inter-industry. However, much international trade, as Section 4 recognised, is intra-industry, that is, it involves trade between countries of goods within the same industrial category – for example, two-way trade in cars between European countries. For example, Adolfo Benavides (2011) estimates that 47% of US trade with 12 other high-income countries in 2008 involved exchange of goods and services in the same product category, measured as trade in goods or services in the same 3-digit Standard International Trade Classification (SITC). However, only 28% of US trade with 12 developing countries was intra-industry in this sense. Table 15.4 shows data from ten of the countries in the study, reflecting the much greater variation in the extent of intra-industry trade in the low- and middle-income group.

Table 15.4   Extent of intra-industry trade between the USA and specified countries, 2008

High-income country	% of trade intra-industry	Low-/middle-income country	% of trade intra-industry
Canada	52.96	China	15.79
Japan	31.47	Mexico	45.45
Germany	54.72	India	29.11
United Kingdom	51.15	Chile	7.74
South Korea	34.80	Vietnam	6.53

(Source: Benavides, 2011)

Intra-industry trade reflects the imperfectly competitive nature of most international markets. One reason for its prevalence is variety:

consumers like a choice within particular goods and services categories, such as cars or airlines, and intra-industry trade provides wider choice. So greater variety on the international market can be seen in itself as a gain from trade.

A second gain from intra-industry trade concerns cost efficiency. If competition is imperfect, then firms will face different downward-sloping demand and average revenue curves in each market, and develop separate sales strategies for each market.

Imperfect international markets may thereby generate pro-competitive gains from trade. If two countries open up to international trade, this enlarges the market served by the firms in each country to include the other country's market. Competition within the larger market may benefit consumers.

The model of monopolistic competition that you studied in Chapter 14 can be used to show how this works (Figure 15.8).

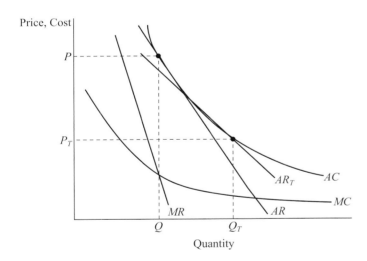

Figure 15.8   Gains from trade with monopolistic competition

In Figure 15.8, a firm in monopolistic competition is serving its domestic market, in the absence of trade. Under monopolistic competition, firms are producing a variety of somewhat differentiated goods for a single market (Chapter 14, Section 4). The demand curve for this firm's product is AR, and its marginal revenue curve is MR. The firm's average and marginal cost curves are AC and MC. The firm is in long-run equilibrium, maximising profit where $MC = MR$ at output Q, at the point where AR is tangent to AC with price P. The firm is making normal profits.

Then the country opens up to trade with another country. Now firms from each country are competing in a larger international market, and there is intra-industry trade. The demand (AR) curve for the firm in Figure 15.8 becomes flatter, shifting to AR_T. If the firm raises its price, it will now lose more sales to competitors than before the market enlarged.

The firm's new long-run equilibrium is at output Q_T with price P_T. This is the point again where the demand curve is tangent to the AC curve, so $AC = AR$ and the firm is again making normal profits. (I have left out the new MR curve, to avoid cluttering the diagram.) Note that the firm has a production technology with increasing returns to scale. It has moved down its average cost curve, so production has become more efficient. Price to the consumer has fallen. The increase in competition has driven down price and cost.

However, not all trading partners necessarily gain from the pro-competitive effect of trade. Suppose that before the opening of trade, there are two firms, each with a monopoly in their own market. Opening trade creates competition, undermining monopoly profits. However, if economies of scale are large enough, then one firm may be able to drive down its costs to the point where it occupies the whole enlarged market as a monopolist. At that point, it can charge monopoly prices again, and consumers lose out anew. Furthermore, the country that loses its producer is particularly damaged, since the monopoly profits now accrue to a firm outside its borders.

Economies of scale therefore affect trade outcomes. Fast-growing Asian countries such as South Korea and later China focused their trade policy on promoting learning-by-doing (Chapter 11), drawing technological expertise from joint ventures with foreign firms, and moving up the technological ladder over time. The gains from trade, and their distribution between countries, depend on technology and market structure.

7.2   Firms and strategic trade policy

'Strategic' trade policy is trade policy that aims to redistribute the gains from trade in the direction of the country using the policy instrument.

Optimal tariffs are one example. This section contains some policy examples that require analysis of links between trade policy and firms' behaviour.

'Infant industry' tariffs

Tariffs can be used to promote economic development through learning-by-doing by firms. If firms in a given industry face a 'learning curve', such that their average costs fall as cumulative output rises (Chapter 11), then when a firm starts production, it will necessarily have average costs above those of more long-standing firms in the industry. In a developing country, this may be a problem facing a large part of its industrial sector. Competition from imports will then wipe out new firms before they have had time to move down their learning curve.

This provides a strong argument for temporary tariff protection for 'young' firms while they learn and grow. Such 'infant industry' protection works best when it protects firms that have a real prospect of 'growing up' to stand full international competition in the medium term – rather than to provide permanent protection to the inefficient. East Asian countries such as South Korea managed to combine protection for emerging industries with strong incentives for individual firms to compete hard in the domestic market and to 'graduate' to international competitiveness over time.

Anti-dumping tariffs

Anti-**dumping** tariffs are permitted under WTO rules if a country can show that a foreign firm is dumping its product in their domestic market.

Dumping
An imported product is dumped if its price is either below its producer's price in its home market or below its producer's average cost of production.

Why would a firm find it profitable to 'dump' its products? Dumping may be profitable when a firm is able to sell its product at different prices in different markets (this is called price discrimination). The markets must be disconnected in the sense that goods sold into a low-price market cannot be re-exported to the higher-price market causing prices in the two markets to converge.

Figure 15.9 builds on the analysis of monopoly in Chapter 14 to show how dumping can be profitable. It shows how a firm that is a monopolist in its domestic market may be able to maximise its profits by dumping part of its output into a competitive export market, rather than selling only on its domestic market.

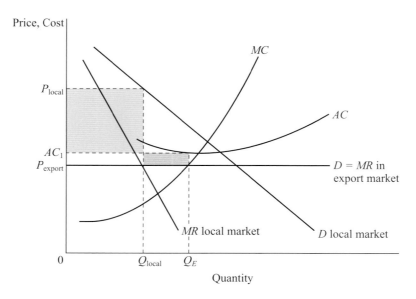

Figure 15.9   A discriminating monopolist dumps its product abroad

Figure 15.9 shows the firm's cost curves, MC and AC. It also shows the firm's revenue curves in two markets. In its domestic market, the firm faces a downward sloping demand curve $D_{local\ market}$ and marginal revenue curve MRlocal market. In its export market the firm is a price taker, so it faces a horizontal demand curve $D=MR$ at price P_{export}.

The firm maximises its profits by producing QE, where $MC = MR$ in the export market, at average cost $AC1$. Why is this so? The firm faces different marginal revenue curves in its domestic and export markets. So it sells each unit of its output in the market that provides the higher marginal revenue. It sells Qlocal in its domestic market, at price P_{local} This is because at sales up to Qlocal, the firm's marginal revenue in the domestic market exceeds the marginal revenue that it could earn in the export market. Beyond Qlocal, the export market provides higher marginal revenue than the domestic market, so the firm turns to exporting.

In the export market, the firm faces a horizontal demand curve, and its export price Pexport is its marginal revenue from exports. The firm continues to produce up to output QE, where its marginal cost MCequals marginal revenue from exports. The firm therefore sells QE − Qlocal overseas at the world price Pexport.

Now here is the puzzle. In the export market, the price Pexport lies wholly below the firm's average cost curve, AC. So why is it profitable for the firm to export at this price? This is because the firm's marginal cost of production of each additional unit above Qlocal, traced by the *MC* curve, up to *Q*E, is below the marginal revenue from exporting those additional units. The firm makes additional profits by continuing to produce above *Q*local up to *Q*E, despite selling on the world market below average cost.

The firm therefore engages in dumping. It charges a lower price abroad than at home, and sells below average cost abroad. The country to which it is exporting would be permitted under WTO rules to impose an anti-dumping duty, that is, a tariff equal to the difference between the exporter's local price and the dumped price.

The extent to which anti-dumping duties work as strategic trade policy depends on the reaction of exporting firms. The aim of the anti-dumping duties is to protect home producers in the import market. However, depending on the market structure, the exporter might raise its export prices to reduce the duty (by reducing the gap between its domestic market price and its export prices, and hence reduce the duty). In that case the importing country's consumers lose out from the higher prices, while the domestic firms are protected but the duty collected by government is reduced. The net benefit may be positive or negative.

7.3   Exchange rate manipulation

> The best (or at least the least problematic) PPP-based estimate for renminbi undervaluation remains about 30 percent.
>
> (Subramanian, 2010, p. 6)

An accusation of dumping can also be made against a country that is accused of manipulating its exchange rate to cheapen its exports. This is a highly controversial topic in trade policy. At the time of writing (2012), China has been repeatedly accused, notably by the USA, of maintaining an undervalued exchange rate in order to promote exports.

One reason for the controversy is the difficulty of knowing what the exchange rate *should be*. One possible benchmark is purchasing power parity (PPP), which was defined in Chapter 2. Purchasing power parity holds when price levels in two countries are equal when expressed in a common currency. For example, suppose that a basket of goods in the

UK costs £100 sterling, and that the exchange rate with the euro is £1 = €1.10. Then PPP holds if the European basket costs €100 × 1.1 = €110.

This example illustrates the relationship between exchange rates and prices. If PPP holds, then the exchange rate between two currencies equals the ratio of the price levels in the two countries.

Activity 15.10

Suppose that in country A, a basket of goods costs 100, while in country B the same basket of goods, bought with country A's currency, costs 90. Is A's currency undervalued or overvalued?

Answer

In this case, A's currency is overvalued using the PPP benchmark, since it can buy more in B than in A. Country B's goods are cheaper than country A's in A's currency.

So how about China? Comparisons of purchasing power in the USA and China show that the renminbi is undervalued relative to the US dollar, as the quotation above (from an economist previously with the IMF) asserts.

This PPP benchmark can be used to assess currency overvaluation and undervaluation only if we assume that exchange rates should adjust through the market to achieve PPP between trading countries. By implication, if they do not, then there is currency manipulation.

However, empirical observation of price levels of similar goods across countries shows that price levels are correlated with GDP per head. Richer countries tend to have higher prices. And it has been persuasively argued that PPP should not be expected to hold between a developing country such as China and a high-income country such as the USA.

Why is this so? The economists Paul Samuelson and Bela Belassa proposed an explanation that depends on productivity differences and the existence of goods and services that are not traded internationally. In countries where productivity is high, wages will reflect this high productivity. Wages in non-traded goods and services (education and health services, for example) will reflect productivity in the traded goods sectors such as manufacturing for export. As a result, wage costs and hence prices will be higher for non-traded goods in richer countries, even when PPP holds in the traded goods sector.

The implication is that PPP would not be expected to hold in 2012 between the USA and China. As China gets richer, we would expect that its exchange rate would increasingly approach a level at which PPP would hold with high-income countries. Meanwhile, PPP-based estimates of the undervaluation of the renminbi may be too large, though there is a consensus that there is some undervaluation and that the valuation promotes Chinese exports. The main losers from this undervaluation are likely to be other developing country exporters that compete directly with China in their export markets.

8   Conclusion

Trade policy displays a complex mixture of win–win – mutual benefits from trade liberalisation – and win–lose – as patterns of inequality are reshaped. This chapter has explained some of the sources of the gains from trade, and some of the policies and market pressures that produce winners and losers. In the process it has shown why trade policy can be so politically explosive – and why it is so important. One question that emerged in Section 6 was the extent to which governments can and should compensate losers from trade liberalisation. The next chapter introduces better measures of inequality than you have studied so far, and explores methods by which governments may act to reduce national income inequality.

References

Baldwin, R.E. (2008) *The Development and Testing of Heckscher–Ohlin Trade Models*, Cambridge, MA, MIT Press.

Benavides, A. (2011) 'The intra-industry structure of the United States' international trade with selected industrialized and developing nations', *International Journal of Business and Social Science*, vol. 2, no. 22, pp. 1–6.

Bhagwati, J. (1958) 'Immiserizing growth: a geometrical note', *Review of Economic Studies*, vol. 25, no. 3, pp. 201–5.

Broda, C., Limão, N. and Weinstein, D.E. (2008) 'Optimal tariffs and market power: the evidence', *American Economic Review*, vol. 98, no. 5, pp. 2032–65.

Bussolo, M., de Hoyos, R. and Medvedev, D. (2011) 'Free trade in agriculture and global poverty', *The World Economy*, vol. 34, no. 12, pp. 2019–43.

Dollar, D. and Kraay, A. (2004) 'Trade, growth and poverty', *Economic Journal*, vol. 114, pp. F22–F49.

Erten, B. (2011) 'North–South terms of trade trends from 1960 to 2006', *International Review of Applied Economics*, vol. 25, no. 2, pp. 171–84.

Lucas, R.E. (2009) 'Trade and the diffusion of the Industrial Revolution', *American Economic Journal: Macroeconomics*, vol. 1, pp. 1–25.

Ricardo, D. (1817) *On the Principles of Political Economy and Taxation*, London, John Murray.

Rodrik, D. (1998) 'Why is trade reform so difficult in Africa?', *Journal of African Economies*, vol. 7, suppl. 1, pp. 10–36.

Sachs, J. and Warner, A. (1995) *Economic Reform and the Process of Global Integration*, Brookings Papers on Economic Activity no. 1, Washington, DC, Brookings Institution Press.

Sawada, Y. (2009) 'The immiserizing growth: an empirical evaluation', *Applied Economics*, vol. 41, pp. 1613–20.

Subramanian, A. (2010) *New PPP-based Estimates of Renminbi Undervaluation and Policy Implications*, Peterson Institute for International Economics Policy Brief, April, [online] www.iie.com/publications/pb/pb10-08.pdf (Accessed 8 December 2012).

UNCTADstat (2012) *Terms of Trade Indices and Purchasing Power Indices of Exports, Annual, 1980–2011*, [online] http://unctadstat.unctad.org/TableViewer/tableView.aspx?ReportId=16421 (Accessed 6 December 2012).

Van Reenen, J. (2011) 'Wage inequality, technology and trade: 21st century evidence', *Labour Economics*, vol. 18, pp. 730–41.

World Trade Organization (WTO) (2007) *Sixty Years of the Multilateral Trading System: Achievements and Challenges*, Geneva, WTO.

World Trade Organization (WTO) (2012) *International Trade Statistics 2011: Appendix Tables*, [online] www.wto.org/english/res_e/statis_e/its2011_e/its11_appendix_e.htm (Accessed 6 December 2012).

Chapter 16
Inequality and redistribution

Martin Higginson

Contents

1   Introduction

Chapter 15 explained how comparative advantage enables trade and specialisation, which increases the consumption possibilities of trading countries and their citizens. It also highlighted how such gains are shared unequally between and also within nations. This chapter continues with the theme of inequality, focusing specifically on inequality of incomes within countries. It discusses how such inequality can be measured, offers reasons why it matters, and considers how governments can influence the level of inequality within a country.

At the start of the second decade of the 2000s, increased levels of inequality became the basis for global protest movements. The 'Occupy' movement saw people occupying landmark sites close to leading financial centres across some of the richest countries in the world. They were trying to highlight what they saw as the injustice of a system that seemed to be sharing the gains of that system in a way that favoured the few over the many.

Protestors outside St Paul's Cathedral in London

(Source: Wells, 2011)

The protestors pointed to how in the years running up to the economic crisis that began in 2008 there were rising levels of inequality, but when faced with the resulting crisis governments responded by implementing policies that were likely to make such inequality more pronounced. But inequality of what? What is the 99% to which the protestors in the picture are claiming to belong? And what exactly is meant by inequality?

This might at first appear straightforward: it seems a simple matter to decide whether or not something is shared equally. I may divide a pie into equal slices, but if not, I have divided it unequally. However, if one thinks a little more about what to assess to measure inequality within a country, things become more complicated.

There are various options from which to choose. I could assess how consumption possibilities are distributed, for example, by variations in levels of wealth or the ownership of certain goods. Alternatively, I could use quality of life measures based on educational experiences, health outcomes or the quality of accommodation. All of these approaches are valid and would say something about how resources are shared within economies, but the main focus in this chapter is on income inequality. Household income tends to be the measure most frequently used to assess inequality, and it also has close associations to other indicators of well-being; people living in low-income households are more likely to consume less and to die younger, although the causation between these factors is complex. Household income is also used to measure poverty levels; whether and how to reduce these is an important policy issue for governments.

The learning outcomes for this chapter are:

- to explain why inequality matters
- to understand different ways of measuring household income
- to interpret different measures of income inequality, including distinguishing between income inequality and poverty
- to describe some of the ways in which governments can affect income inequality
- to understand why there are trade-offs between different economic objectives with respect to welfare policy.

2   Why does income inequality matter?

The economic crisis that began in 2008 renewed the interest of economists and governments in income inequality. The 'Occupy' protestors focused on the unfairness of unequal societies, but increasingly economists are also taking much more interest in the role played by inequality in influencing economic activity. Some argue that inequality is bad for growth; others argue that it encourages growth; still others claim that whatever its effects on growth, it is unfair and governments should do what they can to reduce it. A further line of argument is that inequality produces social problems and for that reason should be reduced.

2.1   Economic growth

Not all income is spent on consumption; some of it is saved. In Part 2, the marginal propensity to consume was defined as the fraction of each extra unit of income that households plan to spend on consumption. It varies with household income, with the marginal propensity to consume being higher in lower-income households.

Recognising that high-income households consume less and save more of their income, a supply-side view argues that higher levels of inequality would lead to greater levels of saving and in turn greater capital accumulation and economic growth. Because more unequal societies channel more resources to those who have a greater propensity to save, inequality improves the prospects for economic growth. It leads to faster savings accumulation, which enables greater investment in productive infrastructure and new industries, and thus promotes economic growth.

However, a Keynesian argument would focus on the demand-side effects of income inequality, saying that because higher-income households have a lower propensity to consume than lower-income households, inequality reduces the multiplier. As you saw in Part 2, this has important effects on the level of output that can be sustained in an economy. Increasing levels of inequality therefore act as a constraint on output and growth. Stewart Lansley (2011) uses similar reasoning based on rising inequality to explain both the Great Depression of the 1930s and the economic and financial crisis that began in 2008.

Dust Bowl refugees during the Great Depression, 1937

(Source: Bettmann/Corbis in Lansley, 2012)

2.2   Inequality and equity

Inequality also matters if one cares about issues of equity or fairness. You saw at the beginning of the chapter that there have been protests arguing that current levels of inequality are unjust.

Equity
Equity refers to a distribution of income (or assets) that a society deems to be fair and just.

The notion of **equity** has an ethical dimension: it means a fair distribution. Some inequality could be considered equitable. If you cut a pie into unequal size slices, then there is clearly inequality. However, is it necessarily an inequitable distribution? For example, should the person who made the pie, or the person who contributed more money to buy the ingredients, be entitled to a larger slice? Or should someone who is particularly hungry be entitled to more? If there are good reasons for the slices to be unequal, then how unequal can still be fair? These questions have no simple answers, and when applied to how income is distributed in a country or between different groups in society, some fundamental policy questions turn on them.

Whether income inequality is equitable is sometimes framed around the extent to which individuals can shape their own economic futures and therefore whether they deserve to be rich or poor. A short story from the days of the Great Depression illustrates this nicely:

A young man asked an old rich man how he made his money. The old guy fingered his worsted wool vest and said, 'Well, son, it was 1932. The depth of the Great Depression. I was down to my last nickel. I invested that nickel in an apple. I spent the entire day polishing the apple and, at the end of the day, I sold the apple for ten cents. The next morning, I invested those ten cents in two apples. I spent the entire day polishing them and sold them at 5 pm for 20 cents. I continued this system for a month, by the end of which I'd accumulated a fortune of $1.37. Then my wife's father died and left us two million dollars.

(Greenspun, 1998)

Did you think that inheriting the fortune that placed the old man towards the top end of the income range was fair or equitable? Would it have been more equitable had he earned his high income through buying and selling apples? There are no simple answers, not least because in the example above the man not only inherited his millions, but he inherited them from his wife's father. Turning this around, is it fair that someone born into a very poor family has the limited opportunities that having less money brings? This highlights how meanings of equity and fairness can be subjective.

2.3   Inequality and its wider social impact

Another reason for caring about inequality is that it might give rise to social problems.

In their influential book *The Spirit Level*, Wilkinson and Picket (2009) argue that more unequal societies fare worse on a range of health and social indicators. Figure 16.1 (overleaf) shows an example of one of many graphs that Wilkinson and Picket present. It shows that societies with higher levels of income inequality tend to have worse societal outcomes, as measured by a mix of health and social indicators listed to the left of the graph. An index of these is measured along the vertical axis, and a measure of income inequality, known as the Gini coefficient, is given along the horizontal axis. (Section 3.2 will show you how Gini coefficients are calculated and what they mean.)

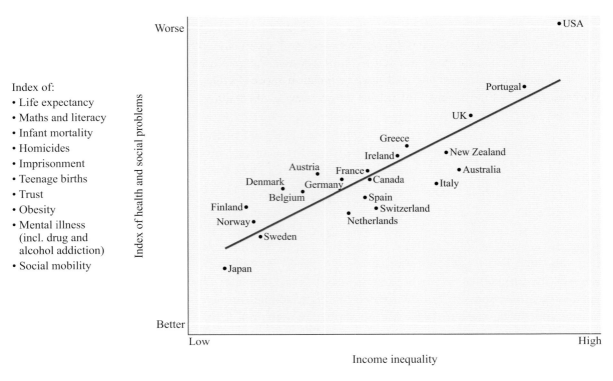

Index of:
- Life expectancy
- Maths and literacy
- Infant mortality
- Homicides
- Imprisonment
- Teenage births
- Trust
- Obesity
- Mental illness (incl. drug and alcohol addiction)
- Social mobility

Figure 16.1   Index of health and social problems (combined measure of health and social problems) and income inequality

(Source: Wilkinson and Picket, 2009)

The analysis in *The Spirit Level* focuses on richer and more industrially developed countries. Its message is that in order to build a better society, governments should focus on reducing income inequality, as well as – or instead of – chasing more conventional goals, such as economic growth. While the message that the authors wanted people to get from their findings was clear, and their book has led to much research into the association between inequality and a range of social indicators, their work has been contested.

One criticism is that drawing the implication that reducing inequality would improve outcomes relies on assuming that income inequality is the cause of the health and social problems with which it is associated. Data alone cannot explain why such an association exists, and O'Connell (2010) argues that there can be many different reasons for the observed outcomes.

For example, Wilkinson and Picket (2009), using Figure 16.2, imply that more unequal societies have lower education scores. Figure 16.2 appears to support their claim. Countries such as the USA and Portugal have high levels of income inequality and lower education scores, while countries such as France and Finland have lower levels of inequality and higher education scores.

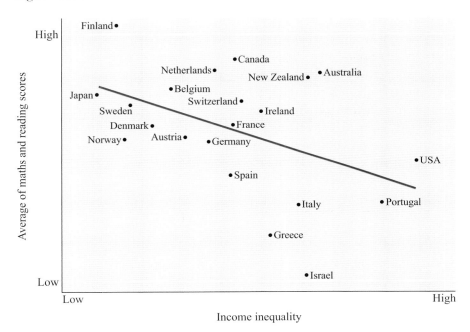

Figure 16.2   Education scores and income inequality

(Source: Wilkinson and Picket, 2009)

its different educational performance. Immigrant children may face
additional barriers of culture and language that might help to explain
lower educational scores in countries with high levels of immigration. And
if immigrants also have lower incomes than other workers, then this will
also make such countries more unequal.

Another criticism of Wilkinson and Picket's approach is that the
measure of income that they use to assess a country's level of income
inequality ignores the benefits of government spending on public
services, such as health care and education. You will see in the next
section that taking account of the value of such services can change
measured levels of income and income inequality significantly. What
counts as income and how income inequality is measured are therefore
significant issues, which are now considered.

3 Measuring income and income inequality

In order to do something about income inequality, one must be able to measure it. One needs to be able to tell whether policies have reduced or exacerbated inequalities, and, to see what alternatives there are, compare the level of inequality in different countries (as Figures 16.1 and 16.2 did in Section 2). To measure inequality, therefore, one needs some way of summarising the distribution of income in a population. How this should be done depends on the particular aspect of inequality that is of interest.

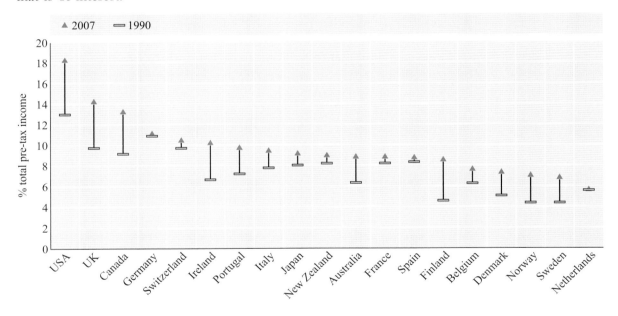

Figure 16.3   Share of the top 1% of incomes in total pre-tax incomes, 1990–2007

(Source: Organisation for Economic Co-operation and Development (OECD), 2011)

One measure that would capture the idea of the gap between the very rich and the rest, that the protestors outside St Paul's in London were emphasising, is the share of total income going to the individuals receiving the top 1% of incomes. Figure 16.3 shows how this changed for selected OECD countries between 1990 and 2007. In relation to the rest (the 99%), the protestors at St Paul's may have a point. The pattern is clear: in every country apart from the Netherlands, the share of pre-tax income going to that top 1% increased. For the USA it increased from around 13% to over 18%, and for the UK it increased from around 10% to just over 14%.

This measure gives quite a good idea of how income inequality at the top end of the distribution increased, but it says nothing about what happened to those lower down. Did the poor also fall behind the median? Measuring inequality by just one number cannot hope to capture all this complexity, so there are a number of different ways to measure inequality: which to use depends on the question being asked.

3.1   Measures of household income

Equivalised household income

Equivalised household income is household income adjusted to account for household size and composition.

Because people within households tend to share their expenditure, their standard of living is usually measured at a household level. This is done by pooling all the different sources of a household's income and then 'equivalising' it to take account of the composition of the household. This equivalisation is necessary because a household with more members will need a larger income to achieve a given standard of living. However, this equivalisation cannot be done simply by dividing household income by the number of household members, because living with others reduces costs through, for example, being able to share household goods and buy in bulk. The box below explains how government statistics that report **equivalised household income** take into account the different compositions of households.

Note that this process inherently assumes that households share resources in such a way that all members enjoy the same standard of living – an assumption that may mask significant inequalities within households.

What is 'equivalised income'?

The income that a household needs to attain a given standard of living will depend on its size and composition. For example, a couple with dependent children will need a higher income than a single person with no children to attain the same material living standards. 'Equivalisation' means adjusting a household's income for size and composition so that we can look at the incomes of all households on a comparable basis. Official income statistics use the 'Modified OECD' equivalence scale, in which an adult couple with no dependent children is taken as the benchmark with an equivalence scale of one. The equivalence scales for other types of households can be calculated by adding together the implied contributions of each household member from the table below.

Modified OECD equivalence scale

Head	0.67
Subsequent adults	0.33
Each child aged 0–13	0.20
Each child aged 14–18	0.33

For example, a household consisting of a single adult will have an equivalence scale of 0.67 – in other words, he or she can typically attain the same standard of living as a childless couple on only 67 percent of its income. In a household consisting of a couple with one child aged three, the head of the household would contribute 0.67, the spouse 0.33, and the child 0.20, giving a total equivalence scale of 1.20. In other words this household would need an income 20 percent higher than a childless couple to attain the same standard of living.

(Source: Institute for Fiscal Studies (IFS), 2012)

Households obtain their income in different ways. Figure 16.4 illustrates this and will be used later in the chapter to consider various ways in which government policies affect inequality. Chapter 1 showed that for most households the largest source of original income comes from participation in the labour market by members of the household, who may be full-time, part-time or self-employed workers. Income from other sources besides earnings includes pensions and income from capital, as interest payments on savings or dividends from owning shares. The combination of income from these sources is referred to as **original income** – sometimes also referred to as market income – in Figure 16.4 (overleaf). Many households also receive income from cash benefits from the government. Examples include Child Benefit, state pensions, disability payments and means-tested support for low-income households. Cash benefits, when added to original income, make up 'gross income' in Figure 16.4. As you will see, such benefits are particularly important for households whose members are not in paid employment or earn low wages.

Original income
Original income is income obtained from the market before any benefits have been added or taxes deducted.

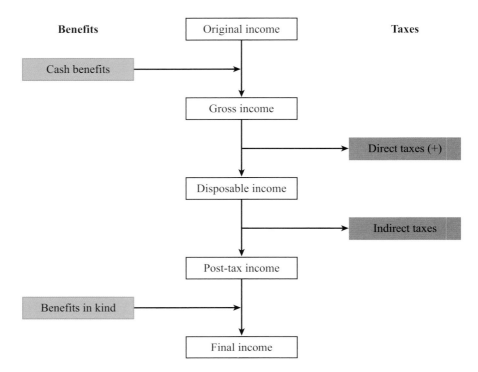

Figure 16.4   Household income, cash benefits, taxes and benefits in kind
(Source: adapted from Office for National Statistics (ONS), 2012)

Gross income
Gross income is measured by adding any government cash benefits to original income.

Disposable income
Disposable income is gross income minus direct taxes such as Income Tax and National Insurance Contributions.

Post-tax income
Post-tax income is the result of deducting indirect taxes such as VAT and excise duties from disposable income.

Final income
Final income is post-tax income adjusted to take into account the consumption of benefits in kind provided by government, such as education and health care.

Gross income   minus the direct taxes that are levied on income or earnings, such as Income Tax and National Insurance Contributions, is referred to as **disposable income**. When the amount going on indirect taxes such as VAT and excise duties is subtracted from disposable income, what is left is referred to as **post-tax income**. Households also benefit from their consumption of public services, for example, health care and education. The value of these 'benefits in kind', measured by the government expenditure needed to finance them, are added to post-tax income to reach **final income**. All these additions to and subtractions from household income due to government policy affect income inequality. Section 4 analyses them in more detail in considering what governments can do about income inequality.

3.2   Measures of inequality: the Lorenz curve and the Gini coefficient

Nearly all measures of income inequality start by ranking households by income. You met a similar technique in Chapter 1, where employees were lined up by their earnings in an 'earnings parade'. The 10th percentile of earnings is the earnings of the person 10% of the way up the line – the one who earns more than 10%, but less than 90%, of the population. The 50th percentile is the earnings of the person in the middle of the parade, with 50% of the population earning more and 50% earning less; the 50th percentile is therefore just the median. And the 99th percentile is the earnings of the person 99% of the way up the line, nearly at the back, for whom 99% of the population earn less, and just 1% of the population earn more.

The earnings parade used in Chapter 1 was based on the more well-known 'income parade' that is used to give a visual representation of how the standard of living of people in an economy is distributed. Instead of using their individual earnings as in Chapter 1, an income parade to illustrate income inequality would line up everyone by the equivalised income of their household. If each person's height represents their equivalised household income, then the first people to go through will be really short, but the last will be gigantically tall. Such an income parade could be drawn up using any of the measures of household income in Figure 16.4.

As you have seen, one measure of inequality is to look at the percentage of total income that goes to the top 1% (the last 1% in the income parade), with higher numbers indicating more inequality. Alternatively, one could look at the percentage of total income that goes to the bottom 1% (the first 1% in the income parade), in which case a lower number would indicate more inequality. But the problem with each of these measures is that they capture inequality only between the very rich (or very poor) and the rest, not what is going on at the other end of the distribution or in the middle.

The Lorenz curve and the Gini coefficient are two measures of inequality that also use the idea of looking at the percentage of total income received by the bottom 1%, 5% or 10%, and so on, but build in information from the full distribution. **The Lorenz curve** is a graphical representation of inequality, from which the Gini coefficient can be derived to provide a numerical summary description.

Lorenz curve
The Lorenz curve is a graphical representation of inequality. It shows the cumulative percentage share of household income plotted against the cumulative percentage of households.

To see how Lorenz curves are constructed, you need first to understand what a decile group is. Recall that the incomes of people in households a certain percentage of the way along the income parade are called percentiles. Every tenth percentile can also be called a decile, with the first decile being the 10th percentile, the second decile the 20th percentile, the fifth decile the 50th percentile (the median), and so on.

Decile and quintile groups
Decile groups divide the total population into ten equally sized groups, ranked from the bottom to the top in terms of a variable such as income. Quintile groups do the same thing but divide the ranked population into five equally sized groups.

We can also construct **decile groups**, ten equally sized slices of the ranked population, and **quintile** groups, when the ranked population is divided into five equally sized slices. In the income parade, the first decile group consists of the first 10% of people, i.e. those with household incomes below that of the first decile; the second decile group is the next 10% of the population, i.e. those with household incomes between those of the first and the second decile; and so on right up to the tenth (or top) decile group, which includes all those with household incomes above that of the ninth decile. (Note that one can also talk about percentile groups: the 99th percentile group is the top 1%, i.e. the very rich whose share of total income Figure 16.3 showed was increasing in many countries in the years before the financial crisis.)

I can now look at the steps needed to derive the Lorenz curve by considering the data shown in Table 16.1. Households must be first ranked in ascending order by their equivalised income, and then divided into equal-sized groups. In Table 16.1, households are divided into decile groups. The second column is a reminder of the cumulative percentage of households, i.e. the percentage of households in each decile group or below.

The third column gives the share of the total income of the whole population received by each income decile group. It tells you that the bottom decile group as a whole received just 1.1% of total original income. The second decile group's income is 2.1% of total original income, and so on, right up to the 32.9% of total income for the top decile group. These shares are used as the basis for calculating the cumulative share of income (fourth column), i.e. the percentage of total income received by households in that decile group or below. To calculate this, the bottom decile group's share of total income (1.1%) is added to the second decile group's share of total income (2.1%) to give 3.2%. So the bottom 20% of households received 3.2% of total original income in 2010/11, and so on.

Table 16.1   UK household original income by decile groups, 2010/11

Decile	Cumulative percentage of households (%)	Share of total income (%)	Cumulative share of total income (%)
Bottom	10	1.1	1.1
2	20	2.1	3.2
3	30	3.1	6.3
4	40	4.2	10.5
5	50	5.7	16.2
6	60	8.3	24.5
7	70	11.0	35.5
8	80	13.7	49.2
9	90	17.9	67.1
Top	100	32.9	100.0
Whole population		100.0	

(Source: ONS, 2012)

In a Lorenz curve, the cumulative percentage share of income is plotted against the cumulative percentage of the population. The cumulative percentage of the population increases in steps of 10 percentage points (as these are decile groups). These plots are shown in Figure 16.5 (overleaf).

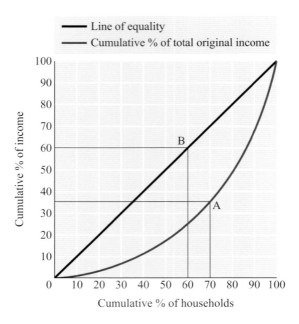

Figure 16.5   UK Lorenz curve (original income) 2010/11

(Source: based on ONS, 2012)

Line of equality

The line of equality shows the Lorenz curve for perfect equality.

So, for example, point A shows that the bottom 70% of the households received about 35% of total original income. The 45-degree line in a Lorenz curve diagram is called the **line of equality** and shows what the Lorenz curve would be if there was perfect equality, that is, if everyone had the same income. This would represent the actual distribution of income only if each decile group of households received 10% of total income. So at point B on the line of equality, 60% of households would have 60% of total income.

The closer the Lorenz curve is to the line of equality, the lower the level of inequality.

One potential difficulty with looking at Lorenz curves is that they don't necessarily give unambiguous answers when used to compare the levels of inequality between different countries or over different time periods. The next activity illustrates this.

Activity 16.2

Lorenz curves can be used to look at inequalities in wealth as well as income. A household's wealth is its stock of assets, such as housing, savings in the bank, and shares in firms. Wealth typically has greater levels of inequality than income. Figure 16.6 gives three curves showing how household wealth was distributed in the UK in the years 1945, 1975 and 2005. How would you rank the years in terms of inequality of wealth?

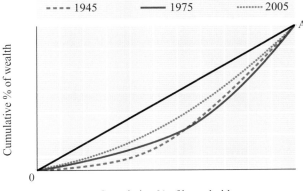

Figure 16.6   Lorenz curves for distribution of wealth in the UK in 1945, 1975 and 2005

(Source: Economics Network)

Answer

Wealth is least unequal in 2005, with the Lorenz curve being closer to the line of equality than the other years. It is not possible to say whether the 1945 curve or the 1975 one is the more unequal. These two Lorenz curves cross at around 50% of the population (where wealth is at its median), with the 1945 curve being further away from the line of equality than the 1975 curve for households whose wealth is below the median, but closer to the line of equality for higher-wealth households.

One way to resolve this dilemma would be to take account of the whole area between the Lorenz curve and the line of equality. The greater this area, the more inequality, as the curve will be further away from the line of equality.

The **Gini coefficient** is a single numerical value that does this. It is calculated by dividing the area between the line of equality and the Lorenz curve (shown by A in Figure 16.7) by the total area under the line of equality in the diagram (A + B).

Gini coefficient
The Gini coefficient measures the extent to which the total distribution of income among individuals or households within an economy deviates from a perfectly equal distribution.

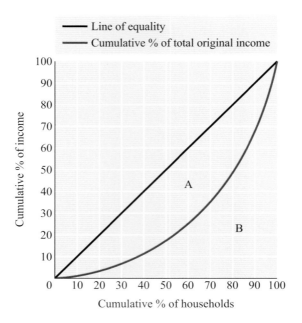

Figure 16.7   The Lorenz curve and the Gini coefficient

The Gini coefficient for original income in Figure 16.7 is 0.52. If there was no inequality and the Lorenz curve was at the line of equality, then the Gini coefficient would be 0. The maximum value that the Gini coefficient can take is 1, Between 0 and 1, the higher the value of the Gini coefficient, the higher the level of income inequality. The detail of calculating the area under the Lorenz curve is not needed here, but you do need to be able to interpret the Gini coefficient as a measure of inequality. These were the measures of inequality used in Figures 16.1 and 16.2 of Section 2.

Between 1985 and the onset of the economic crisis of 2008, income inequality as measured by the Gini coefficient increased in most OECD countries, as shown in Figure 16.8. However, the size of such increases varied, and in two cases, Turkey and Greece, income inequality decreased.

Activity 16.3

Compare Figures 16.3 and 16.8. They are not for exactly the same countries or periods, so you would expect some differences. But for what other reason do you think there are differences?

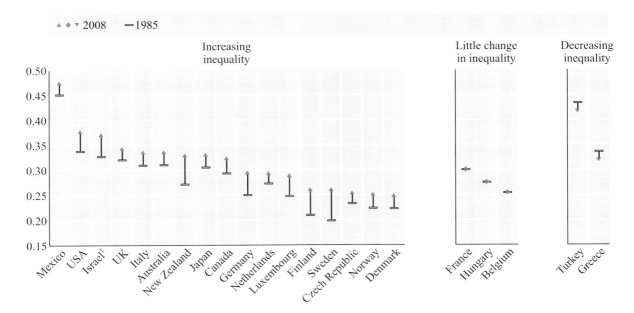

Figure 16.8   Gini coefficients showing changes in inequality in household disposable income (equivalised), mid-1980s and late 2000s. 'Little change in inequality' = < 2%

Answer

Figure 16.3 looks at individual incomes, while Figure 16.8 examines equivalised household incomes. More significantly, perhaps, Figure 16.3 just takes account of the top 1% of incomes compared with the rest, while Figure 16.8, by examining Gini coefficients, takes account of inequality across the whole spectrum of incomes. The countries in which the increases in overall inequality in Figure 16.8 are highest include New Zealand, Germany and Sweden, in none of which did the share of income going to the top 1% increase as much as in the UK or the USA. Only Finland showed unusually large increases in both measures.

3.3   Inequality and poverty

Poverty is a concept related to, but different from, inequality. In the UK you are more likely to hear politicians making the reduction of poverty, or specifically the elimination of child poverty, their goal rather than reducing income inequality. Like inequality, poverty is usually measured at the household level, even though it is recognised that the distribution of resources within households may be far from equal.

Absolute poverty
Absolute poverty is defined as having a level of household income below that needed to consume the basic necessities of life such as food, shelter, water and warmth.

There is also a distinction between absolute and relative poverty. Being in **absolute poverty** means not having the income that is needed to enjoy a physiologically defined minimum standard of living. The anti-poverty campaigner Joseph Rowntree (1901) defined this as the 'level of income necessary for the bare necessities of life'.

In contrast, the concept of relative poverty is concerned with people living in households whose income is below that needed to participate fully in the society in which they live. Unlike meeting the bare necessities with which Rowntree was concerned, the concept of relative poverty takes into account that societies differ in what is required to participate in them. As a result, relative poverty is usually measured by having a household income not too far below the median household income of society – not below 60% of the median, say. The percentage chosen is known as 'the relative poverty line', and where it is drawn will determine the proportion of the population living in households with incomes under that line, that is, in relative poverty. The higher the line is drawn, the greater the percentage of people described as living in relative poverty (see Figure 16.9). (Note that poverty rates can be measured either before or after housing costs. Poverty rates in the UK are higher when using the after housing costs measure because housing costs take up a higher proportion of the income of lower-income households.)

Note that relative poverty rates are always below 50%. This is because only those with incomes below the median can be in relative poverty (and only a proportion of those). So in very poor countries, households who are not in relative poverty could be in absolute poverty. In rich countries, it is the other way around; many of those in relative poverty might not be in absolute poverty.

As discussed above, relative poverty is concerned with the ability to participate in a society, and I have used income as an indicator for this, but such participation does not depend on income alone and can be influenced by a range of social, economic and political factors. For example, someone can be income poor but have access to a range of social and public services (for example, health care and education), or alternatively lack access to such services. Someone may be excluded from participating in a society on grounds of gender, religion, race or age. So poverty can be related to consumption of material goods, but has a broader meaning. In formulating policy, government can target these different aspects of poverty.

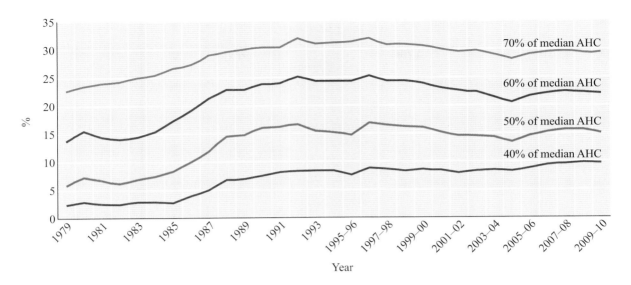

Figure 16.9   Relative poverty: percentage of individuals in households with incomes below various fractions of median income (after housing costs, AHC)

(Source: Jin et al., 2011)

Relative poverty and income inequality are different concepts, but they are related. Changes in income distribution affect relative poverty rates only if they increase or decrease the proportion of households living below the relative poverty line; this can happen only if the median income or incomes well below it are affected. Changes in the income distribution at the top end do not affect poverty rates. That is why the share of the top 1% of incomes could rise as in Figure 16.3, without poverty rates being affected. But suppose, perhaps due to policies introduced by government to reduce poverty, that the share of national income going to the bottom 20% of households increases from 5% to 5.25%. Such a change of just one-quarter of 1% would have a minimal effect on the overall distribution of income as measured by the Gini coefficient, but for the poorest 20% this is an increase of 5% in their income (because 0.25% is 5% of 5%). If, as a result, the incomes of many of these households were raised above the relative poverty line then there would be a substantial drop in the relative poverty rate, but only a very small decrease in inequality.

In practice, there appears to be a strong association between levels of income inequality and relative poverty. Figure 16.10 shows that levels of inequality between countries are closely associated with relative poverty, with countries such as Mexico, Turkey and the USA having higher levels of income inequality and higher poverty rates. Conversely, countries towards the bottom left of Figure 16.10, such as Denmark and Norway, have lower levels of income inequality and lower relative poverty rates.

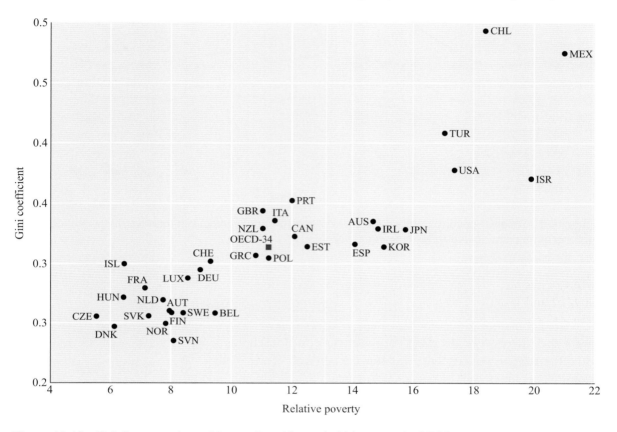

Figure 16.10   Relative poverty and inequality of household incomes in OECD countries, mid/late 2000s

Note: Household income = equivalised household disposable income. Relative poverty = percentage of individuals living in households with income less than 50% of median household income. OECD34 = the average of the 34 OECD countries.

(Source: Pisu, 2012)

While this association appears to be strong, it is possible to have increasing levels of income inequality and falling poverty rates, as the UK experienced in the first decade of the 2000s.

Activity 16.4

How might it be possible for income inequality and relative poverty rates to move in different directions?

Answer

The answer lies in the different things that are measured by income inequality and poverty. Relative poverty measures what happens to people and households towards the bottom of the income distribution. Government policy could target raising the income of households in lower decile groups, while not really worrying about what happens to income at the top end. This is what in effect happened in the UK, where high incomes increased significantly in the late 1990s and at the start of the 2000s until the economic crisis of 2008, but a focus on poverty reduction meant that many households moved above the poverty line. Many governments target poverty rather than levels of income inequality.

Poverty rates and income inequality actually fell between 2009/10 and 2010/11, despite the UK experiencing recession and low levels of economic growth. According to the Institute for Fiscal Studies (IFS) (Cribb et al., 2012), there were 13 million individuals living in poverty in the UK in 2010/11, which is 500 000 fewer than in 2009/10 (as measured by incomes after housing costs below 60% of median income). This represented 21.3% of the UK population. At the same time, the Gini coefficient fell from 0.36 to 0.34, representing the largest fall between two years since 1962.

So does this mean that the poor were catching up with the rich and their incomes were rising to take them out of poverty? This is partly correct. It is true that the gap between high-income earners and low-income earners had narrowed, but rather than being because of rising incomes at the bottom, it was because incomes across the whole income range had fallen. Incomes towards the bottom had fallen less quickly, in part because government support for low-income households was doing its job of protecting living standards. The 10th percentile of incomes fell 1.1%, compared to 5.1% for the 90th percentile (Cribb et al., 2012). This led to some arguing that absolute poverty measures become more important at times of falling incomes, when relative poverty rates can hide falling living standards for individuals on low incomes.

4   Government and inequality

Government actions affect inequality in a number of ways. This can be seen in Figure 16.4, which shows how the government redistributes income between households through taxes, benefits and a range of public services (benefits in kind). These move the distribution from that in the original income box through to that of the final income box in Figure 16.4.

Government policies may also affect the distribution of original income. This, as you will see, produces a dilemma. Governments that are keen to reduce inequality need to decide whether it is more effective to do so through the taxes and benefits that transform original income into final income (the inflows and outflows down the sides of Figure 16.4) or through tackling the original distribution of income (the starting box at the top of Figure 16.4). The dilemma is that the taxes and benefits may themselves affect original income.

I will explore that dilemma in Section 5. Here I first examine the policy tools that governments have at their disposal and consider how effective they are in reducing inequality.

4.1   Original income

Parts 2 and 3 showed how macroeconomic policies aiming to promote economic growth and stabilise economies will also influence how original income is distributed within an economy by affecting employment rates.

Employment rates are important as they give access to wages in the labour market, but are only one aspect of the explanation of how original income is distributed. Inequality within wage earners is also important, as Figure 16.11 shows.

Figure 16.11 highlights how inequality in gross earnings varies between economies. Countries on the left of the chart have lower earnings inequality. Levels of skills are an important determinant of wages, with higher-skilled workers being paid more than workers with lower skills. Koske et al. (2012) find that policies that improve secondary and tertiary education lead not only to increases in economic growth, but also reductions in earnings inequality, through improvements in human capital making workers more highly skilled. Increased productivity results in narrowing earnings differentials.

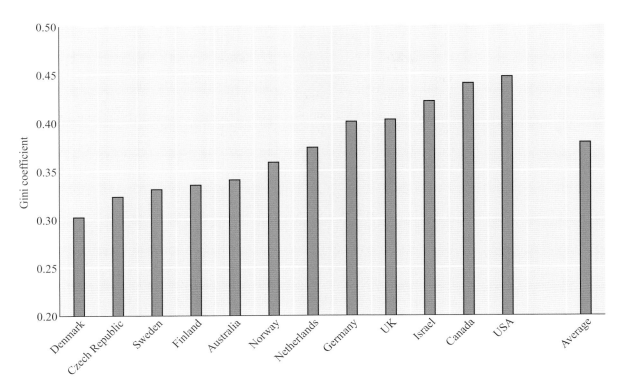

Figure 16.11   Earnings inequality across selected OECD countries: all workers
(Source: OECD, 2011)

However, rising inequality has been linked to the gap between the wages of low- and high-skilled workers widening (OECD, 2011). Wilson et al. (2010) find that while much of the growth in employment in the UK in the early 2000s was for high-skilled occupations, there was also growth for a number of less-skilled workers, but mainly in sectors – for example, the service sector – where tasks are less easily automated. This has led to an increase in inequality, with jobs in the middle disappearing, and employment being polarised between well paid and very poorly paid jobs.

A different explanation for the increase in wage inequality can be linked to changes in labour market regulations. In the UK, and across many other countries, the strength of trade unions and employment protection has diminished. Where minimum wage legislation exists, the level at which minimum wages have been set has tended to fall over time relative to median wages, widening the range of below median earnings. It has been argued that lower wage inequality in Nordic countries can partly be explained by workers having higher levels of employment protection and a stronger bargaining position for wages. Figure 16.11 would seem to support such a claim, with Denmark, Sweden and Finland having lower Gini coefficients. These countries are also characterised by higher shares of employment in the public sector, which has lower wage inequality than the private sector.

Corporate governance structures also vary across countries, with in some countries employee representatives on boards of companies tempering rises in the pay of top executives (as in the case of Germany). In the UK in 2012, there were proposals to give shareholders greater say in setting the pay of executives.

While recognising that the labour market is central to explaining income inequality and poverty levels, there are difficulties in relying on labour market policy to reduce inequality or poverty. Reducing inequality is not the sole objective of labour market policy, and the types of structural changes taking place in the UK are likely to increase polarisation in the labour market. Indeed, an increasing number of people, particularly in the low-paid service sectors, are finding that they can get only part-time jobs or are becoming self-employed. As Figure 16.12 shows, this will impact on inequality.

Activity 16.5

What conclusion might you draw from the data in Figure 16.12 about income distribution and types of employment other than full-time employment?

Answer

Across all countries, the Gini coefficient is lower among full-time employees than among all workers. While there has been increasing representation in the labour market by underrepresented groups, such groups are more likely to work in part-time jobs and have lower wages than other workers (for example, despite equality legislation, there is a persistent gap between men's and women's wages). The earnings of self-employed workers are also more unequal than those of employees. Chapter 7, Section 3 discussed employee representation and bargaining power as one explanation for changes in the labour market, a factor that may also play a role here where part-time workers are less likely to be in a trade union.

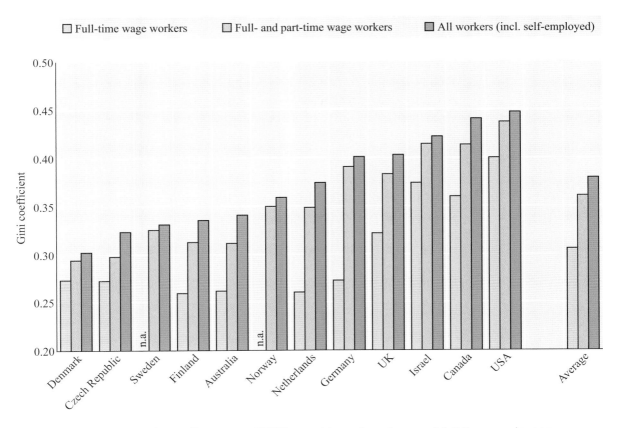

Figure 16.12   Earnings inequality across OECD countries: all workers and full-time employees

The evidence from Figure 16.12 would suggest that labour market policies will not reduce inequalities in original incomes unless they take account of the types of jobs being created, and in particular pay attention to those not in full-time jobs. Without substantial reforms, the current labour market is unlikely to provide a solution to increasing levels of inequality.

4.2   From original income to post-tax income – the role of taxes and benefits

'Cash benefits' are payments made to individuals and households from governments to help them financially in particular circumstances. Such payments can be seen as a form of insurance. Cash benefits can be divided into **contributory benefits** and **non-contributory benefits**. Contributory benefits depend on the contributions that individuals have previously made into the system; in many countries, including the UK

Contributory benefits
Contributory benefits are government benefits paid to those who have made contributions.

Non-contributory benefits
Non-contributory benefits are paid according to need and are not linked to contributions.

in 2012, the state retirement pension is a contributory benefit (linked to National Insurance contributions), although in other countries it is a non-contributory benefit available to all citizens over retirement age. Non-contributory benefits are not linked to contributions, and in many countries are means-tested so that entitlement depends on a household's income; in 2012 in the UK, there were plans to replace nearly all non-contributory benefits by a single means-tested benefit, known as Universal Credit, but a few non-contributory benefits would remain, including Carer's Allowance and Child Benefit.

It can be seen from Table 16.2 that the retirement pension, the cash benefit received by the largest number of people in the UK, is also the one that takes the largest share of total government expenditure.

Table 16.2   UK cash benefits allocated to households, 2010/11

	£ million	% of government expenditure[1]
Contributory benefits		
Retirement	67 540	9.5
Incapacity Benefit	6 550	0.9
Widows' and guardians' allowances	620	0.1
Maternity pay	1 900	0.3
Jobseeker's Allowance	820	0.1
Redundancy benefit and statutory sick pay	240	0.0
Non-contributory benefits		
Social fund	3 680	0.5
Income Support	16 160	2.3
Working and child tax credits	23 150	3.2
Child Benefit	12 040	1.7
War pensions	950	0.1
Other	31 930	4.5
Student support	1 010	0.1
Rent rebates and allowances	21 100	3.0
Total cash benefits	**187 690**	**26.3**

[1] General government expenditure includes expenditure by central and local government.

(Source: ONS, 2012)

The UK government raises the majority of its revenue through taxation. As Figure 16.4 showed, taxes fall into two categories. Direct taxes, such as Income Tax and employees' National Insurance Contributions, are taxes levied directly on individual income. Corporation Tax and employers' National Insurance Contributions are direct taxes on firms' profits and wage bills. Indirect taxes such as VAT or excise duties (for example, taxes on petrol, cigarettes and beer) are paid by firms, who will attempt to recoup as much of this tax as they can by raising the cost of the product for the consumer. Indirect taxes are so called because they tax income only indirectly (by taxing it when it is spent). Table 16.3 shows the breakdown of UK government tax revenue for 2010/11.

Table 16.3   UK taxes (% of GDP, 2010/11)

Income Tax and National Insurance contributions	17.0
VAT	5.8
Onshore Corporation Tax	2.4
UK oil and gas receipts	0.6
Fuel duties	1.8
Business Rates	1.6
Council Tax	1.7
Excise duties	1.3
Capital taxes	1.0
Other taxes	2.5
Total taxes	**35.8**

(Source: Office for Budget Responsibility (OBR), 2012)

Income Tax was the largest source of government revenue, with £151.3 billion collected in 2010/11, and National Insurance Contributions and VAT receipts brought in £105.6 billion and £97.3 billion, respectively (OBR, 2012).

The distributional impact of cash benefits and taxes can be seen by looking at the Lorenz curves in Figure 16.13. The three Lorenz curves move from original income down Figure 16.13 to gross income (which includes cash benefits), and then through the stages to post-tax income.

Activity 16.6

What is the impact on original income inequality of cash benefits and taxes in the UK?

Answer

Cash benefits reduce income inequality, with the Lorenz curve for gross income being nearer the line of equality than that for original income. However, indirect and direct taxes together seem to have a fairly neutral effect on income inequality. The post-tax Lorenz curve is hardly visible in Figure 16.13 as it is so close to the gross income Lorenz curve.

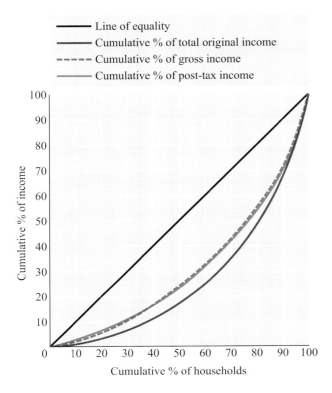

Figure 16.13   Impact of tax and benefits on original income in the UK

The Gini coefficient for original income is 0.52, while for gross income it is 0.37 and for post-tax income it is 0.38, suggesting that the net effect of direct and indirect taxation is to increase overall inequality slightly, though not nearly enough to counteract the effects of cash benefits in reducing it. The difficulty in visually distinguishing the Lorenz curves for gross and post-tax incomes highlights the usefulness of the Gini coefficient as a numerical measure of inequality.

The concepts of progressive and regressive taxation are useful in explaining why taxes overall have so little effect on income distribution. A **progressive tax** is one where proportionally more tax is paid as income increases. A **regressive tax** is the opposite: as income increases, the proportion of income paid in tax falls. (A proportional tax is a tax where the proportion of income paid in tax is the same for all taxpayers regardless of income.)

Progressive tax
For a progressive tax, the proportion of a person's income paid as tax increases as their income increases.

Regressive tax
For a regressive tax, the proportion of a person's income paid as tax decreases as their income increases.

Table 16.4 shows that direct taxes are progressive in the UK, with the bottom quintile group paying 10.5% of their gross income in tax, and the highest quintile group paying 23.6%. However, indirect taxes are highly regressive. The bottom quintile group pay 27.7% of their gross income in indirect taxes, while the top quintile pay just 10.0%. Combining both direct and indirect taxes, the tax system is broadly proportional, although it is noticeable that the bottom quintile pay the highest proportion of their gross income in tax.

Table 16.4   Taxes as a percentage of UK household income, 2010/11

	Quintile groups					
	Bottom	2nd	3rd	4th	Top	All households
Direct taxes	10.5	12.5	16.3	20.6	23.6	19.7
All indirect taxes	27.7	18.6	16.4	13.8	10.0	13.9
All taxes	38.2	31.1	32.7	34.4	33.6	33.7

(Source: ONS, 2012)

4.3   From post-tax income to final income – benefits in kind

Governments make decisions that influence both the overall level of government expenditure and also how that expenditure is divided between benefits in kind and cash benefits. So far, the discussion has focused on taxes and cash benefits as ways of redistributing income, but for some countries, government spending on social services such as health care and education is as high as on cash transfers, and can have more important distributional impacts.

Figure 16.14 shows that retirement pensions and health care are generally the two areas of greatest government expenditure within cash benefits and services, respectively.

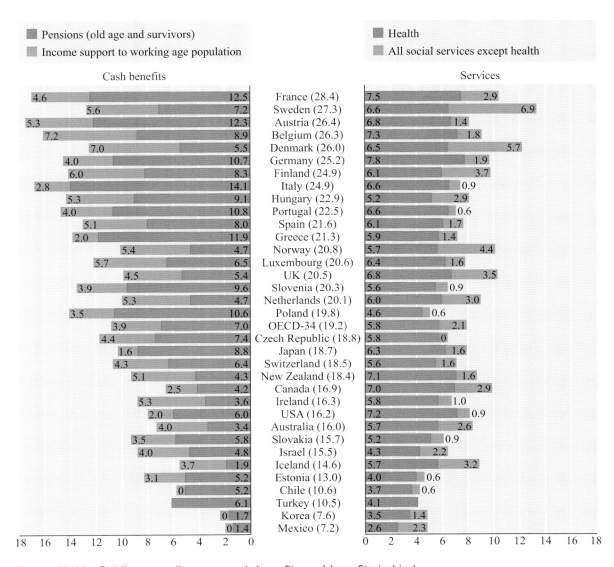

Figure 16.14   Public expenditure on cash benefits and benefits in kind (services) as a percentage of GDP, 2007

(Source: Adema et al., 2011)

Activity 16.7

Which countries had the highest overall expenditure (as measured by percentage of GDP)? Did these countries also spend most on benefits on kind?

Answer

It can be seen that in 2007, France, Sweden and Austria had the highest overall public expenditure, with 28.4%, 27.3% and 26.4% of GDP, respectively. However, while France and Sweden were among the high spenders on benefits in kind, other countries, such as the UK, Canada, Iceland and other Nordic countries, also had relatively high government expenditure on benefits in kind.

Stiglitz (2009) argues that the most meaningful concept of income for measuring a household's standard of living is its final income; this takes into account government interventions through tax, cash transfers and public spending on areas such as education and health care – the last box in Figure 16.4. It is important to consider such services to get a full picture of the impact of government.

One reason for this is that countries differ in how services such as health care and education are provided. In some they need to be paid for from post-tax income; in others they are publicly provided for free (with various in-between systems too). How these services are provided and consumed can have important effects on the standard of living of households, particularly of the poorest households, which tend to gain more from public provision. Measures of post-tax income can mask these differences. As taxes reduce household income and fund public services as well as benefits, it is a more complete analysis of effects on household income to include public services along with the taxes used to fund them.

When measuring the impact of public services, because many of them are free at the point of use (for example, state education and the National Health Service (NHS) in the UK), it is necessary to estimate a monetary value for their use. This is a complex measurement issue, and there are alternative ways of doing it. The box below provides a summary of the method used by the ONS in the UK to estimate the impact of publicly provided education and health care on income.

Estimating the value of education and health care

The current method uses data that are available on the average cost to the Exchequer of providing the various types of health care – hospital inpatient/outpatient care, GP [general practitioner] consultations, and pharmaceutical services, and so on. Each individual ... is allocated a benefit from the National Health Service according to the estimated average use made of these various types of health service by people of the same age and sex, and according to the total cost of providing those services. ... The assigned benefit is relatively high for young children, low in later childhood and through the adult years until it begins to rise from late middle age onwards. ... The benefit given to households for the NHS is estimated to be equivalent to 12 per cent of the average post-tax income for non-retired households, or an average of £3,400 per year.

[...]

Education benefit is estimated from information provided by the Department for Education and, by local authorities, of the cost per full-time equivalent pupil or student in maintained special schools, primary and secondary schools, universities, and other further education establishments.

(Source: ONS, 2011, p. 16)

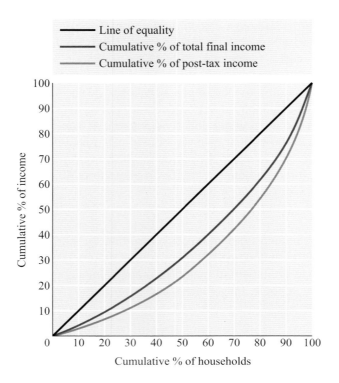

Figure 16.15   Comparing Lorenz curves for final income and post-tax income in the UK, 2010/11

When imputing the financial value of benefits in kind to calculate final income from post-tax income, there is an inwards shift of the Lorenz curve in the UK towards the line of equality (see Figure 16.15), and the Gini coefficient of 0.28 for final income shows a reduction in inequality compared with the post-tax income Gini coefficient of 0.38.

According to the OECD (2011), taking account of benefits in kind such as education, health care and housing has an impact on income inequality across many countries. Figure 16.16 shows the Gini coefficient both before (the blue columns) and after (the grey lines) benefits in kind have been taken into account.

Activity 16.8

What conclusion might you draw from Figure 16.16?

Answer

Across all countries in Figure 16.16, public services (benefits in kind) reduce levels of income inequality. Figure 16.14 showed that the percentage of GDP spent on such services varies between countries,

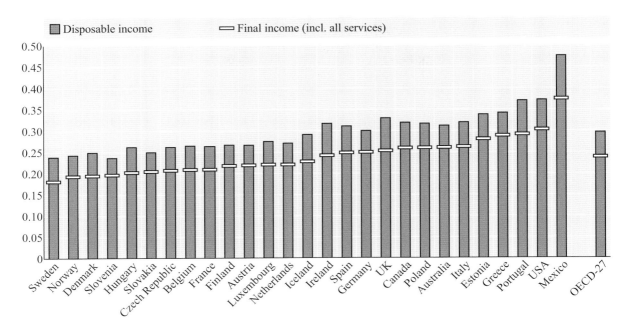

Figure 16.16   The impact of benefits in kind on post-tax income in OECD countries, 2007
(Source: OECD, 2011)

and while the purpose of such expenditure (for example, health care and
education) is not solely for redistribution, its impact reduces the Gini
coefficient on average by one-fifth in the countries in Figure 16.16.

The combination of the three methods to redistribute income discussed
in this chapter can be seen in Figure 16.17. For households in the lower
decile groups, the impact of benefits in kind increases their share of
total final income compared to post-tax income, while after the sixth
decile group the share begins to fall. This suggests that the combination
of cash transfers, tax and benefits in kind reduces overall inequality, by
redistributing income from higher-income decile groups to lower-income
ones, with benefits in kind having the largest redistributive effect.

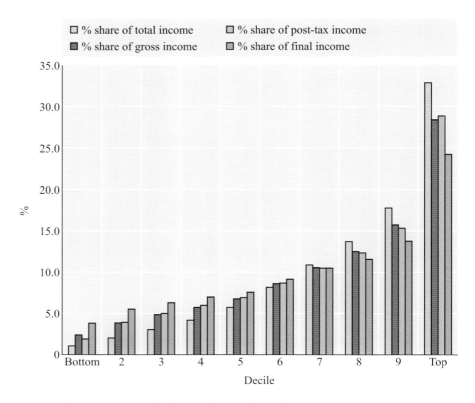

Figure 16.17   Combined effects of cash benefits, tax and benefits in kind in the UK, 2010/11

(Source: ONS, 2012)

That benefits in kind, such as education and health care, redistribute income is an important argument for public provision of such services. And the public may find redistribution through the provision of public services more acceptable than through cash payments. However, redistribution is not the only reason why governments provide such services. It is also because such services have important benefits to society more widely, as well as to the individual who consumes them.

Benefits (or costs) of consumption that affect others besides the individual consumer or producer are known as 'externalities' (discussed in Chapter 17). An individual deciding how much to buy of a good or service does not account for any externalities in their evaluation of how much to consume of it; they will therefore consume less of it than if they took account of any wider social benefits of their consumption. This makes a case for government intervention to encourage the consumption of goods and services that have wider benefits to society.

Musgrave (1959) uses the example of education, which he argued people would underconsume because they would not take into account the wider and longer-term benefits of their education to society as a whole. In such situations, governments have different options available to them to increase consumption. They can enforce consumption by making schooling compulsory to a certain age and/or provide such services free of charge or at a subsidised price. You will meet further discussion of externalities in Chapter 17.

Activity 16.9

What positive externalities might arise from an individual consuming education and training?

Answer

There is a wide choice here, but externalities that have been claimed include:

- higher productivity in the economy
- helping to create new technologies that may increase economic growth
- reduced taxation through fewer benefits having to be paid to that individual in the future through their greater employability and earning power
- increased international competitiveness for the economy as a whole, leading to higher rates of growth and employment
- improved citizenship and social skills, which lead to greater participation in public life
- reduced crime rates making people feel safer
- helping to spread knowledge more widely in society.

Milton Friedman, a powerful advocate of free markets, argues that government needs to have a role in encouraging consumption of education:

> A stable and democratic society is impossible without a minimum degree of literacy and knowledge on the part of most citizens and without widespread acceptance of some common set of values. Education can contribute to both. In consequence, the gain from

education of a child accrues not only to the child or to his parents but also to other members of the society. … Most of us would probably conclude that the gains are sufficiently important to justify some government subsidy.

(Friedman, 1962)

5   Issues in welfare policy

Financial and economic crises often produce re-evaluations of how welfare is organised. As Figure 16.14 showed, before the economic crisis of 2008, social expenditure in most European countries amounted to more than 20% of GDP. For OECD countries as a whole, social expenditure had been increasing from an average of 15.6% of GDP in 1980 to 19.2% of GDP in 2007. Many European governments decided that they could no longer afford such expenditure as they tried to reduce their deficits by introducing 'austerity measures'.

The UK government's response to what they saw as too high levels of government spending was one of the strongest. They introduced a range of changes to tax and benefits, as well as significant cuts in government spending. The argument put forward by the coalition government elected in 2010 was that reforms were needed not only to reduce costs to the taxpayer, but also to increase incentives to work, so that people did not become dependent on the state, while still protecting the most vulnerable in society. David Cameron, the Conservative Prime Minister, put it like this:

Never again will work be the wrong financial choice. Never again will we waste opportunity. We're finally going to make work pay – especially for the poorest people in society.

[…]

I passionately believe that the welfare system should be there to support the needy and most vulnerable in our society and provide security and dignity for those in old age.

[…]

We've made our decision – we will reform welfare and reduce its costs, partly in order to protect vital services and our nation's future.

(Cameron, 2011)

Cameron did not mention reducing inequality as one of his aims, but raising the living standards of the poor is usually seen as the way to do that. As you have seen, poverty and inequality often go together, although the high incomes of the very rich also contribute to inequality, as the 'Occupy' protestors pointed out. However, welfare policy is usually seen as directed towards raising the incomes of the poorest households.

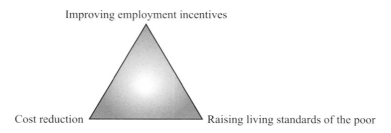

Figure 16.18   The iron triangle of welfare

Figure 16.18 shows the three goals of protecting and raising living standards of low-income households, improving employment incentives, and keeping down the costs of the welfare state, that have been referred to as the 'iron triangle' of welfare reform. There is a conflict between these goals, so that meeting one of them better means achieving worse outcomes with respect to another. In other words, there are inevitable trade-offs between the three aims in the triangle.

At times there has been more emphasis on one of the three aims than the others, with the focus more on poverty reduction in the 1950s and 1960s, on cost reduction in the 1980s, and on employment incentives in the 2000s – albeit with a renewed focus on cost reduction as the 2000s have progressed. It is around the trade-offs between these objectives that many of the arguments about redistribution are framed, and this section explores these. I have already examined how policies can raise living standards of the poor by reducing inequalities, and mentioned that such policies can take a sizeable proportion of GDP. The next subsection examines the issue of improving employment incentives, the top vertex of the iron triangle in Figure 16.18.

5.1 Employment incentives

All taxes and benefits impact on incentives. Benefits increase the incentive to do or be whatever qualifies one for the benefit. Similarly, taxes decrease the incentive to do or have whatever they apply to. A simple example going back a few hundred years can illustrate this.

Between 1696 and 1851, the English government taxed the number of windows in a house. In principle, this could be seen to be equitable, as the wealthy who owned larger houses paid more tax. However, the tax created incentives to alter behaviour. Much is written about tax avoidance, that is, finding legal ways of reducing tax liabilities; to avoid **Window Tax**, people would simply brick over their windows. For poorer households this often meant living in rooms with poor ventilation, increasing the risk of disease and illness. For the government it meant collecting less revenue than they had anticipated.

Such discussions about incentives were also topical issues of debate in 2012 when George Osborne, the Conservative Chancellor of the Exchequer, announced a reduction in the new top rate of Income Tax from 50% to 45%. His argument for the reduction was that the higher tax rate had at best a neutral effect on tax receipts, but was detrimental to the economy. First, just as people bricked over their windows to avoid paying Window Tax, higher-income earners would be able to find ways to avoid paying the higher rate legally, or even illegally evade paying it. Further, the tax created incentives to earn less and therefore be less productive to the economy. Examples of this might include retiring early, working fewer hours or even emigrating. Others argued that it was too early to make such judgements, because the 50% top

Window Tax
Window Tax was introduced in 1696 in England and repealed in 1851. It was a property tax based on the number of windows in a property.

A VISION OF THE REPEAL OF THE WINDOW-TAX.

"HOLLO! OLD FELLOW; WE'RE GLAD TO SEE YOU HERE."

rate of tax had only been in place for two years (since 2010), and more time was needed to see the true impact on incentives.

Incentives do not apply just to high-income earners. Considerable attention has been paid to effects of taxation and cash benefits on the incentives for those not in paid employment to find jobs, and for those in employment with low earnings to earn more.

Teasing out incentive effects is complicated, but a measure of the incentive to take employment that is often used is the **participation tax rate** (PTR), which gives the proportion of earnings that are taken away in tax or through lower benefit entitlements when an individual starts employment.

The formula for calculating a PTR is

Participation tax rate
The participation tax rate (PTR) is the proportion of earnings that are taken away in tax or through lower benefit entitlements when an individual takes employment.

$$\text{PTR} = 1 - \frac{\text{net income in employment} - \text{net income out of employment}}{\text{gross earnings in employment}}$$

For example, consider an unemployed individual whose income after tax and benefits is £60. If he got a job, his gross earnings would be £250, and he would need to pay £40 in income tax. The PTR is calculated as

$$1 - \frac{240(\text{GBP}) - 60(\text{GBP})}{300(\text{GBP})} = 1 - \frac{180(\text{GBP})}{300(\text{GBP})} = 40\%$$

The lower the value of a person's PTR, the greater his incentive to take employment, as he gets to keep a higher proportion of his earnings.

There is also an issue of incentive effects for people already in paid employment to earn more. The **effective marginal tax rate (EMTR)** measures the incentive for people in a household to earn more, for example, by working longer hours or gaining a promotion. The EMTR gives the proportion taken away in tax or through lower benefit entitlements when an individual already in employment earns an extra pound. With an EMTR of 0%, the household keeps all of the increased earnings, whereas with an EMTR of 100%, none of the increased earnings would be retained. High EMTRs for low-income households lead to **poverty traps** where the gain from increasing earnings is so low that it may not be financially worthwhile to make the effort to do so at all.

The following hypothetical example illustrates the poverty trap. Marie, a lone parent, receives an income of £7960 when she is employed for 16 hours per week at her minimum wage job (at £6.20 per hour). This income is made up of £5160 from her part-time job and £2800 of benefits that are means-tested, so that for every £1 that she earns above £5200, Marie loses 80p of benefits.

Unemployment trap
An unemployment trap is a situation where the tax and benefit systems combine to create disincentives to take up employment.

Effective marginal tax rate
The effective marginal tax rate is the percentage that is taken away in tax or through lower benefit entitlements when an employed worker earns an extra unit of income.

Poverty trap
A poverty trap is a situation where the tax and benefit systems combine to make it difficult to escape poverty through creating disincentives to earn more by taking a better-paid job.

Answer

For every £1 that Marie earns, she loses 80p in benefits – her EMTR is 80%. This means that she takes home only 20p for each extra £1 that she earns. It will probably not be financially worth her working longer hours if she also has to pay for childcare. Marie is in a poverty trap.

The UK coalition government's welfare reforms, particularly those introduced in 2013, aimed to increase employment incentives and weaken what was described as a dependency culture. It introduced a Universal Credit to merge nearly all working-age benefits into a single payment, means-tested in such a way that for at least one person in a household employment would always be financially beneficial. As well as trying to boost employment incentives, the government tried to tighten eligibility for benefits and withdraw them in certain situations. Such an approach is not new; indeed, in the 1870s the Borough of Essex withdrew relief to the poor who owned a dog.

In 2013, dog owners escaped but tenants and parents did not, with changes including: cutting benefits in real terms by limiting their increases to well below inflation; restricting the type of accommodation for which families could claim housing benefit; and putting a cap on the total benefit that one family could receive. The personal allowance, the threshold at which people start paying income tax, was also raised by more than the rate of inflation, enabling people in employment to earn more before paying Income Tax, but not helping those with earnings below the previous threshold or those with no earnings at all.

These changes were controversial because they reduced the incomes of some of the poorest in society, increased inequality and worsened employment incentives for second earners in families. Critics also argued that the reductions in welfare spending, on services as well as benefits, would reduce aggregate demand and make recovery from the recession even harder. This serves as a reminder that the policies discussed in this chapter also have macroeconomic effects and cannot be seen in isolation from the policies discussed in Parts 2 and 3.

5.2   The iron triangle

Having discussed why welfare policy inevitably has effects on employment incentives, I can go back to considering the three goals that make up the iron triangle:

- raising living standards of low-income households
- improving employment incentives
- keeping down the costs of the welfare state.

Figure 16.19 illustrates all three goals by showing how different levels of original household income translate into final income. In general, the welfare system redistributes from richer to poorer households. The solid line in Figure 16.19 illustrates this. A dashed 45-degree line showing original income is also drawn, to see which households gain and which lose. Poorer households have a net gain from the system as their final income is higher than their original income, while richer households pay out more in taxes than they gain in benefits and public services.

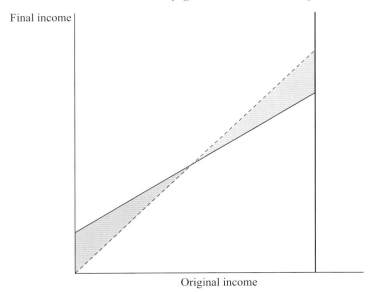

Figure 16.19   Welfare policy: from original to final income

(Source: adapted from Manning, undated, Figure 2)

The slope of the final income line is a measure of employment incentives. It shows how any increase in original income translates into final income; the shallower it is, the smaller the gain in final income for any increase in original income. The intercept of the final income line with the vertical axis is a measure of the welfare system's effect on the poorest households; it gives the final income of households whose original income is zero. The slope of the line is also a measure of how redistributive the system is – that is, how much it reduces inequality; a shallower slope means more redistribution towards greater equality. The extent of the redistributive nature and generosity of the welfare system (and therefore, its net cost) depends on the distribution of original income. To keep things simple, I will assume that original income is distributed along a straight line which starts at zero income, and goes up to a maximum indicated by the vertical line in Figure 16.19: this inaccurate assumption will not affect the argument that I will make about how different types of reforms might affect the cost. Households at the top end of the income distribution are net contributors to the welfare system. In this case the net cost of the welfare system is the difference between the blue area and the pink area, which is the difference between the net tax paid by those whose households contribute more than they receive and the net benefits received by the rest.

Thus Figure 16.19 captures all three points of the iron triangle. I can now examine how the position and slope of the final income line varies depending on the welfare policies adopted by government.

If the government wants to reduce the cost of the welfare system, it could lower final incomes as shown in Figure 16.20, by shifting the final income curve downwards, so that the pink area below the new line shrinks and the blue area above the new line grows, reducing the net cost of the system. This will result in lower incomes for all households, including the poorest at the bottom of the original income range. (This is in practice also an increase in inequality since the same absolute fall in income is a greater percentage fall for poorer households.)

Now consider a different approach, where income is protected for those at the very bottom, but the cost of the system is reduced in a different way. Figure 16.21 provides an example of how this could be done. Again the difference between the new pink and blue areas has been reduced, but this time it is by reducing the slope of the final income line, while keeping its intercept, the amount received by the poorest families, unchanged. This has reduced the net cost and protected the incomes of the poor, but now the slope of the final line has flattened, reducing employment incentives by reducing the amount of final income

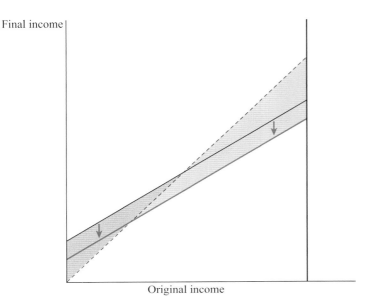

Figure 16.20   Reducing the cost of the welfare system

(Source: adapted from Manning, undated, Figure 3)

that households gain when their original income increases. Inequality has also been reduced.

This is why people talk of those three goals of raising living standards of low-income households (or reducing inequality in this way), improving employment incentives and keeping down the costs of the welfare state as forming an iron triangle: there is an inevitable trade-off between them. Policymakers have to choose between these goals. By making any one their priority, they are inevitably downplaying the others, even if they do not recognise that explicitly.

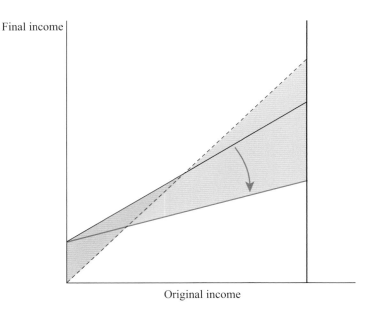

Figure 16.21   Protecting low incomes and reducing the costs of the welfare system

(Source: adapted from Manning, undated, Figure 4)

6   Conclusion

This chapter has considered a wide range of connected aspects of income inequality, from the reasons why it matters, through how we measure it, to considering how governments can reduce it. I have examined a number of reasons why governments must be concerned about not only the overall size and growth of national income, but also how that income is distributed. The next chapter extends this discussion by developing a broader approach to inequality by discussing other measures of well-being besides income.

Making societies more equal presents a range of political challenges for government, as doing it by redistribution may be perceived unfairly to favour one section of the electorate over another since it involves directly or indirectly transferring income from higher-income groups to lower-income groups. While this chapter has discussed how government can reduce inequalities, the next chapter asks more fundamental questions about the role of government in an economy and asks what governments *should* do, not only what they can do.

References

Adema, W., Fron, P. and Ladaique, M. (2011) 'Is the European welfare state really more expensive? Indicators on social spending, 1980–2012; and a manual to the OECD Social Expenditure Database (SOCX)', OECD Social, Employment and Migration Working Papers no. 124, Paris, OECD Publishing.

Cameron, D. (2011) *PM's Speech on Welfare Reform Bill*, 17 February, [online] www.number10.gov.uk/news/pms-speech-on-welfare-reform-bill (Accessed 9 December 2012).

Cribb, J., Joyce, R. and Phillips, D. (2012) *Living Standards, Poverty and Inequality in the UK: 2012*, IFS Commentary C124, London, Institute for Fiscal Studies.

Friedman, M. (1962) *Capitalism and Freedom*, Chicago, IL, University of Chicago Press.

Greenspun, P. (1998) *How to Become as Rich as Bill Gates*, [online] http://philip.greenspun.com/bg (Accessed 8 December 2012).

Institute for Fiscal Studies (IFS) (2012) *Where Do You Fit In?*, [online] www.ifs.org.uk/wheredoyoufitin/about.php (Accessed 8 December 2012).

Jin, W., Joyce, R., Phillips, D. and Sibieta, L. (2011) *Poverty and Inequality in the UK: 2011*, IFS Commentary 118, London, Institute for Fiscal Studies.

Koske, I., Fournier, J. and Wanner, I. (2012) 'Less income inequality and more growth – are they compatible? Part 2. The distribution of labour income', OECD Economics Department Working Papers no. 925, Paris, OECD Publishing; available online at http://dx.doi.org/10.1787/5k9h2975rhhf-en (Accessed 9 December 2012).

Lansley, S. (2011) *The Cost of Inequality*, London, Gibson Square.

Lansley, S. (2012) 'Why economic equality leads to collapse', *The Observer*, 5 February, [online] www.guardian.co.uk/business/2012/feb/05/inequality-leads-to-economic-collapse (Accessed 8 December 2012).

Manning, A. (undated) *Welfare Reform: A Brief Summary*, [online] http://econ.lse.ac.uk/~amanning/courses/ec406/ec406_welfare.pdf (Accessed 9 December 2012).

Musgrave, R. (1959) *The Theory of Public Finance*, New York, McGraw-Hill.

O'Connell, M. (2010) *Affluence Versus Equality? A Critique of Wilkinson and Pickett's Book 'The Spirit Level'*, [online] http://irserver.ucd.ie/bitstream/handle/10197/2475/spirit%20level%20summary%20critique.pdf?sequence=3 (Accessed 9 December 2012).

Office for Budget Responsibility (OBR) (2012) *Economic and Fiscal Outlook*, [online] http://budgetresponsibility.independent.gov.uk/wordpress/docs/March-2012-EFO1.pdf (Accessed 1 February 2013).

Office for National Statistics (ONS) (2011) *The Effects of Taxes and Benefits on Household Income, 2009/2010*, [online] www.ons.gov.uk/ons/rel/household-income/the-effects-of-taxes-and-benefits-on-household-income/2009-2010/index.html (Accessed 9 December 2012).

Office for National Statistics (ONS) (2012) *The Effects of Taxes and Benefits on Household Income, 2010/2011*, [online] www.ons.gov.uk/ons/dcp171778_267839.pdf (Accessed 9 December 2012).

Organisation for Economic Co-operation and Development (OECD) (2011) *Divided We Stand*: *Why Inequality Keeps Rising*, Paris, OECD Publishing; available online at http://dx.doi.org/10.1787/9789264119536-en (Accessed 8 December 2012).

Pisu, M. (2012) 'Less income inequality and more growth – are they compatible? Part 5. Poverty in OECD countries', OECD Economics Department Working Papers no. 928, OECD Publishing; available online at http://dx.doi.org/10.1787/5k9h28tlt0bs-en (Accessed 9 December 2012).

Rowntree, B.S. (1901) *Poverty: A Study of Town Life*, London, Macmillan.

Stiglitz, J.E. (2009) 'Joseph Stiglitz and why inequality is at the root of the recession', *Next Left*, 9 January.

Wells, M. (2011) 'Occupy Wall Street live: march on Times Square', *The Guardian*, 16 October, [online] www.guardian.co.uk/world/blog/2011/oct/15/occupy-wall-street-times-square (Accessed 8 December 2012).

Wilkinson, R. and Picket, K. (2009) *The Spirit Level: Why Equality is Better for Everyone*, London, Penguin.

Wilson, R.A., Kriechel, B., Gardiner, B., Pollitt, H., Ward, T., Livanos, I., Stehrer, R., Chewpreecha, U., Barton, J. and Sauermann, J. (2010) *Forecasting Skill Supply and Demand in Europe: Overview and Synthesis*, Thessaloniki, European Centre for the Development of Vocational Training; available online at http://cedefop.europa.eu/EN/Files/3052_en.pdf (Accessed 9 December 2012).

Chapter 17
Government action, public goods and welfare economics

Paul Anand

Contents

1   Introduction

Governments intervene in the economy for many different reasons. Parts 2 and 3 dealt with intervention at the macro level, often with the aim of stabilising economic activity. Part 4 considered industrial regulation. In Part 5, Chapters 15 and 16 have analysed trade policy and redistribution of income through the tax/benefit system.

This chapter tackles two more important government interventions. Economic activity that has negative impacts not reflected in prices (negative externalities) can lead to overproduction. I examine in Section 3 the use of taxes and other mechanisms to address this problem. Conversely, public goods such as clean air or national defence may be underprovided. Once such goods are provided, it is difficult to exclude people from benefiting, and therefore hard to recoup the costs of production through normal market mechanisms. Section 4 introduces the technique of game theory and then uses it to analyse underprovision of public goods and ways in which this problem might be resolved.

In this chapter, I also take a step back from specific government interventions, and ask more generally what governments *should* do. Can economic analysis shed light on whether some interventions should not happen at all? The branch of economics that addresses this is called welfare economics, introduced in Section 2. Welfare economics evaluates the impact on human well-being of different allocations of resources through the market, and of different actions by government. Welfare economics must therefore consider what increases human well-being – not only economic growth, but also progress in broader aspects of human well-being. There is recent UK government interest in thinking about and monitoring progress in this broader sense (Section 6).

While there is no single definitive classification, a useful starting point for thinking about the proper extent of the functions of government can be found in the national US Council for Economic Education (CEE) summary list (Table 17.1).

Table 17.1   The economic functions of government

1 Maintaining a legal and social framework	Minimal
2 Providing public goods and services	Active
3 Maintaining competition	Active
4 Redistributing income	Active
5 Correcting for externalities	Active
6 Stabilising the economy	Active

(Source: based on Dick et al., 2005)

After studying this chapter, you will have examined issues relating to most of these functions. You will see that I have characterised all the functions in Table 17.1 depending on whether they form part of a *minimal* state, or imply a more *active* interventionist state. The language of government intervention in political debate tends to have mildly or significantly negative connotations, referring to paternalism, interventionism, or 'big government'. A careful distinction between minimal functions and a more engaged state allows a more balanced view. Section 5 of this chapter looks at the philosophical and other arguments that governments might merely maintain a legal framework. Furthermore, in the sections on externalities and public goods, I consider both government and non-governmental solutions. By the end of this chapter, you will have deepened your critical understanding of the arguments for involvement of governments in economic activity.

The learning outcomes for this chapter are:

* to define welfare economics and the concept of Pareto optimality

* to explain why negative externalities create an oversupply problem, and discuss Pigovian taxes as a solution

* to outline Coase's theorem

* to understand the basic concepts of game theory and the prisoners' dilemma game

* to use game theory to explain the problem of market undersupply of public goods

* to explain methods of resourcing the provision of public goods

* to discuss arguments for and against minimal government intervention

* to outline a variety of influences on human well-being.

2   Welfare economics

Welfare economics is the study of the effect on human well-being of different allocations of resources between people, and of different interventions to change those allocations. Welfare economics evaluation focuses on the well-being that a person derives from consuming goods, and begins from the assumption (that may be relaxed later) that consumers seek to maximise the pleasure or satisfaction that they derive from consuming goods.

2.1   The concept of utility

Welfare economics uses the concept of utility, rather than money income, as a starting point (utility was introduced in Chapter 12, Section 2.3. Utility expresses the idea that the welfare derived from consumption is subjective, in the sense that the satisfaction gained by one person from consuming a given amount of a particular good may be quite different from the satisfaction gained by another person from consuming the same amount of the same good. The concept of utility is used by economists to give a numerical summary or representation of the amount of pleasure that a person gets from a good. The concept of utility reflects the fact that personal preference is a key source of value.

One of the oldest ideas in utility theory is the concept of diminishing marginal utility, first discussed by mathematicians in the early 1700s. The idea is that the more units of something that are consumed, the less valuable are successive units to the consumer, as discussed in Chapter 12, Section 2.3. Too much of a good thing can make you bored, sick or drunk. For many goods, for example cups of coffee, the amount of pleasure derived one cup might be high, from the second lower, and from another lower still or even negative. Marginal utility is important for decisions that are made at the margin (many are – should I have one cup of coffee or two?). Marginal utility can helpfully be thought of as being derived from total utility, as in the two parts of Figure 17.1 (overleaf).

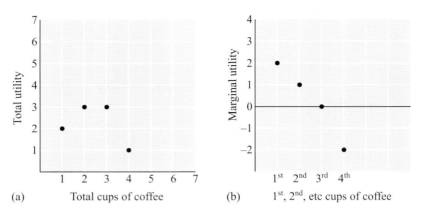

Figure 17.1   (a) Total utility from consuming cups of coffee; (b) marginal utility from consuming cups of coffee

---

Activity 17.1

Figure 17.1a shows the total utility gained from consuming successive cups of coffee. Using Figure 17.1a, calculate the utility gained from each additional cup of coffee.

Answer

One cup of coffee produces 2 units of utility. Two cups of coffee jointly produce 3 units of utility. So the additional utility from the second cup of coffee is 1 unit. Three cups of coffee generate 3 units of utility also. So there is no additional benefit gained from the third cup of coffee over the second. The total utility of consuming four cups of coffee is 1 unit, i.e. 2 units less than consuming only three cups. The added (marginal) utility is negative, i.e. −2 units.

Now that I have established from Figure 17.1a the marginal utility gained from consuming each successive additional cup of coffee, this can be represented in Figure 17.1b. Look, for example, at the move from three to four cups of coffee in each part of the diagram: total utility decreases (Figure 17.1a) because marginal utility is negative (Figure 17.1b). This example also illustrates the fact that more consumption is not always better.

If you drew a line through the points in Figure 17.1b, would the curve remind you of anything? The downward slope of a diminishing marginal utility curve is similar to a downward-sloping demand curve (Chapter 12), and the two ideas are very closely related. One reason why a demand curve might slope downwards is diminishing marginal utility: as you consume more, your willingness to pay for the last unit therefore declines.

Finally, many economists have argued that if society wants to maximise welfare, it should aim to maximise the utility enjoyed by consumers. How can this be done? Suppose that a consumer is choosing between music downloads and sandwiches for lunch. Then she will be maximising her utility if her marginal utility from the last £1 spent on tunes equals the marginal utility from the last £1 spent on sandwiches.

Activity 17.2
Why is that? Think about it before reading on.

Answer
If it were not the case, then she could increase her total utility by shifting some spending towards the good that gives more satisfaction at the margin. When no shift of £1 between tunes and lunch brings more total satisfaction, then utility is maximised.

2.2   Pareto optimality

The idea of utility helps in evaluating benefits to societies as well as individuals. It underpins a key concept in welfare economics: Pareto optimality. Named after the Italian economist Vilfredo Pareto, the concept is simple but useful. If a change is better for some people, in terms of their evaluation of their own utility, but makes no one worse off, then the change is said to be **Pareto improvement**. If a situation is such that no change can make one person better off without damaging another, then the situation is said to be **Pareto optimal**.

An attractive feature of the concept of Pareto improvement is that it does not require you to compare utility (a subjective concept) between consumers; just ask each person if they are better or worse off. Devising situations or policies that make some better off and do no harm to others can often be a good thing.

But are Pareto improvements always desirable?

Pareto improvement
A change is a Pareto improvement if it makes someone better off and no one worse off.

Pareto optimal
A situation is Pareto optimal if no one can be made better off without someone being made worse off.

291

Activity 17.3

Here is an example to consider for yourself. Suppose, in a very unequal society, that a change makes the rich still richer – but does not make anyone poorer. This is a Pareto improvement. Is it necessarily desirable? The Chapter 16 discussion of inequality is relevant here.

2.3   The benefits of free markets

These concepts of marginal utility and Pareto optimality have long been used in economics to demonstrate the benefits of free markets, as shown in Chapter 13, Section 6. Under certain assumptions, it can be shown that free market trading will lead to a Pareto optimal distribution of goods. A market equilibrium at which consumers equate their marginal utility MU to the price of the product P, and producers equate their marginal cost MC to price, is Pareto optimal. This necessary condition for optimal consumption can be written as

$$MC = P = MU$$

This result underpins the arguments for the effectiveness of competition in markets in promoting welfare, and hence for the promotion of competition by industrial regulators (discussed in Chapter 14).

The assumptions required include perfect competition. It must also be the case that all the benefits and costs of a good are reflected in its price; however, this is not always the case. Sometimes an economic transaction can have negative or positive impacts on 'innocent bystanders'. The next three sections focus on two classic examples of this problem, which identify some limits to the benefits of competitive markets, and some reasons why governments might actively engage with economic activity on behalf of a country's citizens. Another way of putting this is to acknowledge that there is much interdependence in the behaviour and welfare that people experience – an idea that I now explore in more depth.

3 Externalities

Chapter 16, Section 4 briefly described positive consumption externalities: consumption that benefits others as well as the consumer. More generally, an **externality** occurs when the activities of an economic agent such as a firm or an individual have effects on others that are not (fully) reflected in market prices.

Externalities may be negative or positive, and may arise in production or consumption. They represent positive or negative utilities that are not completely reflected in the market price. This section examines negative production externalities, such as negative environmental impacts on general citizens.

As explained in Section 2, a general principle in welfare economics is that for a Pareto optimal level of production of a good to be attained, the marginal cost of production should equal the marginal benefit from consumption. It can be shown that generally, under the assumptions of perfect competition, this condition holds, and therefore an appropriate level of production and consumption will emerge in the market.

However, this desirable outcome from a welfare perspective breaks down if the firm's marginal cost of production is not the same as its cost of production to society as a whole. Figure 17.2 illustrates the problem, which I discuss using the example of a firm providing steel for the world market.

Externality
An externality arises in a market when one economic agent's actions affect the welfare of others in ways that are not reflected in market prices.

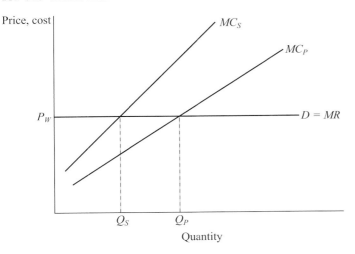

Figure 17.2   Divergence between marginal private costs and marginal social costs

Figure 17.2 shows, for a representative steel producer, output on the horizontal axis, and costs and price on the vertical axis. The firm is producing in conditions of perfect competition, so it faces a horizontal demand curve (Chapter 13). The factory can sell all its production at the world price P_W, which is therefore its marginal revenue from producing each extra unit of steel. The factory's marginal cost of production is assumed to rise as output increases, shown by the marginal cost curve MC_P.

Given these costs and revenues, the factory maximises its profits at Q_P, where $MC_P = P_W$. However, suppose that there are additional costs to society from steel production, not borne by the firm, such as the factory's air pollution from fuel use. In this case, the total costs of production to society are higher than the private costs experienced by the factory. The marginal social cost curve MC_S is above the firm's private marginal cost curve MC_P in Figure 17.2.

From a societal perspective, taking the costs of pollution together with the factory's costs, the output level that equates consumers' marginal benefit with marginal social cost is Q_S. This is the Pareto optimal level of output, and it is lower than Q_P. In the presence of these negative externalities, the profit-maximising firm will produce too much steel. Perfect competition, in the presence of externalities, does not in general give rise to a Pareto optimal level of consumption and production, because consumers' decisions about use of their money are not responding to the full cost of the good to society.

An important question for economists is: what can be done about such overproduction? I consider below several possibilities: Pigovian taxes, regulations, tradeable permits and Coasian negotiations.

3.1   Pigovian taxes

Historically, taxes tended to be levied by the powerful in order to raise revenue. In such cases, the ideal activity or asset to charge is one that cannot be changed to avoid the tax: the Chapter 16 discussion of the window tax illustrates both the principle and what can go wrong.

However, in 1705, the Russian emperor Peter the Great introduced a tax on beards precisely with the aim of encouraging men to go clean-shaven, as was the fashion in western Europe. The idea was that beard-wearing was costless to the wearer but caused a negative externality to others who had to observe it, so the aim of the tax was to discourage it through financial penalty. The move illustrates a quite different motivation for raising tax: changing behaviour.

Arthur Pigou was a British economist writing in the early twentieth century, and a founder of welfare economics. It was he who first analysed extensively the application of behaviour-changing taxes to the problem of overproduction in the presence of negative externalities. Pigou's idea was to reflect the external cost of production to society by applying a tax on production – called a Pigovian tax. The firm will experience the tax as a rise in its costs, and will equate its private marginal cost *plus* the tax with the market price. If correctly calculated, the tax results in the correct amount of steel being produced, taking all costs to society into account.

Activity 17.4

Before reading on, see if you can show graphically, with the aid of Figure 17.2, the Pigovian tax that would be required. (Hint: Remember that the tax is an increase in the firm's costs.)

Answer

Figure 17.3, based on Figure 17.2, shows the answer. A tax t is added to the firm's marginal cost at each level of output. This shifts the firm's marginal cost curve to $MC_P + t$. The firm's profit-maximising point is now A, where $MC_P + t = P_W$ with output Q_S, the socially optimum output.

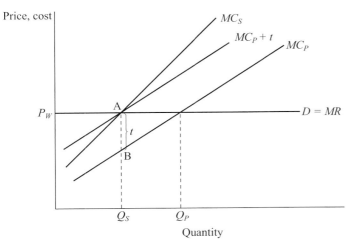

Figure 17.3   A Pigovian tax to reduce a polluting firm's output

The Pigovian tax *t* is shown by the vertical distance AB. It is set to equal the gap between the marginal social cost (shown by MC_S) and the marginal private cost (MC_P) at the optimum output Q_S. The tax has reduced production and consumption to the optimum level.

Globally agreed taxes on carbon emissions, and national taxes on cigarette smoking, are examples of Pigovian taxes. Such taxes are quite commonly regarded as good in theory but difficult to operate in practice, because of the information required to set the correct tax level. For example, those affected by the externality may not know how much it costs them. Even if they do, governments may not have an accurate way of finding out this information, and the affected party might want to exaggerate its costs. A further oft-cited concern is political lobbying by producer interest groups. This may affect how the tax is levied or how it is spent, and both could have substantial welfare implications that outweigh the original desired benefits. (Santos and Fraser (2006) discuss these problems for road pricing.)

That said, Table 17.2 shows some UK examples of taxes that may reflect the government's wish to correct for oversupply and overconsumption caused by the disparity between private and social costs.

Table 17.2   Taxes with a possible Pigovian justification

Selected indirect taxes	Revenue (£bn)	% of government tax receipts
Fuel duties	26.9	4.6
Tobacco duties	9.3	1.6
Alcohol duties	9.7	1.6
Air passenger duty	2.5	0.4
Landfill tax	1.2	0.2
Climate change levy	0.7	0.1
Aggregates levy	0.3	0.1
Bank levy	1.9	0.3 (estimate)

(Source: Adam and Browne, 2011, p. 4, Table 1)

In addition, there are areas where tax exemptions or reduced rates might be taken as evidence of Pigovian subsidies designed to correct for underconsumption. Table 17.3 shows some possibilities.

Table 17.3   Estimated cost of exemptions and reduced rates of VAT, UK 2010–11

Selected items	Estimated tax revenue forgone (£m)
Books, newspapers and magazines	1600
Water and sewerage services	1700
Contraceptives	10
Children's car seats	15
Smoking cessation products	15
Energy-saving materials	50
Health services	1500
Postal services	200
Burial and cremation	150
Cultural admission charges	30

(Source: Adam and Browne, 2011, p. 16)

Tax policies vary internationally, but the data in these two tables suggest that the UK government may be using taxes to address externalities: negative externalities related to the environment and health, and positive externalities concerning education and infrastructure. The idea of having a bank levy or tax on financial transactions to reflect the potential risks imposed on the whole of society is not new, but was attracting growing support following the 2008 financial crisis.

Problems with Pigovian taxes

There are essentially three classes of problems with Pigovian taxes.

First and foremost, there is the question of measuring social costs and benefits as distinct from private ones. Pigou himself recognised the problem, though economists have developed a range of techniques for measuring such costs. For very large decisions, for example to do with climate change, it seems worthwhile to try to apply these techniques to measure, for example, the social gains from policies to alter impact on the environment.

Second, concern has been expressed about the distributional consequences of such taxes. For example, there is increasing interest in the use of fat taxes to bring the private costs of fats and sugars into line with social costs that include costs of health care and reduced life expectancy. However, such taxes often affect the poor most, and this regressive impact is deemed undesirable by many.

Finally, there are those who object to the imposition of taxes of any form, and this view is often expressed keenly by those in the USA. This view might seem a little extreme from other countries' perspectives, but there is certainly some agreement among economists that setting the right level of tax or subsidy is difficult but important if the use of a tax is to be justified. Enforcement can be difficult in practice.

3.2   Auctioning pollution rights and Coase's theorem

A standard Pigovian tax can be imposed on all firms in an industry. The analysis shows how a tax could, in principle, bring about the right adjustment. However, some firms are better at abating pollution than others, so it would be economically efficient if pollution abatement took place in those firms first.

Auctioning pollution rights

One way of achieving this is for the government to auction pollution permits. The following example demonstrates this.

Table 17.4 shows the marginal cost of abatement for two firms. If firm A reduces pollution by one unit, then the cost is £4; if it reduces pollution by two units, then the total cost of its abatement efforts is £10 (= £4 + £6); and so on.

Table 17.4   Marginal cost of abatement of pollution for two firms

Abatement	Firm A	Firm B
1st unit	£4	£6
2nd unit	£6	£8
3rd unit	£8	£10

Now suppose that society wants to abate pollution by one unit. How should this be done most efficiently? One method is to auction a permit (the right) to pollute. If a permit for a unit of pollution is offered, firm A would be willing to pay up to £4. At a price above £4, it is cheaper for firm A to abate. However, because firm B's abatement costs are higher, it would be willing to pay up to £6 to emit a unit of pollution. So in this case, firm B would bid most and carry on polluting, while firm A would reduce its pollution by one unit. To achieve further abatement, such as two units, further permits can be issued. Firm B would be willing to pay £14 to continue to pollute, while at that price firm A would abate two units.

Using a permit auction, society therefore gets its pollution reduction at least cost. Furthermore, although the government still needs to determine what the optimal level of abatement should be, it does not then need to obtain information about the abatement cost functions of individual firms. In markets for carbon emissions, permits once auctioned are also tradeable, which allows them to move over time to the producers with the highest cost of abatement, thereby ensuring that abatement is done by those with the lowest abatement costs.

Coasian negotiation

Another important contribution to debates about Pigovian corrections for externalities derives from work by the British-born American-based Nobel prize-winning economist Ronald Coase. Coase's (1960) idea amounts to an argument for letting parties sort things out without reference to government. His argument is often used by those who prefer the minimal version of government to the more engaged or active approach implied by Pigou's analysis.

An example of Coase's argument is as follows. A confectionery manufacturer and a medical equipment manufacturer have adjacent factories. They find that the vibrations created by the sugar grinder are preventing the careful calibrations required for the medical equipment. The confectionery manufacturer is making a profit of £10 000. The medical equipment manufacturer is only breaking even because of the vibration-linked quality problems, so total profits with both firms operating are £10 000. However, if the confectionery factory were to close down, the equipment maker would have profits of £50 000.

Can negotiation deal with the problem? The socially superior outcome is for the equipment maker to carry on in business while the other manufacturer closes, since this creates higher total profits for society. If the parties can negotiate, then they will come to an agreement on that outcome, since the equipment maker can afford to buy out the confectioner. The Pareto optimal outcome of negotiation is that the equipment maker earns £50 000, out of which he compensates the confectionery manufacturer by at least £10 000 for closing down. Each is at least as well off as in the situation before negotiation, and society is better off.

Coase's insight is now often referred to as a theorem, because in principle it applies widely, and can be given a general mathematical demonstration. There are many different ways of describing it, but for present purposes I describe it as follows:

Coase's theorem (one version)

In situations where two parties are connected by an externality, a Pareto optimal outcome can be reached by private negotiation, and furthermore, this is the case regardless of whom is initially assigned the property rights.

The following example illustrates Coase's theorem. Suppose that there are two companies: Wheat, which produces arable crops, and Salmon, which produces freshwater fish. Wheat uses fertilisers that run off into rivers and negatively affect the water quality required for producing fish.

In this example, I consider the impacts on both companies of different levels of reduction in fertiliser use. In Table 17.5, reducing fertiliser use creates costs for Wheat, but produces benefits for Salmon. The marginal losses to Wheat increase as the pollution reduction rises, whereas the marginal gains to Salmon decrease.

Table 17.5   Example illustrating Coase's theorem

Total reduction in fertiliser use	Marginal loss of profit to Wheat	Total loss of profit to Wheat	Marginal gain in profit to Salmon	Total gain in profit to Salmon
1 ton	£4 000	£4 000	£9 000	£9 000
2 tons	£6 000	£10 000	£7 000	£16 000
3 tons	£8 000	£18 000	£5 000	£21 000
4 tons	£10 000	£28 000	£3 000	£24 000
5 tons	£12 000	£40 000	£1 000	£25 000

(Source: adapted from Goodstein, 2002)

Now suppose that Wheat and Salmon were to negotiate over the possibility of a 1 ton reduction. Suppose further that Wheat owns the right to pollute the water – that is, Wheat has the property rights that matter in this case.

A 1 ton reduction in pollution would cost Wheat £4000 but benefit Salmon by £9000, so the parties should agree this. Any compensation of Wheat by Salmon over £4000 and under £9000 would lead to a Pareto improvement: both will be better off.

Activity 17.5
Should the parties then agree to a further reduction? Consider this before reading on.

Answer
The marginal cost to Wheat from reducing by a second ton is £6000 while the gain to Salmon is £7000. So this reduction is also worth implementing, and will lead to gains for both parties so long as Salmon compensates Wheat by more than £6000 and less than £7000. But what about abating pollution by 3 tons? In this case, the loss to Wheat would be £8000, whereas the gain to Salmon would be £5000. Salmon does not make enough from the reduction to compensate Wheat for its loss. That is, the additional reduction in pollution does not make a net contribution to social outcomes, and the parties do not agree to it. Similar reasoning applies to further reductions up to 5 tons.

This example shows that 2 tons is the efficient level of pollution reduction. Lower and higher levels produce fewer total benefits to society – measured as gains minus losses. Furthermore, this efficient level can be reached by negotiation between the parties, despite the fact that Wheat owns the right to pollute, so long as there are no transaction costs such as high lawyers' bills. I have assumed that the costs of negotiating are zero.

This is the essence of Coase's insight. It is an important insight in economic theory – but does it need to be applied with caution? Coase's theorem has been used to justify the view that industry should be allowed to pollute as it wishes, on the grounds that people who are significantly affected by externalities will pay industry to reduce pollution up to the level that is efficient, i.e. that maximises the gains to society.

Activity 17.6

Can you think of any problems with that argument?

Economists have noted two important problems with or limitations of this argument.

First, there are issues to do with distribution between those negotiating. Notice that there is some room in the negotiations above: a 1 ton reduction in pollution is better for both parties if compensation is more than £4000 and less than £9000. How the property rights are initially assigned is likely to alter where in this space any agreement is settled on. Put another way, the final distribution of benefits is likely to depend on the bargaining power of the parties concerned. Coase's theorem recommends private negotiation but is silent about the distribution of benefits: if society is concerned about distributive issues, as Chapter 16 has suggested is often the case, then private negotiation might not lead to the distribution of outcomes desired by society.

Second, there are issues concerning transaction costs. In practice these may not be zero. Suppose that each party involved in negotiations had to pay £4500 in legal fees for each ton reduction agreed. In that case, the transaction costs would outweigh the benefits from pollution reduction and it would be in neither party's interests to enter into negotiation.

For this reason, it has been suggested that the principle of 'polluter pays' is preferable. If a reduction in externalities leads to environmental benefits that are small but enjoyed by many, transaction costs of negotiation are likely to be prohibitive. In such cases, it has been argued that a charge should be levied on the producer. In many practical cases where the zero transaction costs assumption of Coase's theorem is violated, the use of Pigovian taxes by government appears more satisfactory than assigning property rights and allowing parties to negotiate. There are those, called 'contractarians', who argue that if a solution has been agreed by all, then it is by definition fair. Coase's theorem in contractarian hands could therefore be used to argue that a Pigovian tax is fair because it would be agreed if the negotiation costs were zero.

4   Public goods

National security is often argued to be an example of a pure 'public good' – one that normal markets cannot provide because of the *non-excludability problem*. For markets to provide defence, the argument goes, firms would have to charge those who benefited and exclude those who do not, but exclusion seems to be difficult in the case of goods like defence. So any firm selling defence to members of the public might have difficulty in obtaining sufficient revenue to cover its costs.

Nor does the problem apply just to defence. For example, public health (variously defined, but including the ability to live in an environment free from contagious medical conditions) seems to be a similar kind of good. If the environment minimises risks from contagious disease, then everyone benefits, so obtaining revenue by charging each individual would be difficult. Similarly, it has been suggested that the convention of driving on the left-hand side of the road is a kind of public good – and it is difficult to see how multiple firms would charge drivers for maintaining such a convention!

As these examples illustrate, many public goods are also *non-rival* in consumption – that is, if one person consumes the good, it remains available for others to consume too. Goods that are both non-rival and non-excludable are characterised as 'pure' **public goods**.

Public goods
Public goods are goods that are non-excludable and non-rival.

4.1   Game theory: analysing the underprovision of public goods

Since public goods are hard to supply through the market, some other method of provision is often sought. Voluntary and government provision are possibilities, but because public goods are non-excludable, people are tempted to try to benefit without paying towards provision. Game theory can be used to analyse the problem of reconciling individual and collective interests, and to explore potential solutions.

Game theory

Game theory is a tool that is widely used by economists for studying interdependence between firms, countries or people. Some of the elements of game theory are as follows:

- A *game* is a situation involving interdependence – i.e. decisions and outcomes depend on what others do.

- The *players* are the decision makers who recognise the interdependence.

- A *strategy* is a plan of action available to a player. It defines a list of actions that each player chooses as a best response to the actions of other players. In the games analysed in this book, where all players play at the same time, strategies are equivalent to actions.

- A *payoff* is a player's gain or loss from playing a particular strategy.

In economics, the players are economic agents, and the payoffs are typically profits, output or sales measured in money, though a payoff may equally be utility, or something else that is valued by a player.

Game theory is thus the study of strategic decision making. In recent times, there has been interest in understanding how people actually play games, but the assumptions of traditional game theory have tended to be somewhat more idealised. The approach of a traditional game is:

- *individualistic* – a player is assumed to be self-interested, in that they try to maximise their own payoff, and that payoff is calculated without reference to the benefits or costs of others

- *rationalistic* – a player is deemed able to calculate payoffs correctly and then select the strategy that will maximise his own individual payoff.

In presenting a game, the range of potential payoffs is often presented in a payoff matrix, which is a table showing all the various possible actions available to all players and the payoffs each player gets. The players then individually select their own preferred strategy. In the game examined below, only the relative ordering of the payoffs matters; the numbers themselves are chosen to illustrate particular incentive problems, not realistic benefits and costs.

I first describe how the payoff matrix is constructed, and then examine the players' decisions. The game described is a one-off game, that is, played just once; game theory also studies repeated games.

A prisoners' dilemma game

The 'prisoners' dilemma' is a famous game; the name comes from a version of the game where prisoners decide independently whether or not to confess to a crime, and the game has been applied to many economic situations. Its interest lies in the paradox that it highlights: individual decision making can, in certain circumstances, lead to an outcome that is inferior to the outcome each player would prefer. The application to the problems of resourcing public goods goes back to an analysis by Tucker (1950).

In my example here, there are two players: Robin and Cal. Each player has a choice between two actions: to contribute to the provision of a public good, or to refuse to contribute. Refusal means that the player is trying to 'free ride'. A free rider is a person who succeeds in benefiting without payment from a public good provided by others.

Each player knows their payoff in each cell, that is, the payoff they get when they consider choosing one action *given the action of the other player*. So Robin knows her payoff from contributing, both if Cal contributes and if he does not. She also knows her payoff from refusing, whether or not Cal contributes. Cal similarly knows his payoffs given Robin's possible actions. Players decide simultaneously.

I can set out these payoffs in a matrix such as Figure 17.4, which covers all possible combinations of actions and payoffs.

		Cal	
		Contribute	Refuse
Robin	Contribute	2 , 2	−1 , 3
	Refuse	3 , −1	0 , 0

Figure 17.4   A prisoners' dilemma game demonstrating the problem of resourcing public goods

Robin is the 'row player': you read her decisions along the rows, and her payoff is listed first in each cell. Cal is the column player: you read his decisions down the columns, and his payoff is listed second in each cell.

So, reading along the top row of payoffs, Figure 17.4 tells you that if Robin contributes, then her payoff is 2 if Cal also contributes (the first payoff in column 1). But her payoff is −1 if Cal refuses (the first payoff in column 2). If Robin refuses (the bottom row of payoffs), then she gains 3 if Cal contributes, and 0 if he does not.

Activity 17.7

Now consider Cal. What are his payoffs in all possible outcomes?

To follow Cal, read down the columns. If Cal contributes, then he gains 2 if Robin contributes also (second payoff, column 1 top row), and −1 if she does not (column 1 bottom row). If Cal refuses, then his payoff is 3 if Robin contributes, and 0 if she does not.

How do these payoffs relate to providing a public good? Remember that once a public good is provided, everyone benefits from it, and no one can be excluded. Here, if one player contributes and the other does not, then the refuser gains the best payoff in the game (3) by free riding; however, the contributor finds that the benefit from the public good is outweighed by having to pay its full cost, and actually loses (−1). If both players contribute, then both benefit from the good (2 each) and no one free rides. If neither contributes, then there is no public good hence zero payoffs.

Solving the game

So what will happen in such a game? Which equilibria will be the outcome of the game? And what does this tell you about the difficulties of supplying public goods?

Solving the game means finding out the *strategies* that players will choose. Each player decides separately (i.e. without any discussion or the possibility of making a binding agreement about what to do). Players will want to respond to the strategy of the other player(s) in a way that maximises their own payoff. Once the players' intentions are worked out, it is possible to determine which strategy is played by each player and which payoff they get – which cell (or cells) can be the equilibrium of the game.

One way to solve a game is to see whether each player has a **dominant strategy**.

Dominant strategy
A dominant strategy is one that is best regardless of what the other players do.

If a player finds that there is a strategy that always gives the best payoff, for each possible strategy of other players, then that is a dominant strategy. It will be played regardless of what the other players do. Is that the case here? Look at Robin's options in Figure 17.4. If Cal contributes, then Robin will do best to refuse (she gets 3 instead of 2). If Cal refuses, then Robin will do best to refuse (she gets 0 rather than −1). So to refuse is a *dominant strategy for Robin*.

Activity 17.8

Does Cal have a dominant strategy? Work through the same kind of reasoning as above.

Answer

If Robin contributes, then Cal will do best to refuse (3 instead of 2). If Robin refuses to contribute, then Cal will do best to also refuse (0 rather than −1). So to refuse is also a dominant strategy for Cal.

When both players have a dominant strategy, as is the case here, the game is said to have a dominant strategy solution or dominant strategy equilibrium. Both players will choose Refuse. As Figure 17.4 shows, the equilibrium is the cell where they both refuse (Refuse, Refuse) and get payoffs of zero each: no public good is produced.

So here is the paradox demonstrated by the prisoners' dilemma game. Look back at Figure 17.4. Both players would have preferred the outcome in the top left-hand cell, where both contribute and each has a payoff of 2. Yet each player has been led by their own self-interest to try to free ride, by choosing Refuse. The result is that no public good is produced.

When all players have a dominant strategy, there is one equilibrium outcome, which is always the cell where they play it. Not all games, however, have a dominant strategy equilibrium. A more general way of solving games is to use the concept of **Nash equilibrium**. I introduce it here, then use it to explore further how the players in the prisoners' dilemma game find themselves in an outcome that neither prefers.

The idea here is that the Nash equilibrium of a game is one in which no player has an *individual incentive* to move away from the strategy that led to the Nash equilibrium outcome.

I will now apply this concept to the game in Figure 17.4. To do so, it is necessary to check every cell to see if any player has an incentive to unilaterally move away from it (i.e. to change strategy) or not. I will check in turn to see if any of them is a Nash equilibrium.

Let's start at the cell when the players both decide to contribute. This can be written as the pair of strategies (Contribute, Contribute), giving the players a payoff of 2 each. Is this strategy pair a Nash equilibrium?

Nash equilibrium
A Nash equilibrium solution to a game is a combination of strategies from which no player has an individual incentive to deviate.

307

The answer is no. Consider Cal first. If Robin contributes, then Cal has an incentive to change to Refuse, because he will gain a payoff of 3 rather than 2. Robin faces the same incentive. So for two reasons (Contribute, Contribute) cannot be a Nash equilibrium.

Activity 17.9

Is (Refuse, Refuse) a Nash equilibrium?

Answer

Yes it is. Neither Robin nor Cal has an incentive to change strategy. If Robin changes to Contribute, then her payoff drops to −1, and the same is true for Cal. So the dominant strategy equilibrium in the prisoners' dilemma game is also a Nash equilibrium. The players still face the dilemma that responding to their individual incentives leads to an outcome that is not their preferred one.

Neither of the other two strategies is a Nash equilibrium. In the case where Robin contributes and Cal refuses (Contribute, Refuse), Robin, who earns −1, has an incentive to change to Refuse and earn 0. Similar reasoning applies to Cal in the case of (Refuse, Contribute) – moving from Contribute to Refuse increases his personal payoff from −1 to 0. So neither of these two combinations of strategies can be a Nash equilibrium.

A game without a dominant strategy: a coordination game

I noted above that the rule of everyone driving in the same direction on one side of the road can be seen as a public good. Solving the following game will help you to further understand the Nash equilibrium solution to games and provides an insight into another aspect of the problems of individual provision of public goods. Consider Figure 17.5.

		Cal	
		Drive on left	Drive on right
Robin	Drive on left	1 , 1	−1 , −1
	Drive on right	−1 , −1	1 , 1

Figure 17.5   The 'let's drive on the same side of the road' coordination game

Motorist playing a different strategy

(Source: Robinson, 2010)

This game is also played just once: a one-shot game. In this game, Robin and Cal would both like to follow the same convention for driving. It doesn't matter which side they choose, but there are strong benefits to each from the other's choosing the same convention. The game is played simultaneously, so they cannot know when they choose their strategy what the other player will do.

There are many economic and social interactions where the fact that everyone coordinates brings significant positive benefits to all. For example, two farmers might wish to draw water, and both can do so if they choose to use different wells, whereas the well might dry up completely if they choose to draw from the same well. By coordinating, which might be done at zero cost, each can give a positive benefit to the other (and themselves). The structure of this coordination game is different to that of the prisoners' dilemma game, but the concepts of dominant strategy and Nash equilibrium can be applied to all games.

In the game in Figure 17.5, does anyone have a dominant strategy? Start by reading across the rows for Robin. If Robin chooses to drive on the left, then she will receive 1 if Cal chooses to drive on the left, but a negative payoff if he chooses to drive on the right! Similarly, when Robin considers driving on the right, she gets −1 when Cal drives on the left and a positive payoff of 1 if Cal also drives on the right. Robin prefers to drive on the left if this is what Cal does, and to drive on the right if that is Cal's choice. So Robin does not have a dominant strategy. Exactly the same is true of Cal. Since there are no dominant strategies, I cannot use them to predict the equilibria of the game.

Activity 17.10

Does this game have a Nash equilibrium?

Answer

Consider the situation where both choose 'Drive on left'. Does either have an incentive to deviate unilaterally? If Robin moves to 'Drive on right', then her payoff will drop to −1, so she has no incentive to deviate. If Cal moves to 'Drive on right', then his payoff will also be −1. So neither has an incentive to deviate from the strategy combination (Drive on left, Drive on left), and this combination is therefore a Nash equilibrium. By similar reasoning, (Drive on right, Drive on right) is also a Nash equilibrium.

This game therefore has two Nash equilibria. Nash cannot, however, tell us how players can choose one of them.

Both the prisoners' dilemma and this coordination game illuminate problems of public goods provision. The prisoners' dilemma models a situation where the players end up on an inferior outcome, whereas the coordination game above has multiple (i.e. two) possible equilibria and no mechanism for ensuring that players can coordinate to reach one of them. Moreover, the games do not tell us how the dilemmas can be overcome, but they indicate different challenges – in the prisoners' dilemma the challenge is to get people to contribute more to public goods, and in the coordination game the challenge is to get everyone to follow one of the desirable rules.

4.2   Providing public goods

I have examined some reasons why individual decisions may undersupply public goods. Nevertheless, you can see that such goods are provided in practice, through a range of mechanisms (Sandmo, 2008). In this subsection I briefly discuss some of these mechanisms.

Many public goods are supplied through general taxation. However, this mechanism can suffer from the problems identified by the prisoners' dilemma game: people must be willing to pay taxes, yet many will prefer to free ride if possible on the tax payments of others. Research on willingness to pay taxes, or 'tax morale', goes back to theoretical work by Swedish economist Erik Lindahl (1919) on 'just taxation'. Recent empirical research finds that being satisfied with one's income, and practising some form of religion, are positively related to tax morale.

Perhaps even more significantly, trust in government and national pride play important roles too. It seems that if the state behaves in ways that are regarded as fair and reasonable, voters will be more inclined to contribute to its activities, including the provision of public goods. In general, people appear more willing to contribute to taxes where they value the state as an institution as well as the outcomes that it is trying to pursue. However, narrow self-interest also matters. Agha and Haughton (1996) find that VAT compliance improves not just with a lower VAT rate, but also with fewer rates, a smaller population, and more spending on the smooth administration of tax. That is, financial cost and the 'hassle' factor also influence tax morale.

Associated with tax funding is legal enforcement. 'Drive on the left' is legally enforced in the UK. However, issues of compliance still arise that are similar to tax morale: to be effective, legal rules have to be associated with widespread voluntary compliance, as you know if you have been in countries with more anarchic driving behaviour than in northern Europe.

Another mechanism to provide public goods, to a limited group, is through clubs and associations. If members have to subscribe to join, this offers a way round the free-riding problem, though only to the extent that non-contributors can be excluded. Professional associations that encompass a whole profession are interesting examples of clubs that provide public goods for members, for example by lobbying for good terms and conditions for their members and providing membership services.

A further approach is through charitable activity and volunteering: gifts of time or money. People freely donate blood to help to create a supply that is open to all in the UK, and many people have given funds to support rescue services at sea. To make sense of this method of resourcing public goods, we may need to abandon the assumption of pure self-interest that was modelled in the games studied above.

Altruism
Altruism is a motivational state in which pleasure (utility) can be derived from the well-being of others.

Instead, we might assume that people may act from **altruism**, in the sense that they gain some utility from the welfare of others. The musical *Avenue Q* celebrates the German concept of 'schadenfreude' which one of its songs defines as 'laughing at the misfortune of others'. Models of altruistic behaviour assume, by contrast, that it is possible to obtain utility from positive outcomes that others enjoy. If people gain utility from both their own welfare and the welfare of others, then they may donate to public goods if doing so generates enough perceived well-being for other people (Roy and Ziemek, 2000; Meier, 2006). If in addition a person gets a **warm glow** from themselves being the donor, the donating is in itself a source of utility and worth the loss of utility from the personal income donated (Andreoni, 1990). In short, there are mechanisms at play within us that can be used to overcome the incentives to free ride and provide a resource for funding public goods.

Warm glow
A warm glow is a motivational state in which a person's utility depends on bringing about benefits to others.

Finally, a possible mechanism for providing public goods can be found in the development of social networking sites such as Facebook and LinkedIn. Such sites are not public goods in the same sense as national defence. But they choose to operate in ways that do not exclude people, and tend to have cost structures and offerings such that one person's use of the service barely reduces what is available to others.

Typically, such websites operate by 'bundling' the 'public' good with another item that can be sold. They set up a two-stage decision (or game): one in which people choose to join or not, for no cost, and then a second game in which they choose whether or not to buy in additional services. The purchase of higher-value goods cross-subsidises the provision of the zero-cost service. It is possible to discern a similar trend in the funding of music. As recorded music has increasingly taken on the characteristics of a public good by virtue of difficulties in excluding people from hearing it, so artists have increasingly relied on bundling their music with live performances from which non-contributors can be excluded.

5   Arguments for and against a minimal state

There is quite a long history in economics, politics and philosophy of arguments about the proper economic functions of the state. Economists have tended to focus on efficiency as a criterion for assessing whether government involvement is desirable, although justice and fairness have also been important and appear to be increasingly so. As discussed, few people like taxes, but people do pay them when they are for things that they value – and are difficult to avoid!

5.1   Rawls vs. Nozick

So how active should the state be? What is its proper role? Philosophers who have tackled this question have focused on the enduring themes of fairness and freedom, and the extent of conflict between them. These are issues of both theory and practical economic policy. Two leading philosophers who have influenced this debate in economics are John Rawls and Robert Nozick.

In 1971, the Harvard philosopher Rawls published *A Theory of Justice* in which he draws together ideas from philosophy and economics to produce a modern theory of justice. As his research question, Rawls asks what principles of justice people would choose if they were prevented by a 'veil of ignorance' from knowing where they were located within the economy. They might be born privileged – or not.

Rawls argues that from behind this 'veil of ignorance', people would 'play safe' and try to ensure, for entirely self-interested reasons, that the worst position that they might be in would be as good as possible. Rawls calls this the 'maximin' principle:

> Social and economic inequalities are to be arranged so that they are … to the greatest benefit of the least advantaged.
>
> (Rawls, 1971, p. 83)

This is a justification for an active state. Rawls focuses on the provision of what he calls 'primary goods': goods and services needed by everyone to live a reasonable life. His theory implies quite an egalitarian distribution of goods and services. Questions of how this would be arranged and enforced were not part of Rawls' project, but even as an ideal, his theory of justice suggests a significant redistributive role for government.

Around the same time, another Harvard philosopher, Nozick, produced an equally large volume (Nozick, 1974) that articulates a justification for a much reduced role for government. Nozick argues that governments should exist to protect property rights and maintain law and order, and not much else. He argues that people are self-owners (ruling out slavery) and have rights to their 'lives, liberty and fruits of their labour'. These rights impose duties on others not to harm us.

Nozick then argues that it follows from this that taxation, and government redistribution, are immoral since they force us to labour on behalf of the general collective and thereby violate the principle of self-ownership. Given this position, only a 'night-watchman' state can be justified, i.e. one that protects individuals via police, military and legal means from being harmed by others. This is a fairly extreme doctrine, but it presents one of the most popular modern accounts of a libertarian tradition that goes back at least to the work of John Locke.

5.2   Government failure vs. market failure

I have argued that market failures such as externalities are a basic starting point for justifying government intervention. However, for this to be a convincing justification, governments must be effective. A critical economic literature highlights the possible failures of government. One key theme is the idea that regulatory bodies may be ineffective if they are 'captured' by the industries that they are supposed to regulate, so they begin to operate in the private interests of those industries. The problem may be more pronounced in economies where there is a lot of interaction between business, politics and administration, as there is in the USA, but the dangers are worldwide.

Another, older idea is that government administrators may maximise the size of their budgets, since government organisations do not have to make profits. This may lead to larger governments than might be optimal. A third argument is that public sector bodies may be less efficient than private firms because of the absence of competition, and there is some supporting evidence for this in a number of sectors. Governments may therefore try to introduce markets within government, or to subcontract government services through competitive tender to the private sector, in order to create competitive pressures.

In short, the size and scope of economic functions of the state have been subject to much ideological debate over the years. However, these debates are not just about political preferences: there is much relevant empirical economic evidence to help one to think about the questions raised by philosophers.

6   From growth to progress

I began this chapter with a list of economic functions of government. The list did not explicitly include promoting growth, but this is often regarded as an uncontroversial government economic role, especially as governments clear up after the 2008 financial crisis. However, promoting growth is perhaps an issue that is more unresolved than first appears. Early economic models of growth developed from the mid-1950s tended to focus on the problem of how to maximise growth by getting the right balance between saving and consumption, and the right mix of capital and labour.

However, this begs the question as to whether we indeed want to maximise growth as measured by Gross National Income. Environmentalists have argued since the 1960s that the traditional national income accounting framework is increasingly deficient, as it does not reflect the growing drain on environmental goods and services that are treated as 'free' but are not in fact renewable. Furthermore, the social indicators movement starting in the 1970s, perhaps as an analytical response to the rise of humanism, highlighted the wide range of issues from crime rates to spiritual matters that might be influenced by economic growth.

Economists have long been aware of these issues and have tended, historically, to give one of the following responses:

1   Economic growth is positively related (correlated) to improvement of well-being in other areas.

2   Economic welfare should not be mistakenly understood as a measure of human welfare.

If (1) is true, then we should be able to pursue other objectives by maximising economic growth. However, if (2) is true, then the message seems to be that raising national income may be legitimate but other approaches should be used to measure human welfare.

In fact, within the group of high-income countries, there is little empirical evidence of a relationship between economic income and, say, life expectancy. So there are good reasons for wanting to move 'beyond GDP', and since the 1990s, economists in policy and research have been involved in just this kind of work. In one of the major international projects in this field, the OECD (undated) talks about the 'measurement of progress', and this provides a useful way of thinking about these developments. In the rest of this section, I examine some of the key strands in recent economic thinking about progress, as opposed to growth.

6.1   The sources of happiness

In 1974 the economist William Easterlin noticed that despite decades of growth, American citizens were – according to surveys – no happier than they were before the growth took place. Subsequently, economists have argued that this reflects the results of adaptation – a phenomenon that is well theorised in psychology. As people earn more, so their aspirations adapt upwards, and this leaves them feeling no better off than before, despite being materially better off.

There is substantial evidence from Europe and the USA that people on higher incomes are happier than others (Frey and Stutzer, 2002). However, a number of factors other than income also seem to be important for happiness. These factors include the ways in which we compare ourselves to others. As long ago as 1899, Thorstein Veblen (1915) argued that some consumption was inherently conspicuous, designed merely to signal the fact of a higher status in society. People may tend to look upwards when making comparisons, so wealthier people tend to impose a negative externality on poorer people.

The category of 'positional goods' (Hirsch, 1978) builds on this insight: these are goods that cannot be increased in number by definition (for example, being the richest person in the town). Hirsch argues that such goods impose logical limits on the extent to which economic growth can make people happy. If the production of positional goods, like expensive watches, makes more people unhappy than happy, then it can be argued to be hugely wasteful of resources (Frank, 2008).

So does happiness provide a new outcome-based method for evaluating government expenditure, to compare with approaches that traditionally measure its cost (Frey and Stutzer, 2002)? Santos (2013) shows, for example, that when the costs of domestic violence are measured by their effects on life satisfaction, they are much higher than the costs of policing and legal services. (This is done by treating life satisfaction as a measure of utility, and estimating the willingness to pay for a violence-free life, i.e. how much, on average, individuals are willing to pay to keep themselves safe from domestic violence. It trades off the amount of income that people are willing to give up to have a life without violence.) Using data on happiness or its absence, one might explore directly the levels of income that make people miserable, and identify the specific issues associated with low income that really make people unhappy. Is it lack of material goods, lack of opportunities to socialise, something else and/or some combination of these?

There may also be implications for the *type* of growth and economic activity that we seek. Happiness research suggests that unemployment reduces happiness, at both personal and national levels. This finding runs against economic theories that treat unemployment as voluntary (Frey and Stutzer, 2002). In relation to inflation, people focus on its harms rather than its benefits, fearing political and economic chaos and a fall in national prestige (Schiller, 1996). Links between happiness and democracy suggest that collective decision-making procedures that allow for involvement do lead to happier populations (Frey and Stutzer, 2002).

6.2   Capabilities and well-being

An increasingly influential strand of economic thinking, deriving from work by the Nobel prize-winning economist Amartya Sen, argues that conventional welfare economics ignores the fact that people have rights, and the violation of those rights has negative impacts on their well-being. Sen (1985) formulated three principles:

1   A person's *functionings* (that is, what they do and what they are) depend on the resources to which they have access, and different people convert resources into functionings at different rates.

2   A person's experienced happiness depends on their functionings.

3   A person's overall well-being depends, in addition, on their *capabilities* – that is, what it is that they could do, given their resources and abilities.

Compared with traditional welfare economics, which focuses on identifying the correct allocation of goods and services, this is quite a radical alternative view of the economics of welfare.

The first principle implies that income should be seen as an input into the generation of human welfare, not as a measure of the welfare output produced by economic activity. It also recognises that people have different skills and abilities, and therefore different needs. For example, Kuklys (2005) found that that disabled people in the British Household Panel Survey required on average around 40% more income than the general UK population to make them equally satisfied with their income.

The second principle is compatible with the happiness literature just discussed. The third principle is highly innovative. It holds that in addition to how happy a person is, their 'doings and beings' (that is, everyday activities and aspects of a person's status that contribute to well-being) and *potential* to do things also provide a measure of their level of advantage. The concept of capabilities, in this principle, reflects concerns about equality of opportunity and the distribution of opportunities within society more generally.

Opportunity may not be directly measurable, unlike happiness or functionings, but fairness in this regard matters just as much as, say, the distribution of growth. An example might be the so-called 'glass ceiling' – those invisible constraints to promotion within firms that can face people in particular segments of the labour market (often women). Furthermore, people adapt to their constraints, and subjective reports on happiness may reflect that adaptation. In that case, data on, for example, promotions by gender within firms may be preferable to asking men and women directly about promotion prospects.

6.3   Measuring well-being

The United Nations (UN) has a created a Human Development Index (HDI) to reflect some of the above considerations. This gives rise to summary scores by which countries can be measured (see United Nations Development Programme (UNDP), 2010). The score is an index summarising life expectancy, education and income per head. The highest possible score is 1, and the lowest is 0 (Table 17.6), and it can often be represented as a percentage from 0% to 100%.

Table 17.6   HDI scores for selected countries, 2010

Country	HDI score
USA	0.902
Italy	0.854
UK	0.849
Brazil	0.699
Bangladesh	0.469
Ethiopia	0.328

(Source: UNDP, 2010)

By highlighting health and education as well as income, the HDI has helped people in developing countries to think systematically about different outcomes of development and to measure whether those are being delivered. Higher-income countries, however, all have rather high and similar scores. So to develop a more refined picture, I have, with colleagues, created a series of indices that measure well-being in terms of what people are able to do, as capabilities relate to home, work, community, the environment, service access and health – forming a 'capabilities dashboard' (Figure 17.6). These scores combine data on several capabilities, and normalise each score into a number from 0 to 100 to create an index. The scores are based on answers to a variety of questions of the form 'I am able to …' where higher total scores indicate that people feel able to do a wider variety of things.

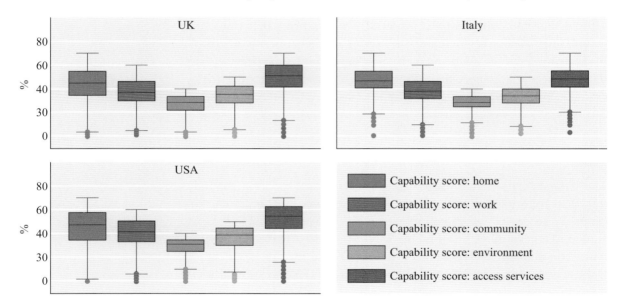

Figure 17.6   A capabilities dashboard (2012 data)

(Source: author's Oxwell Survey of 3000 20–60-year-olds in the UK, the USA and Italy)

Figure 17.6 gives a glimpse of a multi-dimensional approach to capabilities. The scores have been graphed using boxplots. The box contains 50% of the scores: the top of the box is the 75th percentile; the line within the box is the median, and the bottom of the box is the 25th percentile; the lines or 'whiskers' show the extent of most of the scores except extremes.

Activity 17.11

Describe some of the results shown in Figure 17.6.

Answer

In all three countries, highest average capabilities are associated with home and access to services, though the variations are large in both cases. People are least happy, on average, with capabilities associated with their community. Perhaps this reflects the fact that a positive community atmosphere is a kind of public good, or that some negative externalities, such as crime, operate at the community level.

Additional results of the study that are not shown in Figure 17.6 suggest that access to services is more closely linked to personal income in the USA than it is in the UK or Italy – as one might perhaps expect, given that the development of the welfare state is greater in Europe than in the USA.

7   Conclusion

Support for the minimal view of government is far from disappearing, but this chapter has shown how interactions in economic and social life give rise to efficiency problems that cannot be solved by free markets working on their own. There is a significant degree of consensus around the world on the need to address externalities and the provision of some public goods, even in countries where political ideology seems to warn against active government.

Beyond this consensus, increasing government efforts to monitor well-being directly, rather than just through money income, raise some new challenges and questions. What governments do with this information remains to be seen, but one should not assume that government policies must be the result. Well-being at work, the ability to achieve a good work–life balance, being treated as an equal by work colleagues, and living in healthy environments: these all depend heavily on the actions of employers and businesses.

References

Adam, S. and Browne, J. (2011) *A Survey of the UK Tax System*, Institute for Fiscal Studies Briefing Note 9, London, IFS.

Agha, A. and Haughton, J. (1996) 'Designing VAT systems: some efficiency considerations', *Review of Economics and Statistics*, vol. 78, no. 2, pp. 303–8.

Andreoni, J. (1990) 'Impure altruism and donations to public goods: a theory of warm-glow giving', *Economic Journal*, vol. 100, no. 401, pp. 464–77.

Coase, R.H. (1960) 'The problem of social cost', *Journal of Law and Economics*, vol. 3, no. 1, pp. 1–44.

Dick, J., Blais, J. and Moore, P. (2005) *Civics and Government: Focus on Economics*, New York, Council for Economic Education.

Easterlin, R.A. (1974) 'Does economic growth improve the human lot?', in David, P.A. and Reder, M.W. (eds) *Nations and Households in Economic Growth: Essays in Honor of Moses Abramovitz*, New York, Academic Press.

Frank, R.H. (2008) 'Consumption externalities', in Durlauf, S.N. and Blume, L.E. (eds) *The New Palgrave Dictionary of Economics*, Basingstoke, Palgrave Macmillan.

Frey, B. and Stutzer, A. (2002) *Happiness Economy and Institutions*, Princeton, NJ, Princeton University Press.

Goodstein, E.S. (2002) *Economics and the Environment*, Hoboken, NJ, John Wiley.

Hirsch, F. (1978) *Social Limits to Growth*, London, Routledge.

Kuklys, W. (2005) *Amartya Sen's Capability Approach*, Berlin, Springer.

Lindahl, E.R. (1919) *Die Gerechtigkeit der Besteuerung (Just Taxation: A Positive Solution)*, Lund, Gleerup.

Meier, S. (2006) 'A survey of economic theories and field evidence on pro-social behaviour', Federal Reserve Bank of Boston Working Paper no. 06-6.

Nozick, R. (1974) *Anarchy, State and Utopia*, New York, Basic Books.

OECD (undated) 'Better life initiative: measuring well-being and progress', [online] www.oecd.org/statistics/

betterlifeinitiativemeasuringwell-beingandprogress.htm (Accessed 22 March 2013).

Rawls, J. (1971) *A Theory of Justice*, Boston, MA, HarvardUniversity Press.

Robinson, G. (2010) 'Living life in the (wrong) fast lane!', 28 September, [online] www.carrentals.co.uk/blog/living-life-in-the-wrong-fast-lane.html (accessed 19 March 2013).

Roy, K. and Ziemek, S. (2000) 'On the economics of volunteering', ZEF Discussion Papers on Development Policy no. 31, [online] www.zef.de/fileadmin/webfiles/downloads/zef_dp/zef_dp31-00.pdf (Accessed 15 December 2012).

Sandmo, A. (2008) 'Public goods', in Durlauf, S.N. and Blume, L.E. (eds) *The New Palgrave Dictionary of Economics*, Basingstoke, Palgrave Macmillan.

Santos, C. (2013) 'Costs of domestic violence: a life satisfaction approach', *Fiscal Studies*, forthcoming.

Santos, G. and Fraser, G. (2006) 'Road pricing: lessons from London', *Economic Policy*, vol. 21, no. 46, pp. 263–310.

Schiller, R.J. (1996) *Why Do People Dislike Inflation?*, Cowles Foundation Discussion Paper no. 1115, New Haven, CT.

Sen, A.K. (1985) *Commodities and Capabilities*, Amsterdam, North-Holland.

Tucker, A.W. (1950) 'A two-person dilemma', unpublished notes, Stanford University, May 1950. Reproduced in Rasmusen, E. (2001) *Readings in Games and Information*, Oxford, Blackwell.

United Nations Development Programme (UNDP) (2010) *Human Development Reports*, Geneva, UNDP.

Veblen, T. (1915 [1899]) *Theory of the Leisure Class: An Economic Study of Institutions*, London, Macmillan.

Chapter 18
Global public goods

Simon Halliday

Contents

1 Introduction

Euro uncertainty 'undermining recovery'

BBC News 2012

World Bank's Jim Yong Kim: 'I want to eradicate poverty'

Guardian 2012

Lagarde: Huge legacy of public debt could sink [global] recovery

Guardian 2012

Threat of US-China trade war hangs over dealings of century's superpowers

Guardian 2012

Oceans on brink of catastrophe

Independent 2012

While governments make decisions about how to run their own economies, some of the most worrisome problems affecting our societies and economies these days cannot be solved within the borders of each country. Their impacts are global and have far-reaching consequences. Failing to stabilise the euro and public debt in developed countries affects the global economy. Failing to preserve fish and fauna and their reproduction will eradicate a natural resource for future generations, and create worldwide starvation and inflation. Failing to establish trade policies that allow countries to find demand for their products will reduce worldwide output and create imbalances, poverty and instability, affecting all countries, even exporting countries, adversely. This book ends with an appraisal of the limits and opportunities that these global problems impose on governments: how can they cooperate in seeking solutions to these problems, and what are the difficulties in doing so?

One of the recurring themes throughout both books is the question: what can governments do? In Parts 2 and 3, you examined how governments use fiscal and monetary policy to influence unemployment, inflation and economic growth. In Part 4, you saw how government policy influences the actions and performance of firms and markets; and in Part 5, you have seen how government policy shapes international trade, income inequality and the distribution of public goods. This chapter moves beyond thinking about what governments can do, towards a position of what governments can do, or should do, together, and why they have to.

With constant advances in technology, communication and transportation, there is increased interdependence between economies. It will be argued that solutions to many current economic problems require a more collective response through governments cooperating with each other; or perhaps on a gloomier note, solutions cannot be found without this cooperation.

To examine the possibilities for such cooperation, I use the notion of public good to develop what is meant by a global public good, and I use game theory to represent economic situations where global public goods are at stake. I will therefore develop the material on public goods and game theory that was initiated in Chapter 17 in order to understand better some of the greatest challenges faced by national economies today.

The learning outcomes for this chapter are:

- to understand global public goods and global commons problems as applications of the prisoners' dilemma
- to know and be able to identify global public goods and the free rider problem
- to develop further understanding of the notion of Nash equilibrium, and use it in solving games
- to understand collective action games as games with many players
- to understand how outcomes may change when players interact more than once

- to recognise that outcomes and payoffs may vary when games are played by different players with their own cultures, experiences, beliefs and norms.

2   Understanding global public goods

> What is at stake … is not the stability of Greece. It's not the stability of the Eurozone. It's not the future of the Euro. It's actually the stability of the global economy. Because, if things go south, all economies will be affected.
>
> (Lagarde, 2011)

Chapter 17 distinguishes between private goods and public goods. It explains that the distinction between private goods and pure public goods rests in two properties of public goods: non-rivalry and non-excludability. Public goods tend to benefit everyone, and preventing people from using them can be very costly, if this is even possible. At the same time, this means that each individual person's benefit cannot exclude others or reduce the benefit of others. Every Eurozone country is connected, through trade, investments, charities or migration, so every Eurozone country is affected by financial instability. But the Eurozone does not exist in isolation – an unstable euro and a financially unstable Eurozone can cause spillovers to other countries: demand for Eurozone exports may decrease, Eurozone imports may decline, and tourists, investors and migrants may go elsewhere. What happens in the Eurozone affects many countries far beyond its borders. The Eurozone's connectedness and the global nature of the financial crisis is the essence of Christine Lagarde's (2011) message: the collapse of Greece or the disruption of the financial stability of the Eurozone has far-reaching implications. The Eurozone's connectedness makes financial stability a global public good – a public good that is non-excludable and non-rival on a global scale. As the Nobel laureate Paul Samuelson once described global public goods:

> What great blessings or scourges have befallen humanity? Consider issues as disparate as greenhouse warming and ozone depletion, the Internet and William Shakespeare, terrorism and money laundering, the discovery of antibiotics and nuclear proliferation. Each is an example of a complex system whose effects are global and resists the control of individuals and even the most powerful governments. These are examples of global public goods, which

are goods whose impacts are indivisibly spread around the entire globe.

(Paul Samuelson quoted in Nordhaus, 2005)

Activity 18.1

The Samuelson quote highlights several important features of global public goods. List the ones that you can identify.

Answer

Samuelson gives examples of public goods that are global in their impact: though they may arise from the actions of individuals they affect everyone across the world. His examples include public 'bads', such as global warming, and public goods that are beneficial, such as the decline in deaths from infections after the invention of antibiotics. Because public goods like these are non-excludable, cannot be appropriated or owned, their provision or control cannot rely on any single group of countries or people, but must emerge from collective awareness and effort that crosses national borders. These dynamics lead to the main difference between a public good that has local or national effects, as discussed in Chapter 17, and a global public good. While national policies and government incentives can lead societies to produce or consume the right level of national and local public goods, they are much less successful when it comes to global public goods. These goods are global not just in their effects, but also in the solutions that they require.

Debates rage over whether the solution to some of today's global public goods problems should be left for countries with a historical responsibility to solve, or whether Coase's theorem (which you met in Chapter 17) should be applied and countries who benefit the most from public goods be left to negotiate with others to sustain the global public good. In this chapter, I steer clear of the long debate about the ethics of public good provision. However, the debate highlights one of the fundamental problems in providing global public goods: who should contribute to their provision, and are incentives in place to ensure that countries contribute? I turn to this problem next.

3   Revisiting the prisoners' dilemma

If costs of a global public good are borne by a few, but benefits remain non-excludable, then those who bear the costs will see their own benefits decreased by having to pay for its provision. But if they don't bear the costs, then there is a chance that the global public good does not get produced. You came across this problem when you analysed the prisoners' dilemma in Chapter 17.

Recall the game between Robin and Cal where they have to decide whether or not to contribute to a public good. The rules are simple: as long as one player contributes, the public good is provided to both players. The contributor bears the whole cost of the public good if the other does not contribute, and being the only one bearing the whole cost is the worst possible scenario for either player. No player wants to be the 'sucker'. Each player's most preferred scenario is the opposite: to free ride and benefit from the public good while the other player foots the bill. The best outcome for society is when both players contribute. The payoff matrix analysed in Chapter 17 is reproduced in Figure 18.1.

		Cal	
		Contribute	Refuse
Robin	Contribute	2 , 2	−1 , 3
	Refuse	3 , −1	0 , 0

Figure 18.1   A prisoners' dilemma game demonstrating the problem of resourcing public goods

I will start from the socially optimal scenario where both players contribute. As discussed in Chapter 17, this cannot be an equilibrium of this game because, individually, both players would want to change their strategy and avoid contributing. Consider what Robin would do. Robin's payoffs show up first in each cell (the red player, with red payoffs). The payoff received by Robin depends on what Cal does. So when Cal is contributing (first column), Robin gets 2 if she contributes, but she gets 3 (bottom left cell) if she moves away from the socially optimum scenario and tries to free ride. If you now look at what Cal will want to do (the blue player, with blue payoffs, after the comma), you can see that it works in the same way. When Robin contributes (first row), Cal gets 2 when he contributes but 3 (top right cell) if he tries to free ride.

So both players would want to unilaterally change their strategies and would not end up in (Contribute, Contribute).

3.1 Finding the Nash equilibrium of a game using best responses

The example in Figure 18.1 shows that the temptation to free ride can undermine socially optimal outcomes, but it does not reveal the solution of the game. In Chapter 17, Section 4, you learned how to solve the game by checking for each cell whether either player (or both) wants to unilaterally deviate. If not, then the combination of strategies related to that cell is a Nash equilibrium. You also learned that when both players have a dominant strategy, there is one and one only Nash equilibrium, which is when players choose their dominant strategy.

Activity 18.2

Is (Refuse, Refuse) an equilibrium in dominant strategies?

Answer

An equilibrium in dominant strategies occurs when each player's strategy does not depend on what the other player might do. This means that each player will always do the same thing, regardless of what the other player is doing. Consider what that means for the payoff matrix here. Robin will have a dominant strategy if she always prefers to contribute, or always prefers to refuse, whether Cal chooses to contribute (first column) or to refuse (second column). So to find out what Robin will want to do, I have to concentrate on how Robin strategically responds to Cal (what is Robin's best response to each of Cal's actions), and see if these responses are the same regardless of what Cal does.

If Cal contributes, then Robin prefers to refuse (Robin prefers to free ride), getting 3 instead of 2. When Cal refuses, Robin prefers to refuse too, getting 0 instead of −1. The red numbers corresponding to these two responses (3 and 0 along the bottom row) are underlined in Figure 18.2 to show they are both in the same row, namely Robin's Refuse row. Visually, I have established that the way Robin's strategy depends on what Cal does is given by best responses along the same row. This is how one identifies dominant strategies: the row player has a dominant strategy when the best responses are along the same row. Correspondingly, the column player has a dominant strategy when the best responses are in a column. In fact, Cal will also prefer to refuse no matter what Robin does. This can be seen in Figure 18.2 by the underlining for the column player of the blue payoffs corresponding to Cal's best responses.

		Cal	
		Contribute	Refuse
Robin	Contribute	2 , 2	−1 , $\underline{3}$
	Refuse	$\underline{3}$, −1	$\underline{0}$, $\underline{0}$

Figure 18.2 Solving a prisoners' dilemma, underlining best responses

So (Refuse, Refuse) seems to be the dominant strategy equilibrium of this game, because that is what both players will do no matter what.

You can see that (Refuse, Refuse) is also a Nash equilibrium. To show this, I will check whether Robin or Cal will want to unilaterally change strategy at (Refuse, Refuse). If Robin changes to contribute, her payoff will drop to −1, and the same is true for Cal. So the dominant strategy equilibrium is also a Nash equilibrium, as you saw in Chapter 17. You can see that the Nash equilibrium of the game is also found when both payoffs in the same cell are underlined: both players' best responses intersect at points of equilibrium from which neither player wants to deviate. This suggests another way of identifying Nash equilibria:

- Find the best responses of each player to what the other is doing, and underline the payoffs of these best responses.
- Check which cells have both players' payoffs underlined.
- *All* cells with *both* payoffs underlined are Nash equilibria.

This method of finding Nash equilibria applies to all games that are played simultaneously and only once. It can be used when players do not have a dominant strategy, when there is more than one equilibrium in the game, or to find that there is no equilibrium at all. Throughout this chapter, I will use this method of solving games to illustrate the difficulties in sustaining and preserving some important examples of global public goods. The three examples of free trade, fisheries and financial stability will be used.

Activity 18.3

To what extent do you think free trade, international fisheries and financial stability are global public goods?

Answer

All of these examples could be argued to be global public goods, but with different characteristics and different problems. Free trade has the characteristics of a global public good because free trade can promote growth worldwide with the potential for all to benefit. Countries that are open to trade can expand the markets for their products and their economies can grow; and, due to comparative advantage, resources can be used more efficiently worldwide when countries specialise in the production of goods and services in which they have a comparative advantage, and import goods where they do not. Apart from the direct benefits from trade, by stimulating growth in trading countries, trade generates more output and income worldwide (despite the difficulties regarding effective redistribution of the gains from trade across countries, discussed in Chapter 15).

International fisheries are a different type of a global public good. Because fishing and the use of the sea is a non-excludable good, all individuals can catch as much fish as they want. Fish is, however, a rival good: the fish caught by one fishing boat prevents another fishing boat catching that same fish. This type of public good is called more precisely a common resource good or commons.

Financial stability could also be argued to be a global public good. At the level of an individual bank, its actions lead to profits (or losses) for that institution, yet a bank's actions can also affect others outside its trading network. In a financial system that is globally connected, there are significant negative externalities when individual banks collapse, and these negative externalities take the form of public 'bads' – as one bank does worse, it calls in the loans that it gave to other banks, which means that other banks must call in their loans, and so on until a systemic banking collapse may result and no-one can avoid the effects. In recent years, many of us have experienced first-hand the troubles of interconnected banks and financial instability, or of individual banks undermining global financial stability.

There are other global public goods that present more fundamental challenges to governments, such as maintaining peace and eradicating hunger and preventable disease, as well as reducing global poverty.

However, the focus in this chapter is on these three examples – a less ambitious aim, but nevertheless very challenging, as each case has its own particular features that need to be explained in the context of global cooperation.

3.2   Free trade

In the final decades of the twentieth century and early decades of the twenty-first century, the insight that free trade is beneficial is at the heart of the EU's internal market. The member states of the EU have each committed not to impose tariffs on the other member states of the union. Free trade in the internal market is a good – a public good – that provides benefits to all the member states of the EU. Each member can access the markets of the other states without tariffs impeding their trade.

Worldwide, a majority of countries are currently members of the World Trade Organization (WTO). At the time of its creation, the WTO's predecessor body, the General Agreement on Tariffs and Trade (GATT), had succeeded in reducing worldwide tariffs by one-third, had made some progress at reducing agricultural subsidies in developed countries, and had succeeded in having Japan and South Korea agree to lower barriers on rice imports (Wydick, 2008, p. 240). The WTO was created with the following five principles in mind:

- Trade would not discriminate between domestic- and foreign-produced products.
- Freer trade is ultimately better for the world.
- There should not be any uncertainty in the terms of trade and trade policy.
- Trade should foster competition.
- Priorities of developing countries can allow for privileges in setting trade agreements.

With the WTO having 157 members in 2012, and all decisions being agreed unanimously, it is impressive that there are still several success stories in reducing barriers to trade. But not all initiatives have been successful. As discussed in Chapter 15, governments have strong national interests in protecting some of their producers and their own labour force from worldwide competition. Countries will more likely be net importers if world prices for goods consumed domestically are lower than domestic prices, and more likely to be net exporters if world prices for goods consumed domestically are higher than domestic prices. Reducing barriers to trade means that consumption can occur at lower world prices rather than at higher domestic prices.

As Chapter 15 discussed, freeing trade can therefore raise global social welfare, but there are major redistributive effects within and between countries. As Figure 15.5 in Chapter 15 showed, when world prices are below domestic prices, consumers benefit from free trade through lower prices. However, domestic producers lose out, as sales fall. If producers do not improve productivity or find new markets, unemployment may rise.

The political pressure in import countries to protect domestic producers is often the main argument leading countries to implement protectionist measures and undermine free trade. But the response to this incentive, by compromising trade flows between countries, will dictate how open to trade all countries decide to be. Trade policy thus involves a strong element of strategic behaviour. These strategic choices in trade policy can be explained using a payoff matrix, such as the one shown in Figure 18.3.

		USA	
		Low tariffs	High tariffs
China	Low tariffs	400 , 400	200 , 500
	High tariffs	500 , 200	300 , 300

Figure 18.3 China and the USA choosing tariffs (payoffs in billions of dollars)

In this hypothetical example, China and the USA could raise tariffs on each other's traded goods. Let each country have the option of keeping low tariffs or imposing high tariffs on the other country. The outcomes for the two countries are interdependent because the best action for each one depends on what the other country does. There are four possible outcomes in Figure 18.3, with payoffs to each country in billions of dollars. You can think of these payoffs as the social welfare gained by each country in each situation.

When both countries choose low tariffs, this is the socially optimum free trade scenario with benefits in both countries. However, each country will have an incentive to free ride and unilaterally impose high tariffs. If one country imposes high tariffs and the other does not, then the country that keeps its tariffs low will be in the worst possible scenario. When both countries impose high tariffs, they both lose the benefits from free trade.

Activity 18.4

Find the Nash equilibrium or equilibria of this game.

Answer

The easiest way to look for a Nash equilibrium is to find each player's best responses to each of the other player's actions and see which cells, if any, have both payoffs underlined. So starting with the row country, China, I will look at what it prefers when the USA keeps tariffs low (comparing first red payoffs in the first column) and when the USA imposes high tariffs (comparing first red payoffs in the second column). In both cases, China prefers to impose high tariffs. To impose high tariffs is therefore China's dominant strategy. Similarly, to impose high tariffs is the USA's dominant strategy (comparing second blue payoffs first in the first row, then in the second). It turns out that the only cell where both payoffs are underlined is when both countries play their dominant strategy (High tariffs, High tariffs). Thus to impose high tariffs is each player's best response to their opponent. (High tariffs, High tariffs) is therefore the Nash equilibrium of the game. The best responses of each player and the equilibrium of the game are presented in Figure 18.4.

		USA	
		Low tariffs	High tariffs
China	Low tariffs	400 , 400	200 , $\underline{500}$
	High tariffs	$\underline{500}$, 200	$\underline{300}$, $\underline{300}$

Figure 18.4   China and the USA choosing tariffs – best responses and Nash equilibrium

The choices that China and the USA face in the tariff game mirror the structure of the prisoners' dilemma. In games that have the structure of a prisoners' dilemma, players can choose to Cooperate or to Defect. In the public good game that you saw above and in Chapter 17, players cooperate if they contribute to the public good and defect if they don't.

In the tariff game, 'Low tariffs' is equivalent to Cooperate, and 'High tariffs' is equivalent to Defect. The socially optimal outcome where both countries keep tariffs low (cooperate) cannot be reached because individually each country has an incentive to raise tariffs (defect) and try to free ride. If the other country is imposing high tariffs, then there is also an incentive to choose high tariffs to avoid being the sucker bearing all the costs of doing the right thing. In games with the prisoners' dilemma structure, these two forces – the free-riding incentive and the sucker payoff – lead to very gloomy outcomes in which global public goods are not provided and global cooperation is undermined.

3.3 Fisheries

The discussion of free trade as a global public good led to a conclusion that the likely outcome was that free trade would be undersupplied. A variation on public goods is that of commons goods or a commons. A commons is a good that no one individual owns, and consequently that many people have access to and can use. Commons goods are non-excludable and so share some properties of public goods. However, their benefits are rivalrous because as one person, state, firm or organisation consumes a common good, the benefits to others or the total stock of the good decreases. So even though commons can benefit anyone, whoever benefits from consuming the good reduces the benefit of others. Commons are like private goods that anyone can access.

Commons problems have a long history in political philosophy and economics. During the twentieth century, these problems were made notorious by Garrett Hardin in his 1968 paper 'The tragedy of the commons'. Hardin was an ecologist. He argued that if many people all used the same common resource, then the resource would deplete over time. Where the dynamics of public goods like free trade would lead to undersupply, commons goods would lead to overuse.

Hardin's original example involved a common resource – land – where herders could take their cattle to graze because the land was non-excludable. A herder receives private benefits from his cow grazing on the common land because his cow is fed and feeding the cow on the common land costs the herder nothing but time – he does not incur a cost to produce the grass on the common land. But common land is rivalrous, so when a herder allows his cow to graze the common land, he decreases the amount of grass available to others for their cattle, therefore decreasing the potential benefit to other herders. Eventually, given how tempting it is to use a common land for cow grazing, all herders will do so, overgrazing the land and deteriorating the quality of the land for future use until the grass no longer grows and the commons good disappears. Hardin argues that overgrazing on common land highlights a problem of overexploitation more generally:

> [T]he inherent logic of the commons remorselessly generates tragedy … Ruin is the destination toward which all men rush, each pursuing his own best interest in a society that believes in the freedom of the commons. Freedom in a commons brings ruin to all.

> (Hardin, 1968)

The international waters of the large oceans of the world offer a different example of a resource that no one owns, but which fishers from every country can exploit if they so choose. Fisheries in international oceans are common property and non-excludable, but as explained above they exhibit rivalry. As more and more fishers catch the fish, the total stock of fish decreases. Identifying the global commons and analysing the incentives that people face – the costs and the benefits – shows the ways in which over-fishing can emerge as a consequence of each fisher following their self-interest. Though no individual fisher plans to over-fish, over-fishing emerges on aggregate from the incentives faced by all fishers.

For example, as Vidal (2012) argues in *The Guardian*, for many years the seas off the coast of Mauritania in West Africa have provided local fishermen with the resources that they need to sustain their daily lives: enough fish for their families and some to be sold at local markets. But the number of boats on the seas has begun to change. Trawling the Mauritanian waters are massive Russian, Chinese, Korean, Japanese and EU fishing boats. These international fishing boats scour the Mauritanian seas for fish to be sold on international markets. The Mauritanian government reassures its people that as the international fishing fleets trawl deep waters, they cannot affect the fish caught by the locals. The local fishermen, however, claim that they are catching fewer and fewer fish as the number of international fishing boats increases. The challenge that a country like Mauritania faces is a consequence of the tragedy of the commons – the destination of ruin that Hardin

describes when property is common and society permits free access to all.

According to the United Nations Environment Programme (UNEP) report *Towards a Green Economy* (2011, p. 85), the top five fishing countries are Russia, China, the USA, Japan and Taiwan. As shown in Figure 18.5, the amount of fishing along the coasts of China, Japan and Korea is incredibly large and has been intensifying over the decades.

The UNEP (2011) report argues that in order for there to be any kind of concerted control of fisheries, the 'top fishers' must be involved. Game theory and the prisoners' dilemma can illustrate why cooperation between these countries will not happen unless additional mechanisms are put into place. Consider a game between two of the world's top five fishing countries, Japan and China. In estimates from data in 2005, China and Japan 'land' the most valuable fish, at $15.2 billion (China) and $14.4 billion (Japan) in 2005 US dollars.

But, as also discussed in the UNEP (2011) report, because so much fishing goes on in the areas close to Japan and China, the risk of the fish populations along those coastlines 'crashing' is very high. When a fish population crashes, the population suddenly disappears and the likelihood that it will recover in the near future is very low. So China and Japan need to choose whether or not to adopt sustainable fishing policies, i.e. choose between the two actions 'Limit fishing' and 'Over-fish'. Because the outcome depends on whether or not populations will

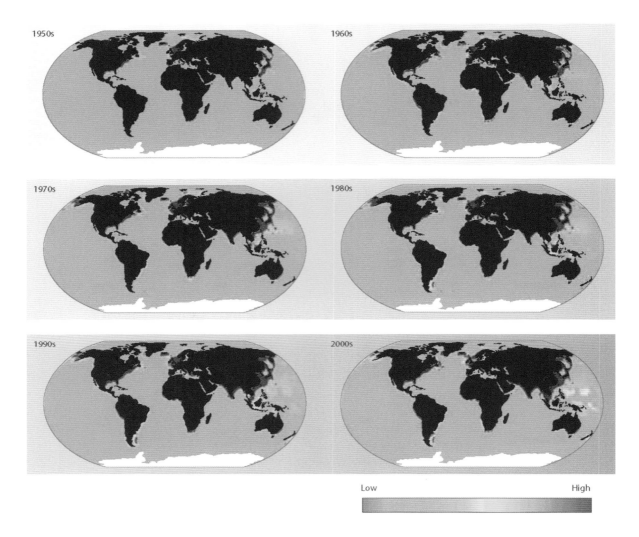

Figure 18.5   The distribution of the value of fish caught internationally, 1950–2010

(Source: Sumaila, 2011, Figure 2)

crash, I will consider a simplified game for the sake of illustration. Suppose that it is known that the fish populations on the coasts of China and Japan will crash if both countries continue to over-fish. If one country limits fishing and the other does not, then the country that limits fishing will lose the profit of not having fished more, and it will lose its own fish population because the other country will take over its coast. If both countries limit fishing, then they will make lower profits in the present, though their profits might be more sustainable and therefore higher over the long run. So the payoffs of this game might be as shown in Figure 18.6.

		China	
		Limit fishing	Over-fish
Japan	Limit fishing	8 , 8	2 , <u>10</u>
	Over-fish	<u>10</u> , 2	<u>3</u> , <u>3</u>

Figure 18.6   Japan and China fishing game (US$ billions)

This game also has the structure of a prisoners' dilemma. The social optimum occurs when both countries adopt sustainable fishing policies and limit fishing, but there is an incentive to unilaterally deviate from this optimum and try to free ride by choosing to over-fish. Over-fishing, no matter what your opponent does, is the dominant strategy for both countries, which leads to an outcome where countries continue to fish to the tragic end of fish commons.

3.4   Financial stability in the Eurozone

You have seen examples that explain why free trade may be undersupplied and international oceans over-fished. A third example refers to the global public good that collapsed in 2008 – financial stability. At the time of writing, the Eurozone has been caught in a crisis of its own, which several critics consider to be self-created:

> The crisis 'is having tremendous impact in the state of affairs, it is pushing the EU into a lasting depression, and it is entirely self-created,' Soros, Chairman of Soros Fund Management, said at a luncheon hosted by the National Association for Business Economics.
>
> (Wearden, 2012)

When countries joined the Eurozone, they signed a pact that required low public deficits. With the crisis of 2008, a lot of countries saw their public deficit pass the threshold, and several countries were finding it hard to pay off the debt. Greece and Portugal were two of the first countries that showed signs of unsustainable structural deficits and thus high levels of debt. For the sake of financial stability across the whole Eurozone, a dominant view was that a country should reduce its deficit and pay off its debts; then it would regain its reputation in the financial world and contribute to the Eurozone's financial stability. However, if a country were to adopt 'austerity measures' and pay off its debts too quickly, then doing so might initiate a recession or even a depression, with consequent unemployment and lower provision of social services. The country's government would find it very difficult to decrease unemployment without further public spending, which would once more contribute to increasing the country's deficit, overall debt and threaten Eurozone stability. But high unemployment and decreased access to social services could trigger social upheaval and political unrest. So while the global public good of financial stability (and the terms of the Eurozone agreement) would require a country like Greece or Portugal to endure economic hardship while paying its debts, the country may experience political and socio-economic pressures within its own borders to avoid paying the debt.

To illustrate the dilemma faced by these countries and their difficulties in paying their debts, consider another game with two players, Greece and Portugal, where each player has two actions to choose from: to pay debts or to not pay debts. It is assumed that the failure to pay its debt could be sufficient to trigger a Eurozone crisis but probably falling short of total collapse. If neither pays, then the Eurozone collapses and financial markets worldwide are affected. If both countries pay, then they do what is socially optimal and preserve financial stability, the integrity of the Eurozone. The stability of the Eurozone will help them to recover from the economic sacrifice of having paid. In the meantime, the countries have to deal with political unrest and social upheaval. If only one country pays, then the paying country has the worst possible outcome, with social upheaval within its own borders and financial instability just the same, which prevent quick recovery. The free rider, however, is in its best position, because it avoids internal problems and the Eurozone does not collapse completely.

The payoffs shown in Figure 18.7 provide a simple illustration with numbers that are ranked consistently with the economic situation. This game still has a prisoners' dilemma structure, with a free-riding incentive to defect, and the sucker effect of being cooperative when the other player is not.

		Portugal	
		Pay debt	Don't pay debt
Greece	Pay debt	1 , 1	–3 , 2
	Don't pay debt	2 , –3	–1 , –1

Figure 18.7   To pay or not pay your debts

So as long as countries weigh the consequences of their actions in the way described, both countries would always choose not to pay, regardless of what the other country does. The Eurozone collapses.

4   Strategies for cooperation

People often think: 'I don't behave like that – I cooperate with my family, friends and even people I don't know.' This section discusses some of the reasons why you may indeed cooperate, and strategies that may help to get governments and communities working together.

4.1   Rewards and punishment

Governments, societies and families all come up with ways to reward and punish people playing everyday games or complicated and politically important games. You may ask why the punishments and rewards that you have experienced are relevant to economics. The answer is that rewards and punishments change the payoffs and rules of the game, and can increase the appeal of outcomes that are better for society.

Returning to the problem of international over-fishing, Khan et al. (2006) discuss subsidies in fishing industries, saying that there are 'good', 'bad' and 'ugly' subsidies. Subsidies can act as rewards for the players in a game: good subsidies create incentives to enhance cooperation, while poorly designed subsidies can jeopardise cooperation.

Subsidies are not the only method by which government can change the incentives that fisheries and players in other prisoners' dilemmas face. For example, with fisheries, many governments have instituted systems of fines for fishers who are caught with too many fish or fish that are protected. These kinds of penalties are meant to reduce the free-riding incentive, and to discourage fishers from over-fishing.

Activity 18.5

Recall the Japan and China fishing game. What would be the equilibrium or equilibria of this game if fines of US$5 billion were subtracted from the payoffs of countries that fish beyond their quotas? The payoff matrix is shown in Figure 18.8.

Answer

If fines are subtracted from the payoffs, then the payoffs from fishing over quota are much lower.

Now, when China remains within the quota, Japan also prefers to remain within the quota because the incentive to free ride disappears when the fine is high enough. When China breaches its quota, Japan continues to

		China	
		Limit fishing	Over-fish
Japan	Limit fishing	<u>8</u> , <u>8</u>	<u>2</u> , 5
	Over-fish	5 , <u>2</u>	–2 , –2

Figure 18.8   Japan and China fishing game with fines (US$ billions)

prefer to stick to the rules. China will want to respond in the same way and stick to the rules by limiting fishing. The game is not a prisoners' dilemma any more because there is no longer an incentive to free ride. The players have a different dominant strategy, which is to always cooperate and remain within quotas. So the game has a unique Nash equilibrium (Limit fishing, Limit fishing), and that equilibrium is socially optimal.

You might wonder who would administer a system of fines like those described in the activity above. Typically, when two agents play a game like this within national borders, it is the state – the police, judiciary, etc. – that enforce fines and punishment. Globally, the problem is more complex and requires multilateral institutions like the UN and the WTO. International organisations like the WTO, by not responding to the interests of a single country, and by having interests that transcend national borders, can more easily enforce fishing quotas and punish countries that breach them. As long as an institution like the WTO can credibly enforce punishment, countries may come together and achieve the socially optimal outcome.

4.2   Collective action

The problem with penalties and rewards, or fines and subsidies, is that the regulatory bodies – often the government or international institutions – have to spend lots of money on the subsidies and on monitoring, detecting and meting out the rewards or punishment. In this subsection, I want you to reflect on the generic strategies of the prisoners' dilemma game: Cooperate and Defect. As you saw in Section 3.2, the strategies Contribute and Refuse used in the public good game can be interpreted as Cooperate and Defect. Contribute is renamed Cooperate in order to convey the sense that there exists an agreement to cooperate between the players, but from which players can choose to defect. Defection undermines cooperation, rather than players simply refusing to contribute to a public good. If you are one of many players in a game, then it can be very difficult to detect when one of your opponents defects. In global commons problems there are many, many players who are simultaneously trying to monitor each other and understand each player's behaviour. In this context, what might help to solve the commons problem? In this subsection, I discuss some *decentralised* solutions for when centralised institutions like the WTO or UN are unable to monitor all the players all the time to ensure that all players cooperate. The centralised institutions recognise that there are many factors outside of their control, and that sometimes delegating control to local communities can help to solve commons problems.

Activity 18.6

Read the following extract from a *New York Times* article. Explain what certain countries are trying to do to create a 'win–win' scenario to overcome the problem of over-fishing.

How to catch fish and save fisheries

The good news is that many large commercial fisheries are already benefiting from the improved management of the last decade. The harder problem is with smaller-scale fisheries that local communities rely on for food and income. The fact is that small-scale fishers – who fish within 10 miles of their coast – account for nearly half of the world's global catch and employ 33 million of the world's 36 million fishermen, while also creating jobs for 107 million people in fish processing and selling. Mostly poor, they live mainly in areas lacking fisheries management, monitoring and enforcement. No one is in a position to formally declare their fisheries 'disasters.' They must just endure their situation. Or – take control of it.

A rising tide of local communities is doing just that. Here's the emerging recipe proposed in [a study in the journal *Science*]: Give local fishers exclusive access to their fishing grounds in the form of territorial use rights, or TURF.

In exchange for the privilege of exclusivity, local fishermen agree to establish and protect no-take zones. Results include increased fish populations, richer marine habitats, and coastlines less vulnerable to climate change – and more food for people.

Unleashing the self-interest of local fishermen to advance both conservation and economic development can create one of those rare win–win scenarios.

A growing body of research shows that fish populations inside a no-take zone can more than quadruple. Fish numbers outside the reserve can double. And, exclusive access enables investment and better management, increasing the catch's value.

It works. We've visited several local fisheries in Mexico and the Philippines this year – with heads of leading research institutions, NGOs [non-government organisations] and government agencies – and in each case, we witnessed increasing fish populations, increased catch value and better-protected reefs.

TURF reserves are not a silver bullet. They might, however, be the silver buckshot. With nearly one billion people reliant on the ocean for their primary source of protein, stakes are high. If the most fish-dependent nations adopted widespread networks of TURF Reserve, they can potentially create enough fish recovery to feed hundreds of millions of people.

(Source: Safina and Jenks, 2012)

Answer

The start of the *New York Times* article says that in order to face the disastrous evolution of fisheries head on, many communities are adopting local institutions of monitoring and punishment. These institutions – called TURFs – delegate to each community the ability to monitor and evaluate their own fisheries, while also allocating to them the rights of control and 'residual claimancy' over the products of their local fisheries. A residual claimant on production is entitled to the profits on the output of that production process. Hence the name TURF – territorial use rights fisheries. Already seeing success in Mexico and the Philippines, TURFs help local communities to take control of their own destinies, while also aligning their incentives with preserving global populations of fish.

Why might a solution like this work? I discuss the problem in general below, and also describe why the proposed solutions seem to be succeeding.

The communities that took control of their local fisheries had to agree to a condition: to establish and protect 'no-take' zones in which the local fishers would not fish. Consequently, it would be in the local fishers' interests to maintain the no-take zones and ensure that the local fisheries did not get over-fished. In maintaining no-take zones, the local fishers would be able to maintain the rights over local fisheries. The no-take zones are occasionally checked by third party observers. These third parties judge whether or not the zones have been adequately cared for. If the no-take zones are not cared for, then the third parties revoke the local fishers' rights to fish. The study published in the journal *Science* (Costello et al., 2012) concluded that local fish populations have grown, richer marine habitats have flourished, and the coastlines appear to be less vulnerable to climate change. If only all commons problems could have so simple a solution.

Commons problems and global public goods problems tend to be more complex than our example of fisheries and TURFs. For instance, global commons and global public goods problems tend to involve many countries, many governments, or many organisations. In these cases, often called collective action games, it is more difficult to achieve a socially optimal solution. The collective nature of the outcome means that the accountability of each player to the final outcome decreases as the number of players increases. When there are more players, it is easier for players to defect and for their defection to go unnoticed, which makes the problem all the more challenging. A solution like the TURFs described above makes sense because a third party decentralises the challenge that it faces by delegating the solution to communities. In small communities, people can monitor each other more easily and defection is much more likely to be noticed. Internationally, if lots of communities monitor themselves, then society will be more likely to obtain a win–win outcome. No third party by itself can monitor everyone, so if each community self-monitors, then the third party's job is a lot easier.

Consequently, in collective action games, players may invest in technologies to detect players who defect so that the players who cooperate can punish the players who defect. Alternatively, when players are unable to detect defection, the players may delegate the role of policing and enforcing cooperation to a third party. International institutions such as the International Maritime Organization, which monitors international fishing, aim to police member states. Similarly, the WTO, which monitors and tries to regulate multilateral trade agreements, uses the Dispute Settlement Mechanism to examine situations in which one government claims that another government has contravened the rules of the organisation – for example, by imposing an unfair tariff on a foreign country or by allowing firms to dump subsidised goods at low prices in foreign countries. In all of these organisations, being a member state requires the members to adhere to judgements made by the enforcement arm of the organisation. For cooperation to succeed, enforcement must involve punishing players who defect (or rewarding those who cooperate). Within society, citizens delegate enforcement to third party institutions – like the police and the judiciary – because the players themselves are unable to sustain cooperation without these institutions.

4.3 Changing beliefs and norms

Did you know?

Harambee is a Swahili word denoting a project to which everyone – originally everyone in a rural Kenyan village – ought to contribute. Consequently, many Kenyans view public goods as harambee – as something that they should support.

In contrast to the large third party monitoring and enforcement operations of the WTO and the UN, TURFs in communities in the Philippines and Mexico exemplify how people in communities can come together and agree on the 'rules of the game' that will govern their behaviour when it comes to common or global public goods. Such agreement often occurs when communities are homogeneous and composed of people who are similar in the way they perceive the problem and its challenges. For many Kenyans, the notion of free riding on the contribution to a public good is not part of their language, and therefore is not likely to be part of the way they would respond to the challenges faced worldwide about sustaining global public goods with individual contributions. In such societies, cooperation is more likely to occur, and to be ensured by social norms that condition the way people want to behave.

Similar norms appear in many societies, from who gets to graze their sheep and how long they may do so in villages in the Swiss Alps, to the Amish raising barns in rural North America, to the division of meat among the Lamalera whale hunters in Indonesia. Institutions can play a role in supporting cooperation by influencing the evolution of social norms.

The trade and tariff example of China and the USA – two countries with a long, antagonistic history – provides a different set of problems. Political scientists and historians might say that interactions between China and the USA cannot be understood only as a prisoners' dilemma; they must be understood in the political and historical context that shaped current norms of behaviour. Similarly, norms play a role in how people in each country believe they ought to act, and how politicians on either side need to maintain a reputation in the context of these histories. No cultural, historical or political details are captured in the concise but clear model of the prisoners' dilemma.

4.4   A credible leader

The example of China, a major export country, and the USA, a major import country, also highlights a problem with which economists still grapple: what happens when the costs and benefits in an interaction are different? That is, what happens when some groups get large benefits while other groups get smaller benefits, or when some groups incur high costs while others incur low or no costs? What happens when groups have different incentives? It is easy to see how this problem is magnified when the costs and benefits of many countries have to be considered. The negotiations between Eurozone members over the sovereign debt crisis at the beginning of the second decade of the 2000s were drawn out in part because the different members faced different costs and benefits of finding solutions. The European Commission or the European Central Bank (ECB) acting as a third party could monitor and set rules that member states should abide by, but individually countries could not agree on a solution. Each country's interests were not reconcilable in a way that allowed the countries to negotiate a solution.

The Eurozone example also illustrates an alternative solution to encourage a cooperative outcome: the nomination of a country or a group of countries to act as leaders. Leaders typically bear more of the costs of cooperating while others may gain more of the benefits. In the Eurozone, it might be argued that Germany is such a leader when it comes to stability of the euro and of the Eurozone economies.

As the economic powerhouse of the Eurozone, Germany is the source of much of the Eurozone's wealth. But as a leader, it must also shoulder the responsibility of sustaining the euro currency when other countries are either unwilling or unable to bear the costs of cooperation. For example, in the case of countries like Greece, Ireland, Italy, Portugal and Spain that did poorly during and in the aftermath of the financial crisis, their sovereign debt problems at the time of writing were at the core of the instability in the Eurozone, and in global finance. As the leader, Germany has had to help to 'bail out' the finances of countries with sovereign debt problems. Why would Germany bail out other countries? Germany might do so because the overall financial stability of the euro, from which Germany benefits greatly, requires the cooperation of the Eurozone's largest producer.

A similar argument about leadership can be made about the ECB's declaration of the Outright Monetary Transactions scheme. The scheme guaranteed that the ECB would buy unlimited amounts of European debt in order to ensure the monetary stability of the euro and therefore the economic stability of the Eurozone. Unlike Germany, the ECB does not have an economy producing final goods, but the ECB's continued existence depends on the Eurozone remaining financially stable.

The idea of leadership – like that of Mario Draghi for the ECB or Angela Merkel in Germany – also illustrates the idea that sometimes players' payoffs may not be symmetric, like they have been in most of the examples used in this chapter. Sometimes, the payoffs may be structured so that the benefits and costs received by one player may be very different to those received by other players. In the case of the Eurozone, the benefits from having a stable euro received by Germany may be greater than those received by Greece. Consequently, Germany may be more willing than Greece to incur costs to maintain the large benefits of financial stability. Greece, however, might even be willing to drop the euro as its currency if the costs of retaining the euro become too high. It is a delicate balance of costs and benefits for each country, with each country recognising that the eventual outcomes are not dependent on any one of them alone. The countries of the Eurozone acting in concert are more likely to cooperate and produce a stable euro than each country trying to maximise its own national interests and undermining cooperation.

5   Conclusion

In his book *The Logic of Collective Action*, Mancur Olson (1965) argues that large groups attempting collective action will likely fail. However, since the book's publication, we have seen many examples of situations in which people in dire circumstances can join together and overcome public goods problems. Yes, public goods problems and commons problems present challenges to the most stalwart and generous of countries and people; but with rewards and punishments, monitoring and collective action, norms and leadership, people, organisations and countries can join together to overcome problems that, were they divided, isolated and merely self-interested, they might never have hoped to defeat.

Kofi Annan, former Secretary-General of the UN, provides an optimistic thought that is perhaps an apt end to this book:

> It is not beyond the powers of political volition to tip the scales towards more secure peace, greater economic well-being, social justice and environmental sustainability. But no country can achieve these global public goods on its own, and neither can the global marketplace. Thus our efforts must now focus on the missing term of the equation: global public goods.
>
> (Kaul et al., 1999)

References

Costello, C., Ovando, D., Hilborn, R., Gaines, S., Deschenes, O. and Lester, S. (2012) 'Status and solutions for the world's unassessed fisheries', *Science*, vol. 338, no. 6106, pp. 517–20.

Hardin, G. (1968) 'The tragedy of the commons', *Science*, vol. 162, no. 3859, pp. 1243–8.

Kaul, I., Grunberg, I. and Stern, M.A. (eds) (1999) *Global Public Goods: International Cooperation in the 21st Century*, Oxford, Oxford University Press.

Khan, A., Sumaila, U.R., Watson, R., Munro, G. and Pauly, D. (2006) 'The nature and magnitude of global non-fuel fisheries subsidies', in Sumaila, U.R. and Pauly, D. (eds) *Catching More Bait: A Bottom-up Re-estimation of Global Fisheries Subsidies (2nd Version)*, Fisheries Centre Research Report vol. 14, no. 6, University of British Columbia, Vancouver, Canada, pp. 5–37.

Lagarde, C. (2011) *New Global Economics*, November, audio available online. Programmme by Martin Wolf, and this particular quote is from 14 November. It is the first programme in the series.

Nordhaus, W.D. (2005) 'Paul Samuelson and global public goods', Yale University Discussion Paper, 5 May.

Olson, M. (1971) *The Logic of Collective Action*, Cambridge, MA, Harvard University Press.

Safina, C. and Jenks, B. (2012) 'How to catch fish and save fisheries', *New York Times*, 19 October, [online] www.nytimes.com/2012/10/20/opinion/how-to-catch-fish-and-save-fisheries.html (Accessed 16 December 2012).

Sumaila, U.R. (2011) *Fisheries: Investing in Natural Capital*, [online] www.unep.org/greeneconomy/Portals/88/documents/ger/3.0_Fisheries.pdf (Accessed 30 April 2013).

United Nations Environment Programme (UNEP) (2011) *Towards a Green Economy*, [online] www.unep.org/greeneconomy/greeneconomyreport/tabid/29846/default.aspx (Accessed 16 December 2012).

Vidal, J. (2012) 'Is the EU taking its over-fishing habits to west African waters?', *The Guardian*, 2 April, [online] www.guardian.co.uk/

environment/2012/apr/02/eu-fishing-west-africa-mauritania (Accessed 16 December 2012).

Wearden, G. (2012) 'Eurozone crisis live: hopes of imminent Greek cuts deal dashed – as it happened', *The Guardian*, 15 October, [online] www.guardian.co.uk/business/2012/oct/15/eurozone-crisis-eu-summit-greece-spain (Accessed 16 December 2012).

Wydick, B. (2008) *Games in Economic Development*, Cambridge, Cambridge University Press.

Acknowledgements

Grateful acknowledgement is made to the following sources:

Cover photo

Kuala Lumpur, Malaysia © Mark Henley

Illustrations

P. 22 © PA Photos; p. 23 (top) © Dariusz Kuzminski; p. 23 (bottom) © Dan Gilwood/Getty Images; p. 100 © iStockphoto/Nastco; p. 229 © Guy Bell/Alamy; p. 232 © Bettman/Corbis; p. 272 © Image Asset Management Ltd/Super Stock; p. 309 © Dirk van Malinckrodt/Alamy; p. 343 © Greenpeace/Gavin Newman; p. 354 © Palani Mohan.

Cartoon

P. 269 © CartoonStock.

Text

P. 5 © The Financial Times Ltd; p. 239 © The Institute for Fiscal Studies, May 2011.

Figures

P. 6 UNCTAD; p. 9 US Bureau of Labor Statisitics; p. 138 US Census Bureau; p. 212 © Elsevier, 2011; p. 234 The Eqality Trust; p. 235 The Equality Trust; p. 237 © OECD, 2011; p. 240 © reproduced under the terms of Open Government Licence for public sector information; p. 247 © OECD, 2011; p. 250 © OECD, 2012; p. 253 OECD, 2011; p. 255 © OECD, 2011; p. 261 OECD, 2011; p. 265 © OECD, 2011.

Tables

P. 258 © reproduced under the terms of Open Government Licence for public sector information; p. 260 © reproduced under the terms of Open Government Licence for public sector information.

Index

state-owned firms in 158
employment incentives
    and welfare policy 270, 271–4, 275–6
EMTR (effective marginal tax rate) 273–4
environmental disasters 329
equality of opportunity
    and well-being 319
equilibrium *see* market equilibrium
equity
    and inequality 232–3
equivalised household incomes 238–9, 242
    in OECD countries 247
European Commission
and trading standards 100–1 European Exchange
    Rate Mechanism 84 European Union (EU)
        Common Agricultural Policy (CAP) 80
        competition policy 168
        and free trade 198, 338
Eurozone crisis 329, 332
    and leadership 355–6
    and the prisoners' dilemma game 345–7
exchange rates 79
    manipulation, and strategic trade policy 219–21
    and price controls 84
    and trade policy 198, 203
expected future prices
    and market demand 61–2
export commodities
    and market power 203
export market power
    and immiserising growth 205–8
external economies
    and China 41–3
externalities 287, 288, 322
    defining 293
    and government intervention 314
    positive 266–7, 297
    see also negative externalities

fast-moving consumer goods 165
final income of households 240, 262
financial crisis *see* crisis (2008)
financial stability
    and global public goods 336, 337, 345–7
        in the Eurozone 345–7
        the Eurozone crisis 329, 332, 345–7
fines
    for international over-fishing 348

Finland
    earnings inequality 254, 255
    education scores and income inequality 235–6
firms
    competition through innovation 170–5
    defining 13
    entry and exit of
        and monopolistic competition 153–4
        oligopolistic markets and barriers to entry 164–7
        and perfect competition 101–3, 122–4
    factors of production 13
    and market interaction 75
    modelling costs 16–26
        total and average costs 16–19
    in monopolistic competition 153–6, 215–16
    negative production externalities 293–302
        and Pigovian taxes 294–8
    oligopolistic markets 160, 161–9
        and competition policy 167–9
        network industries 166–7
    and perfect competition 95–6, 127–9, 131
        compared with monopoly 149–52
        demand curve of a competitive firm 104–6
        freedom of entry and exit 101
        homogeneous products 99–100, 104
        the invisible hand 129–30
        loss-making firms 114–15
        normal and supernormal profits 111–13
        profit-maximisation and supply in the long run 119–26
        profit-maximising output 108–11
        profits in the short run 111–17
        short-run supply curves 117–18
        the shut-down rule 115–17
        size relative to the market 97–9, 104
    and price ceilings 83
    and the production function 13–15
    promotion and the 'glass ceiling' 319
    size of 137, 138
    state-owned 158
    and strategic trade policy 216–19
    see also high-technology companies; large firms;
        manufacturing firms; monopolies; small firms
fisheries
    and cooperative behaviour
        collective action games 350–2, 353
        rewards and punishment 348–9

and welfare policy 270, 274, 275, 278
location
    and monopolistic competition 154
Locke, John 314
long-run equilibrium
    and monopolistic competition 155–6, 215–16
    output decisions and profit of firms 121–4
long-run marginal cost curves (LRMC) 119–20
long-run supply curve
    and perfect competition 120, 124–6
long-run time period
    modelling a firm's costs 18, 19
        see also LRAC (long-run average cost)
    and price elasticity of demand 67–8
    profit-maximisation and supply 119–26
Lorenz curves 241–5
    for final income and post-tax income 264
    and the Gini coefficient 245–6
    impact of cash benefits and taxes 258–9
    line of equality in 244, 245
    and wealth inequality 244–5
loss-making firms
    and perfect competition 114–15
low-income countries
    and comparative advantage 189–91
    export market power and immiserising growth
      205–8
    gains from trade 191–3
    terms of trade 194
    and welfare policy 275
    see also developing countries
low-income households
    government support for 251
    and marginal propensity to consume 231
    raising living standards of 270, 274, 275, 278
    and well-being 230
    see also poverty
LRAC (long-run average cost) 19, 20–6
    curves
        and China 43
        and economies of scale 21–5, 30, 140
        in the long-run equilibrium 122
        and LRMC curves 119–20
        monopolies 140, 141
        and monopolistic competition 155
        and profit-maximisation 119–20
        and Schumpeterian competition 172–3
        and SRAC curves 38–9

and technological change 27, 29
LRMC (long-run marginal cost curves) 119–20
Macleod, C. 40
male wage inequality
    and trade within countries 210–13
manufacturing firms
    and monopolistic competition 154
    offshore production 5–6
        and economies of scale 23–4
        and labour costs 8–12, 16
    and the production function 13–15
manufacturing, trade in
    China 5–6, 185, 186, 195, 203
    terms of trade 195, 196
marginal costs
    analysis 34–6
    and anti-dumping tariffs 218
    and average cost 36–8
    long-run marginal cost curves (LRMC) 119–20
    and marginal utility 129
    for a monopolist 146, 149, 150, 153
    monopolistic competition and intra-industry trade
      215–16
    and negative production externalities 293–4
        Pigovian taxes 295–6
    and oligopolistic markets 163
    and perfect competition 96, 150
        marginal cost curves 117–19, 122
        profit-maximisation 107, 108, 109–11
    of pollution abatement 298–9
marginal product of labour 33–4
marginal revenue
    and anti-dumping tariffs 217–18
    curves
        and market equilibrium 76–7
        monopolistic competition and intra-industry
          trade 215–16
    for a monopolist 142, 144–5, 146
    and profit-maximisation 107, 108, 109–11, 131
marginal utility
    diminishing 289–91
    and free markets 292
    and market demand 64
    and perfect competition 128–9
market demand 54–6, 89
    and the *ceteris paribus* assumption 55, 62, 63
    and consumer incomes 52, 58–60
    and consumer preferences 61